INTENTIONALITY

An essay in the philosophy of mind

FOR DAGMAR

INTENTIONALITY

An essay in the philosophy of mind

JOHN R. SEARLE

CAMBRIDGE
UNIVERSITY PRESS

Published by the Press Syndicate of the University of Cambridge
The Pitt Building, Trumpington Street, Cambridge CB2 1RP
40 West 20th Street, New York, NY 10011-4211, USA
10 Stamford Road, Oakleigh, Victoria 3166, Australia

First published 1983
Reprinted 1983, 1984, 1985, 1987, 1988, 1989, 1990, 1991,
1993

Printed in the United States of America

Library of Congress catalog card number: 82-19849

British Library Cataloguing in Publication Data

Searle, John R.
Intentionality.
1. Intentionalism
I. Title
121   BF311

ISBN 0 521 22895 6 hardback
ISBN 0 521 27302 1 paperback

CONTENTS

ACKNOWLEDGEMENTS

I am indebted to a large number of people and institutions for help
with this book. I want first to thank the John Simon Guggenheim
Memorial Foundation, the University of California Humanities
Institute, the Est Foundation, the Committee on Research of the
University of California Academic Senate, and the A. P. Sloan
Foundation for financial assistance at various times in the
preparation of this and other related works. All of this material has
been presented in lectures and university courses at Berkeley and
other universities, and I am grateful to my students in Berkeley,
Boulder, and Campinas, for their reactions. Special thanks are due
to Ami Kronfeld, David Reier, Jim Stone, Vanessa Whang, Steven
White, and Steve Yablo. Several colleagues and friends read
portions of the manuscript and made helpful comments: I
especially want to thank Ned Block, Sylvain Bromberger, Tyler
Burge, Alan Code, Donald Davidson, Dagfinn Føllesdal, David
Kaplan, Benjamin Libet, George Myro, Thomas Nagel, William
Reinhardt, and Hans Sluga. For comments which affected the
content of the text my greatest debts are to Hubert Dreyfus and
especially to Christine Skarda. Most of all I thank my wife Dagmar
Searle for her constant help and advice.

INTRODUCTION

The primary aim of this book is to develop a theory of Intentionality. I hesitate to call it a general theory because a large number of topics, e.g., the emotions, are left undiscussed, but I do believe the approach here presented will prove useful for explaining Intentional phenomena generally.

This book is the third in a series of related studies of mind and language. One of its objectives is to provide a foundation for my two earlier books, *Speech Acts* (Cambridge University Press, 1969) and *Expression and Meaning* (Cambridge University Press, 1979), as well as for future investigations of these topics. A basic assumption behind my approach to problems of language is that the philosophy of language is a branch of the philosophy of mind. The capacity of speech acts to represent objects and states of affairs in the world is an extension of the more biologically fundamental capacities of the mind (or brain) to relate the organism to the world by way of such mental states as belief and desire, and especially through action and perception. Since speech acts are a type of human action, and since the capacity of speech to represent objects and states of affairs is part of a more general capacity of the mind to relate the organism to the world, any complete account of speech and language requires an account of how the mind/brain relates the organism to reality.

Since sentences – the sounds that come out of one's mouth or the marks that one makes on paper – are, considered in one way, just objects in the world like any other objects, their capacity to represent is not intrinsic but is derived from the Intentionality of the mind. The Intentionality of mental states, on the other hand, is not derived from some more prior forms of Intentionality but is intrinsic to the states themselves. An agent uses a sentence to make a statement or ask a question, but he does not in that way *use* his beliefs and desires, he simply has them. A sentence is a syntactical object on which representational capacities are imposed: beliefs and desires and other Intentional states are not, as such, syntactical objects (though they may be and usually are expressed in sentences), and their representational capacities are not imposed but are intrinsic. All of this is consistent with the fact that language is essentially a social phenomenon and that the forms of Intentionality underlying language are social forms.

This study began as an investigation of that part of the problem of meaning which concerns how people impose Intentionality on entities that are not intrinsically Intentional, how they get mere objects to represent. I originally planned to include a chapter on this question in *Expression and Meaning*, but, in the way of such things, the chapter grew into a book of its own. In attempting to analyze the Intentionality of mental states (Chapter 1) I found I had to investigate the Intentionality of perception (Chapter 2) and action (Chapter 3). But there is no understanding of perception and action without an understanding of Intentional causation (Chapter 4), and various investigations led to the conclusion that Intentionality in all its forms functions only against a background of nonrepresentational mental capacities (Chapter 5). I reached my original goal of explaining the relations between the Intentionality of the mental and the Intentionality of the linguistic only in Chapter 6. But that still left me with a bushel of problems: Chapter 7 concerns the relationships between Intentionality-with-a t and intensionality-with-an-s; Chapters 8 and 9 use the theory developed in prior chapters to criticize several currently influential views on reference and meaning and to present an Intentionalistic account of indexical expressions, natural kind terms, the *de re–de dicto* distinction, and proper names. Finally, Chapter 10 presents a solution (more accurately, a dissolution) of the so-called "mind–body" or "mind–brain" problem.

In urging that people have mental states which are intrinsically Intentional I part company with many, perhaps most, of the currently influential views in the philosophy of mind. I believe people really do have mental states, some of them conscious and some unconscious, and that, at least as far as the conscious ones are concerned, they pretty much have the mental properties they seem to have. I reject any form of behaviorism or functionalism, including Turing machine functionalism, that ends up by denying the specifically mental properties of mental phenomena. I do not criticize these other views in this book as I have discussed them at length elsewhere.[1] I believe that the various forms of behaviorism and functionalism were never motivated by an independent investigation of the facts, but by a fear that unless some way was found to eliminate mental phenomena naively construed, we would be left with dualism and an apparently insoluble mind–body problem. On my view mental phenomena are biologically based: they are both caused by the operations of the brain and realized in the structure of the brain. On this view, consciousness and Intentionality are as much a part of human biology as digestion or the circulation of the blood. It is an *objective* fact about the world that it contains certain systems, viz., brains, with *subjective* mental states, and it is a *physical* fact about such systems that they have *mental* features. The correct solution to the "mind–body problem" lies not in denying the reality of mental phenomena, but in properly appreciating their biological nature. More about this in Chapter 10.

Part of the fun of writing about speech acts is that there is no heavy philosophical tradition weighing down on the investigation. Except for a few favorites such as promises and statements, most types of speech acts have been ignored by the great philosophers of the past; and one can investigate, for example, thanking, apologizing and requesting without looking over one's shoulder to see what Aristotle, Kant or Mill had to say about them. But when it comes to Intentionality the situation is quite different. Entire philosophical movements have been built around theories of Intentionality. What is one to do in the face of all this distinguished past? My own approach has been simply to ignore it, partly out of ignorance of most of the traditional writings on Intentionality and partly out of the conviction that my only hope of resolving the worries which led me into this study in the first place lay in the relentless pursuit of my own investigations. It is worth pointing this out because several people who read the manuscript claimed to

---

1 'Minds, brains and programs', *Behavioral and Brain Sciences*, vol. 3 (1980), pp. 417–24; 'Intrinsic Intentionality', *Behaviorial and Brain Sciences*, same issue, pp. 450–6; 'Analytic philosophy and mental phenomena', *Midwest Studies in Philosophy*, vol. 5 (1980), pp. 405–23. 'The myth of the computer', *New York Review of Books* (1982), vol. XXIX, no. 7, pp. 3–6.

find interesting agreements and disagreements with their favorite authors. Perhaps they are right in their understanding of the relation between this book and the Intentionalist tradition, but with the exception of my explicit responses and my obvious debts to Frege and Wittgenstein, it has not been my aim in this book to respond to that tradition.

Where questions of style and exposition are concerned I try to follow a simple maxim: if you can't say it clearly you don't understand it yourself. But anyone who attempts to write clearly runs the risk of being 'understood' too quickly, and the quickest form of such understanding is to pigeonhole the author with a whole lot of other authors that the reader is already familiar with.

Some of the ideas in this book have appeared in preliminary versions in articles by me. Since several reviewers of *Speech Acts* complained that some of the ideas had already appeared in articles, a word of explanation is in order. I find it very useful to try out ideas in a preliminary form, both for the sake of formulating the ideas and to elicit comments and criticism. Such articles are like an artist's preliminary sketches for a larger canvas. They can stand on their own, but they also function as stages on the way to the larger picture. The hard work comes not only in trying to get each part right, but also in making all the parts cohere in the general conception.

One nagging problem remains that is not addressed directly in the book, but was one of my main reasons for wanting to write it. Ordinary human behavior has proven peculiarly recalcitrant to explanation by the methods of the natural sciences. Why? Why is it that the methods of the natural sciences have not given results comparable to physics and chemistry when applied to the study of individual and collective human behavior? There are many attempts to answer this question in contemporary philosophy, none of them in my view completely satisfactory. I believe that the direction of the correct answer lies in seeing the role of Intentionality in the structure of action; not just in the description of action, but in the very structure of human behavior. I hope to discuss the explanation of human behavior at greater length in a subsequent study. This book gives only some of the tools for such a discussion.

Chapter 1

THE NATURE OF INTENTIONAL STATES

I. INTENTIONALITY AS DIRECTEDNESS

As a preliminary formulation we might say: Intentionality is that property of many mental states and events by which they are directed at or about or of objects and states of affairs in the world. If, for example, I have a belief, it must be a belief that such and such is the case; if I have a fear, it must be a fear of something or that something will occur; if I have a desire, it must be a desire to do something or that something should happen or be the case; if I have an intention, it must be an intention to do something. And so on through a large number of other cases. I follow a long philosophical tradition in calling this feature of directedness or aboutness "Intentionality", but in many respects the term is misleading and the tradition something of a mess, so at the very beginning I want to make it clear how I intend to use the term and in so doing to dissociate myself from certain features of the tradition.

First, on my account only some, not all, mental states and events have Intentionality. Beliefs, fears, hopes, and desires are Intentional; but there are forms of nervousness, elation, and undirected anxiety that are not Intentional. A clue to this distinction is provided by the constraints on how these states are reported. If I tell you I have a belief or a desire, it always makes sense for you to ask, "What is it exactly that you believe?" or "What is it that you desire?"; and it won't do for me to say, "Oh I just have a belief and a desire without believing anything or desiring anything". My beliefs and desires must always be about something. But my nervousness and undirected anxiety need not in that way be *about* anything. Such states are characteristically accompanied by beliefs and desires, but undirected states are not identical with beliefs or desires. On my account if a state *S* is Intentional then there must be an answer to such questions as: What is S about? What is S of? What is it an S that? Some types of mental states have instances which are Intentional and other instances which are not. For example, just as there are forms of elation, depression and anxiety where one is simply elated, depressed, or anxious without being elated, depressed, or anxious about anything, so, also, there are forms of these states where one is elated that such and such has occurred or depressed and anxious at the prospect of such and such. Undirected anxiety, depression, and elation are not Intentional, the directed cases are Intentional.

Second, Intentionality is not the same as consciousness. Many conscious states are not Intentional, e.g., a sudden sense of elation, and many Intentional states are not conscious, e.g., I have many beliefs that I am not thinking about at present and I may never have thought of. For example, I believe that my paternal grandfather spent his entire life inside the continental United States but until this moment I never consciously formulated or considered that belief. Such unconscious beliefs, by the way, need not be instances of any kind of repression, Freudian or otherwise; they are just beliefs one has that one normally doesn't think about. In defense of the view that there is an identity between consciousness and Intentionality it is sometimes said that all consciousness is consciousness *of*, that whenever one is conscious there is always something that one is conscious of. But this account of consciousness blurs a crucial distinction: when I have a conscious experience of anxiety, there is indeed something my experience is an experience of, namely anxiety, but this sense of "of" is quite different from the "of" of Intentionality, which occurs, for example, in the statement that I have a conscious fear of snakes; for in the case of anxiety, the experience of anxiety and the anxiety are identical; but the fear of snakes is not identical with snakes. It is characteristic of Intentional states, as I use the notion, that there is a distinction between the state and what the state is directed at or about or of (though this does not exclude the possibility of self-referential forms of Intentionality – as we will see in Chapters 2 and 3). On my account the "of" in the expression "the experience of anxiety" cannot be the "of" of Intentionality because the experience and the anxiety are identical. I will have more to say about conscious forms of Intentionality later; my aim now is just to make clear that, as I use the term, the class of conscious states and the class of Intentional mental states overlap but they are not identical, nor is one included in the other.

Third, intending and intentions are just one form of Intentionality among others, they have no special status. The obvious pun on "Intentionality" and "intention" suggests that intentions in the ordinary sense have some special role in the theory of Intentionality; but on my account intending to do something is just one form of Intentionality along with belief, hope, fear, desire, and lots of others; and I do not mean to suggest that because, for example, beliefs are Intentional they somehow contain the notion of intention or they intend something or someone who has a belief must thereby intend to do something about it. In order to keep this distinction completely clear I will capitalize the technical sense of "Intentional" and "Intentionality". Intentionality is directedness; intending to do something is just one kind of Intentionality among others.

Related to the pun on "intentional" and "Intentional" are some other common confusions. Some authors describe beliefs, fears, hopes, and desires as "mental acts", but this is at best false and at worst hopelessly confused. Drinking beer and writing books can be described as acts or actions or even activities, and doing arithmetic in your head or forming mental images of the Golden Gate Bridge are mental acts; but believing, hoping, fearing, and desiring are not acts nor mental acts at all. Acts are things one *does*, but there is no answer to the question, "What are you now doing?" which goes, "I am now believing it will rain", or "hoping that taxes will be lowered", or "fearing a fall in the interest rate", or "desiring to go to the movies". The Intentional states and events we will be considering are precisely that: states and events; they are not mental acts, though I will have something to say about what are properly called mental acts in Chapter 3.

It is equally confused to think of, for example, beliefs and desires as somehow intending something. Beliefs and desires are Intentional states, but they do not intend anything. On my account "Intentionality" and "Intentional" will occur in these noun and adjective forms, and I will speak of certain mental states and events as having Intentionality or as being Intentional, but there is no sense attaching to any corresponding verb.

3

Here are a few examples of states that can be Intentional states: belief, fear, hope, desire, love, hate, aversion, liking, disliking, doubting, wondering whether, joy, elation, depression, anxiety, pride, remorse, sorrow, grief, guilt, rejoicing, irritation, puzzlement, acceptance, forgiveness, hostility, affection, expectation, anger, admiration, contempt, respect, indignation, intention, wishing, wanting, imagining, fantasy, shame, lust, disgust, animosity, terror, pleasure, abhorrence, aspiration, amusement, and disappointment.

It is characteristic of the members of this set that they either are essentially directed as in the case of love, hate, belief, and desire or at least they can be directed as in the case of depression and elation. This set raises a rather large number of questions. For example, how can we classify its members, and what are the relations between the members? But the question I now want to concentrate on is this: What exactly is the relation between Intentional states and the objects and states of affairs that they are in some 'sense about or directed at? What kind of a relation is named by "Intentionality" anyhow and how can we explain Intentionality without using metaphors like "directed"?

Notice that Intentionality cannot be an ordinary relation like sitting on top of something or hitting it with one's fist because for a large number of Intentional states I can be in the Intentional state without the object or state of affairs that the Intentional state is "directed at" even existing. I can hope that it is raining even if it isn't raining and I can believe that the King of France is bald even if there is no such person as the King of France.

II. INTENTIONALITY AS REPRESENTATION: THE SPEECH ACT MODEL

In this section I want to explore some of the connections between Intentional states and speech acts in order to answer the question, "What is the relationship between the Intentional state and the object or state of affairs that it is in some sense directed at?" To anticipate a bit, the answer that I am going to propose to that question is quite simple: Intentional states represent objects and states of affairs in the same sense of "represent" that speech acts represent objects and states of affairs (even though, as we will see in

4

Chapter 6, speech acts have a derived form of Intentionality and thus represent in a different manner from Intentional states, which have an intrinsic form of Intentionality). We already have fairly clear intuitions about how statements represent their truth conditions, about how promises represent their fulfillment conditions, about how orders represent the conditions of their obedience, and about how in the utterance of a referring expression the speaker refers to an object; indeed, we even have something of a theory about these various types of speech acts; and I am going to tap this prior knowledge to try to explain how and in what sense Intentional states are also representations.

There is one possible misunderstanding I need to block at the start of the investigation. By explaining Intentionality in terms of language I do not mean to imply that Intentionality is essentially and necessarily linguistic. On the contrary it seems to me obvious that infants and many animals that do not in any ordinary sense have a language or perform speech acts nonetheless have Intentional states. Only someone in the grip of a philosophical theory would deny that small babies can literally be said to want milk and that dogs want to be let out or believe that their master is at the door. There are, incidentally, two reasons why we find it irresistible to attribute Intentionality to animals even though they do not have a language. First, we can see that the causal basis of the animal's Intentionality is very much like our own, e.g., these are the dog's eyes, this is his skin, those are his ears, etc. Second, we can't make sense of his behavior otherwise. In my effort to explain Intentionality in terms of language I am using our prior knowledge of language as a heuristic device for explanatory purposes. Once I have tried to make clear the nature of Intentionality I will argue (in Chapter 6) that the relation of logical dependence is precisely the reverse. Language is derived from Intentionality and not conversely. The direction of pedagogy is to explain Intentionality in terms of language; the direction of logical analysis is to explain language in terms of Intentionality.

There are at least the following four points of similarity and connection between Intentional states and speech acts.

1. The distinction between propositional content and illocutionary force, a distinction familiar within the theory of speech acts, carries over to Intentional states. Just as I can order you to

leave the room, predict that you will leave the room, and suggest that you will leave the room, so I can believe that you will leave the room, fear that you will leave the room, want you to leave the room, and hope that you will leave the room. In the first class of cases, the speech act cases, there is an obvious distinction between the propositional content *that you will leave the room* and the illocutionary force with which that propositional content is presented in the speech act. But equally in the second class of cases, the Intentional states, there is a distinction between the representative content *that you will leave the room*, and the psychological mode, whether belief or fear or hope or whatever, in which one has that representative content. It is customary within the theory of speech acts to present this distinction in the form "$F(p)$", where the "F" marks the illocutionary force and the "p" the propositional content. Within the theory of Intentional states we will similarly need to distinguish between the representative content and the psychological mode or manner in which one has that representative content. We will symbolize this as "$S(r)$", where the "S" marks the psychological mode and the "r" the representative content.

It would perhaps be better to confine the term "propositional content" to those states that are realized linguistically, and use the terms "representative content" or "Intentional content" as more general terms to include both linguistically realized Intentional states and those that are not realized in language. But as we also need to distinguish between those states such as belief whose content must always be expressible as a whole proposition and those such as love and hate whose content need not be a whole proposition, I will continue to use also the notion of propositional content for Intentional states, to mark those states that take entire propositions as contents, whether or not the state is realized linguistically. I will use the notations of speech act theory in representing the content of an Intentional state inside parentheses and the form or mode in which the agent has that content outside. Thus, for example, if a man loves Sally and believes it is raining his two Intentional states are representable as

Love (Sally)
Believe (It is raining).

Most of the analyses in this book will be about states which have whole propositional contents, the so-called propositional attitudes. But it is important to emphasize that not all Intentional states have an entire proposition as Intentional content, though by definition all Intentional states have at least some representative content, whether a whole proposition or not; and indeed this condition is stronger for Intentional states than for speech acts, since some (very few) expressive speech acts do not have any content, e.g., "Ouch!", "Hello", "Goodbye".

2. The distinction between different directions of fit, also familiar from the theory of speech acts,[1] will carry over to Intentional states. The members of the assertive class of speech acts – statements, descriptions, assertions, etc. – are supposed in some way to match an independently existing world; and to the extent that they do or fail to do that we say are true or false. But the members of the directive class of speech acts – orders, commands, requests, etc. – and the members of the commissive class – promises, vows, pledges, etc. – are not supposed to match an independently existing reality but rather are supposed to bring about changes in the world so that the world matches the propositional content of the speech act; and to the extent that they do or fail to do that, we do not say they are true or false but rather such things as that they are obeyed or disobeyed, fulfilled, complied with, kept or broken. I mark this distinction by saying that the assertive class has the word-to-world direction of fit and the commissive and directive classes have the world-to-word direction of fit. If the statement is not true, it is the statement which is at fault, not the world; if the order is disobeyed or the promise broken it is not the order or promise which is at fault, but the world in the person of the disobeyer of the order or the breaker of the promise. Intuitively we might say the idea of direction of fit is that of responsibility for fitting. If the statement is false, it is the fault of the statement (word-to-world direction of fit). If the promise is broken, it is the fault of the promiser (world-to-word direction of fit). There are also null cases in which there is no

---

1 For further discussion of the notion of "direction of fit" see J. R. Searle, 'A taxonomy of illocutionary acts', in *Expression and Meaning* (Cambridge: Cambridge University Press, 1979), pp. 1–27.

direction of fit. If I apologize for insulting you or congratulate you on winning the prize, then though I do indeed presuppose the truth of the expressed proposition, that I insulted you, that you won the prize, the point of the speech act is not to assert these propositions nor to order that the acts they name be carried out; rather, the point is to express my sorrow or my pleasure about the state of affairs specified in the propositional content, the truth of which I presuppose.[2] Now something very much like these distinctions carries over to Intentional states. If my beliefs turn out to be wrong, it is my beliefs and not the world which is at fault, as is shown by the fact that I can correct the situation simply by changing my beliefs. It is the responsibility of the belief, so to speak, to match the world, and where the match fails I repair the situation by changing the belief. But if I fail to carry out my intentions or if my desires are unfulfilled I cannot in that way correct the situation by simply changing the intention or desire. In these cases it is, so to speak, the fault of the world if it fails to match the intention or the desire, and I cannot fix things up by saying it was a mistaken intention or desire in a way that I can fix things up by saying it was a mistaken belief. Beliefs like statements can be true or false, and we might say they have the "mind-to-world" direction of fit. Desires and intentions, on the other hand, cannot be true or false, but can be complied with, fulfilled, or carried out, and we might say that they have the "world-to-mind" direction of fit. Furthermore there are also Intentional states that have the null direction of fit. If I am sorry that I insulted you or pleased that you won the prize, then, though my sorrow contains a belief that I insulted you and a wish that I hadn't insulted you and my pleasure contains a belief that you won the prize and a wish that you won the prize, my sorrow and pleasure can't be true or false in the way that my beliefs can, nor fulfilled in the way my desires can. My sorrow and pleasure may be appropriate or inappropriate depending on whether or not the mind-to-world direction of fit of the

---

2 Since fitting is a symmetrical relationship it might seem puzzling that there can be different *directions* of fit. If *a* fits *b*, *b* fits *a*. Perhaps it will alleviate this worry to consider an uncontroversial nonlinguistic case: If Cinderella goes into a shoe store to buy a new pair of shoes, she takes her foot size as given and seeks shoes to fit (shoe-to-foot direction of fit). But when the prince seeks the owner of the shoe, he takes the shoe as given and seeks a foot to fit the shoe (foot-to-shoe direction of fit).

belief is really satisfied, but my sorrow and pleasure don't in that way have any direction of fit. I will have more to say about these complex Intentional states later.

3. A third connection between Intentional states and speech acts is that, in the performance of each illocutionary act with a propositional content, we express a certain Intentional state with that propositional content, and that Intentional state is the sincerity condition of that type of speech act. Thus, for example, if I make the statement that *p*, I express a belief that *p*. If I make a promise to do *A*, I express an intention to do *A*. If I give an order to you to do *A*, I express a wish or a desire that you should do *A*. If I apologize for doing something, I express sorrow for doing that thing. If I congratulate you on something, I express pleasure or satisfaction about that something. All of these connections, between illocutionary acts and expressed Intentional sincerity conditions of the speech acts are internal; that is, the expressed Intentional state is not just an accompaniment of the performance of the speech act. The performance of the speech act is necessarily an expression of the corresponding Intentional state, as is shown by a generalization of Moore's paradox. You can't say, "It's snowing but I don't believe it's snowing", "I order you to stop smoking but I don't want you to stop smoking", "I apologize for insulting you, but I am not sorry that I insulted you", "Congratulations on winning the prize, but I am not glad that you won the prize", and so on. All of these sound odd for the same reason. The performance of the speech act is *eo ipso* an expression of the corresponding Intentional state; and, consequently, it is logically odd, though not self-contradictory, to perform the speech act and deny the presence of the corresponding Intentional state.[3]

Now to say that the Intentional state which constitutes the sincerity condition is expressed in the performance of the speech act is not to say that one always has to have the Intentional state that one expresses. It is always possible to lie or otherwise perform

---

3 The exceptions that one can construct to this principle are cases where one dissociates oneself from one's speech act, as in, e.g., "It is my duty to inform you that *p*, but I don't really believe that *p*" or "I order you to attack those fortifications, but I don't really want you to do it". In such cases it is as if one were mouthing a speech act on someone else's behalf. The speaker utters the sentence but dissociates himself from the commitments of the utterance.

an insincere speech act. But a lie or other insincere speech act consists in performing a speech act, and thereby expressing an Intentional state, where one does not have the Intentional state that one expresses. Notice that the parallelism between illocutionary acts and their expressed Intentional sincerity conditions is remarkably close: In general, the direction of fit of the illocutionary act and that of the sincerity condition is the same, and in those cases where the illocutionary act has no direction of fit the truth of the propositional content is presupposed, and the corresponding Intentional state contains a belief. For example, if I apologize for stepping on your cat, I express remorse for stepping on your cat. Neither the apology nor the remorse has a direction of fit, but the apology presupposes the truth of the proposition that I stepped on your cat, and the remorse contains a belief that I stepped on your cat.

4. The notion of conditions of satisfaction applies quite generally to both speech acts and Intentional states in cases where there is a direction of fit. We say, for example, that a statement is true or false, that an order is obeyed or disobeyed, that a promise is kept or broken. In each of these we ascribe success or failure of the illocutionary act to match reality in the particular direction of fit provided by the illocutionary point. To have an expression, we might label all of these conditions "conditions of satisfaction" or "conditions of success". So we will say that a statement is satisfied if and only if it is true, an order is satisfied if and only if it is obeyed, a promise is satisfied if and only if it is kept, and so on. Now, this notion of satisfaction clearly applies to Intentional states as well. My belief will be satisfied if and only if things are as I believe them to be, my desires will be satisfied if and only if they are fulfilled, my intentions will be satisfied if and only if they are carried out. That is, the notion of satisfaction seems to be intuitively natural to both speech acts and Intentional states and to apply quite generally, wherever there is a direction of fit.[4]

What is crucially important to see is that for every speech act that has a direction of fit *the speech act will be satisfied if and only if the expressed psychological state is satisfied*, and *the conditions of satisfaction of*

---

4 There are some interesting puzzling cases like doubting that *p* or wondering whether *p*. Shall we say that my doubt that *p* is satisfied if *p*? Or if not *p*? Or what?

speech act and expressed psychological state are identical. Thus, for example, my statement will be true if and only if the expressed belief is correct, my order will be obeyed if and only if the expressed wish or desire is fulfilled, and my promise will be kept if and only if my expressed intention is carried out. Furthermore, notice that just as the conditions of satisfaction are internal to the speech act, so the conditions of satisfaction of the Intentional state are internal to the Intentional state. Part of what makes my statement that snow is white the statement that it is, is that it has those truth conditions and not others. Similarly part of what makes my wish that it were raining the wish it is, is that certain things will satisfy it and certain other things will not.

All of these four connections between Intentional states and speech acts naturally suggest a certain picture of Intentionality: every Intentional state consists of a representative content in a certain psychological mode. Intentional states represent objects and states of affairs in the same sense that speech acts represent objects and states of affairs (though, to repeat, they do it by different means and in a different way). Just as my statement that it is raining is a representation of a certain state of affairs, so my belief that it is raining is a representation of the same state of affairs. Just as my order to Sam to leave the room is about Sam and represents a certain action on his part, so my desire that Sam should leave the room is about Sam and represents a certain action on his part. The notion of representation is conveniently vague. As applied to language we can use it to cover not only reference, but predication and truth conditions or conditions of satisfaction generally. Exploiting this vagueness we can say that Intentional states with a propositional content and a direction of fit represent their various conditions of satisfaction in the same sense that speech acts with a propositional content and a direction of fit represent their conditions of satisfaction.

If we are going to allow ourselves to use notions like "representation" and "conditions of satisfaction" they will require some further clarification. There is probably no more abused a term in the history of philosophy than "representation", and my use of this term differs both from its use in traditional philosophy and from its use in contemporary cognitive psychology and artificial intelligence. When I say, for example, that a belief is a representation I am most emphatically not saying that a belief is a kind of picture, nor am I endorsing the *Tractatus* account of meaning, nor am I saying that a belief re-presents something that has been presented before, nor am I saying that a belief has a meaning, nor am I saying that it is a kind of thing from which one reads off its conditions of satisfaction by scrutinizing it. The sense of "representation" in question is meant to be entirely exhausted by the analogy with speech acts: the sense of "represent" in which a belief represents its conditions of satisfaction is the same sense in which a statement represents its conditions of satisfaction. To say that a belief is a representation is simply to say that it has a propositional content and a psychological mode, that its pro-positional content determines a set of conditions of satisfaction under certain aspects, that its psychological mode determines a direction of fit of its propositional content, in a way that all of these notions – propositional content, direction of fit, etc. – are explained by the theory of speech acts. Indeed, as far as anything I have so far said is concerned, we could in principle dispense with the terms "representation" and "represent" altogether in favor of these other notions, since there is nothing ontological about my use of "representation". It is just a shorthand for this constellation of logical notions borrowed from the theory of speech acts. (Later on I will discuss some differences between Intentional states and speech acts.)

Furthermore, my use of the notion of representation differs from its use in contemporary artificial intelligence and cognitive psychology. For me a representation is defined by its content and its mode, not by its formal structure. Indeed, I have never seen any clear sense to the view that every mental representation must have a formal structure in the sense, for example, in which sentences have a formal syntactic structure. Leaving out some complications (concerning Network and Background) which will emerge later, at this preliminary stage of the investigation the formal relations between these various notions can be stated as follows: every Intentional state consists of an *Intentional content* in a *psychological mode*. Where that content is a whole proposition and where there is a direction of fit, the Intentional content determines the *conditions of satisfaction*. Conditions of satisfaction are those conditions which, as determined by the Intentional content, must obtain if the state is to be satisfied. For this reason the *specification* of the content is already a *specification* of the conditions of satisfaction. Thus, if I have a belief that it is raining, the content of my belief is: that it is raining. And the conditions of satisfaction are: that it is raining – and not, for example, that the ground is wet or that water is falling out of the sky. Since all representation – whether done by the mind, language, pictures or anything else – is *always* under certain aspects and not others, the conditions of satisfaction are represented under certain aspects.

The expression "conditions of satisfaction" has the usual process–product ambiguity as between the *requirement* and the *thing required*. So, for example, if I believe that it is raining then the conditions of satisfaction of my belief are that it should be the case *that it is raining* (requirement). That is what my belief requires in order that it be a true belief. And if my belief actually is a true belief then there will be a certain condition in the world, namely the condition *that it is raining* (thing required), which is the condition of satisfaction of my belief, i.e., the condition in the world which actually satisfies my belief. I think this ambiguity is quite harmless, indeed useful, provided that one is aware of it from the start. However, in some of the commentaries on my earlier works on Intentionality, it has led to misunderstandings;[5] so in contexts where the two senses might seem to lead to misunderstandings, I will mark the two senses explicitly.

Leaving out the various qualifications we might summarize this brief preliminary account of Intentionality by saying that the key to understanding representation is conditions of satisfaction. Every Intentional state with a direction of fit is a representation of its conditions of satisfaction.

III. SOME APPLICATIONS AND EXTENSIONS OF THE THEORY

As soon as one states these views a whole host of questions come crowding in: What shall we say about those Intentional states that do not have a direction of fit? Are they representations too? And, if

---

5 In, e.g., J. M. Mohanty, 'Intentionality and noema', *Journal of Philosophy*, vol. 78, no. 11 (November 1981), p. 714.

so, what are their conditions of satisfaction? And what about fantasy and imagination? What do they represent? And what about the ontological status of all this stuff – are these Intentional states mysterious mental entities and have we not also populated the world with 'states of affairs' in order to satisfy these mental entities? And what about intensionality-with-an-s, how does it fit in? And what about the traditional notion of an "Intentional object" with its alleged "intentional inexistence" (Brentano)? Furthermore there are some more skeptical objections. Surely, one might object, every representation requires some intentional act on the part of an agent who does the representing. Representing requires a representer and an intentional act of representation and therefore representation requires Intentionality and cannot be used to explain it. And more ominously, haven't the various arguments about the causal theory of reference shown that these mental entities 'in the head' are insufficient to show how language and mind refer to things in the world?

Well, one can't answer all questions at once, and in this section I will confine myself to answering a few of these questions in such a way as to extend and apply the preliminary statement of the theory. My aim is double. I want to show how this approach to Intentionality answers certain traditional philosophical difficulties and in so doing I want to extend and develop the theory.

1. One advantage to this approach, by no means a minor one, is that it enables us to distinguish clearly between the logical properties of Intentional states and their ontological status; indeed, on this account, the question concerning the logical nature of Intentionality is not an ontological problem at all. What, for example, is a belief really? The traditional answers to this assume that the question asks about the ontological category into which beliefs fit, but what is important as far as the Intentionality of belief is concerned is not its ontological category but its logical properties. Some of the favorite traditional answers are that a belief is a modification of a Cartesian ego, Humean ideas floating around in the mind, causal dispositions to behave in certain ways, or a functional state of a system. I happen to think that all of these answers are false, but for present purposes the important thing to note is that they are answers to a different question. If the question "What is a belief really?" is taken to mean: what is a belief *qua belief*?,

then the answer has to be given, at least in part, in terms of the logical properties of belief: a belief is a propositional content in a certain psychological mode, its mode determines a mind-to-world direction of fit, and its propositional content determines a set of conditions of satisfaction. Intentional states have to be characterized in Intentional terms if we are not to lose sight of their intrinsic Intentionality. But if the question is "What is the mode of existence of beliefs and other Intentional states?" then from everything we currently know about how the world works the answer is: Intentional states are both caused by and realized in the structure of the brain. And the important thing in answering this second question is to see *both* the fact that Intentional states stand in *causal* relations to the neurophysiological (as well as, of course, standing in causal relations to other Intentional states), and the fact that Intentional states are *realized in* the neurophysiology of the brain. Dualists, who correctly perceive the causal role of the mental, think for that very reason they must postulate a separate ontological category. Many physicalists who correctly perceive that all we have in our upper skulls is a brain think that for that reason they must deny the causal efficacy of the mental aspects of the brain or even the existence of such irreducible mental aspects. I believe that both of these views are mistaken. They both attempt to *solve* the mind–body problem when the correct approach is to see that there is no such problem. The "mind–body problem" is no more a real problem than the "stomach–digestion problem". (More about this in Chapter 10.)

At this stage the question of how Intentional states are realized in the ontology of the world is no more a relevant question for us to answer than it is relevant for us to answer the analogous questions about how a certain linguistic act is realized. A linguistic act can be realized in speaking or in writing, in French or in German, on a teletype or a loudspeaker or a movie screen or a newspaper. But such forms of realization do not matter to their logical properties. We would, with justification, regard someone who was obsessed by the question whether speech acts were identical with physical phenomena such as sound waves as having missed the point. The forms of realization of an Intentional state are just as irrelevant to its logical properties as the forms in which a speech act is realized are irrelevant to its logical properties. The logical properties of Intentional states arise from their being representations, and the point is that they can, like linguistic entities, have logical properties in a way that stones and trees cannot have logical properties (though statements about stones and trees can have logical properties) because Intentional states, like linguistic entities and unlike stones and trees, are representations.

Wittgenstein's famous problem about intention – When I raise my arm what is left over if I subtract the fact that my arm goes up?[6] – resists solution only as long as we insist on an ontological answer. Given the non-ontological approach to Intentionality suggested here, the answer is quite simple. What is left is an Intentional content – that my arm goes up as a result of this intention in action (see Chapter 3) – in a certain psychological mode – the intentional mode. To the extent that we find ourselves dissatisfied with this answer I believe that our dissatisfaction reveals that we have a mistaken model of Intentionality; we are still searching for a thing to correspond to the word "intention". But the only thing that could correspond is an intention, and to know what an intention is, or what any other Intentional state with a direction of fit is, we do not need to know its ultimate ontological category but rather we need to know: first, what are its conditions of satisfaction; second, under what aspect(s) are those conditions represented by the Intentional content; and third, what is the psychological mode – belief, desire, intention, etc. – of the state in question? To know the second of these is already to know the first, since conditions of satisfaction are always represented under certain aspects; and a knowledge of the third is sufficient to give us a knowledge of the direction of fit between the representative content and the conditions of satisfaction.

2. A second advantage of this approach is that it gives us a very simple answer to the traditional ontological problems about the status of Intentional objects: an Intentional object is just an object like any other; it has no peculiar ontological status at all. To call something an Intentional object is just to say that it is what some Intentional state is about. Thus, for example, if Bill admires President Carter, then the Intentional object of his admiration is

6 *Philosophical Investigations* (Oxford: Basil Blackwell, 1953), Part I, para. 621.

President Carter, the actual man and not some shadowy intermediate entity between Bill and the man. In both the case of speech
acts and the case of Intentional states, if there is no object that
satisfies the propositional or the representative content, then the
speech act and the Intentional state cannot be satisfied. In such
cases, just as there is no "referred-to object" of the speech act, so
there is no "Intentional object" of the Intentional state: if nothing
satisfies the referential portion of the representative content then
the Intentional state does not have an Intentional object. Thus, for
example, the statement that the King of France is bald cannot be
true, because there is no King of France, and similarly the belief
that the King of France is bald cannot be true, because there is no
King of France. The order to the King of France to be bald and the
wish that the King of France were bald both necessarily fail of
satisfaction and both for the same reason: there is no King of
France. In such cases there is no "Intentional object" of the
Intentional state and no "referred-to object" of the statement. The
fact that our statements may fail to be true because of reference
failure no longer inclines us to suppose that we must erect a
Meinongian entity for such statements to be about. We realize that
they have a propositional content which nothing satisfies, and in
that sense they are not "about" anything. But in exactly the same
way I am suggesting that the fact that our Intentional states may
fail to be satisfied because there is no object referred to by their
content should no longer puzzle us to the point where we feel
inclined to erect an intermediate Meinongian entity or Intentional
object for them to be about. An Intentional state has a representative content, but it is not about or directed at its representative
content. Part of the difficulty here derives from "about", which
has both an extensional and an intensional-with-an-s-reading. In
one sense (the intensional-with-an-s), the statement or belief that
the King of France is bald is about the King of France, but in that
sense it does not follow that there is some object which they are
about. In another sense (the extensional) there is no object which
they are about because there is no King of France. On my account
it is crucial to distinguish between the *content* of a belief (i.e., a
proposition) and the *objects* of a belief (i.e., ordinary objects).

Of course, some of our Intentional states are exercises in fantasy
and imagination, but analogously some of our speech acts are

fictional. And just as the possibility of fictional discourse, itself a product of fantasy and imagination, does not force us to erect a class of "referred to" or "described" objects different from ordinary objects but supposedly the objects of all discourse, so I am suggesting that the possibility of fantasy and imaginative forms of Intentionality does not force us to believe in the existence of a class of "Intentional objects", different from ordinary objects, but supposedly the objects of all our Intentional states. I am not saying there are no problems about fantasy and imagination, what I am arguing rather is that the problems are of a piece with the problems of analyzing fictional discourse.

In fictional discourse we have a series of pretended (as if, make-believe) speech acts, usually pretended assertives, and the fact that the speech act is only pretended breaks the word-to-world commitments of the normal assertive. The speaker is not committed to the truth of his fictional assertions in the way that he is committed to the truth of his normal assertions. Now similarly in imagination the agent has a series of representations, but the mind-to-world direction of fit is broken by the fact that the representative contents are not contents of beliefs but are simply entertained. Fantasies and imaginings have contents and thus they are as if they had conditions of satisfaction, in the same way that a pretended (i.e., fictional) assertion has a content and therefore is as if it had truth conditions, but in both cases the commitments to the conditions of satisfaction are deliberately suspended. It is not a failure of a fictional assertion that it is not true and it is not a failure of a state of imagination that nothing in the world corresponds to it.[7]

3. If I am right in thinking that Intentional states consist of representative contents in the various psychological modes, then it is at least misleading, if not simply a mistake, to say that a belief, for example, is a two-term *relation* between a believer and a proposition. An analogous mistake would be to say that a statement is a two-term relation between a speaker and a proposition. One should say rather that a proposition is not the *object* of a statement or belief but rather its *content*. The content of the statement or belief

---

7 For further discussion of the problems of fiction, see 'The logical status of fictional discourse', in Searle, *Expression and Meaning*. pp. 58–75.

that de Gaulle was French is the proposition that de Gaulle was French. But that proposition is not what the statement or belief is about or is directed at. No, the statement or belief is about de Gaulle and it represents him as being French, and it is about de Gaulle and represents him as being French because it has the propositional content and the mode of representation – illocutionary or psychological – that it has. In the way that "John hit Bill" describes a relation between John and Bill such that John's hitting is directed at Bill, "John believes that *p*" does not describe a relation between John and *p* such that John's believing is directed at *p*. It would be more accurate to say in the case of statements that the statement is *identical* with the proposition, construed as stated; and in the case of belief the belief is *identical* with the proposition construed as believed. There is indeed a relation ascribed when one ascribes an Intentional state to a person, but it is not a relation between a person and a proposition, rather it is a relation of representation between the Intentional state and the things represented by it; only remember, as with representations in general, it is possible for there to be the Intentional state without there actually being anything that satisfies it. The muddled view that statements of propositional attitudes describe a relation between an agent and a proposition is not a harmless manner of speaking; it is rather the first step in the series of confusions that leads to the view that there is a basic distinction between *de re* and *de dicto* Intentional states. I will discuss this view in Chapter 8.[8]

4. An Intentional state only determines its conditions of satisfaction – and thus only is the state that it is – given its position in a *Network* of other Intentional states and against a *Background* of practices and preintentional assumptions that are neither themselves Intentional states nor are they parts of the conditions of satisfaction of Intentional states. To see this, consider the following example. Suppose there was a particular moment at which Jimmy Carter first formed the desire to run for the Presidency of the United States, and suppose further that this Intentional state was realized according to everybody's favorite theories of the ontology of the mental: he said to himself "I want to

---

8 Indeed, the Russellian terminology of 'propositional attitude' is a source of confusion since it implies that a belief, for example, is an attitude toward or about a proposition.

run for the Presidency of the United States"; he had a certain neural configuration in a certain part of his brain which realized his desire, he thought wordlessly and with fierce resolve: "I want to do it", etc. Now suppose further that exactly these same type-identical realizations of the mental state occurred in the mind and brain of a Pleistocene man living in a hunter-gatherer society of thousands of years ago. He had a type-identical neural configuration to that which corresponded to Carter's desire, he found himself uttering the phonetic sequence, "I want to run for the Presidency of the United States", etc. All the same, however type-identical the two realizations might be, the Pleistocene man's mental state could not have been the desire to run for the Presidency of the United States. Why not? Well, to put it as an understatement, the circumstances were not appropriate. And what does that mean? To answer that, let us explore briefly what has to be the case in order that Carter's state could have had the conditions of satisfaction that it did. In order to have the desire to run for the Presidency, that desire has to be embedded in a whole Network of other Intentional states. It is tempting but wrong to think that these can be exhaustively described as logical consequences of the first desire – propositions that have to be satisfied in order that the original be satisfied. Some of the Intentional states in the Network are in that way logically related, but not all of them. In order that his desire be a desire to run for the Presidency he must have a whole lot of beliefs such as: the belief that the United States is a republic, that it has a presidential system of government, that it has periodic elections, that these involve principally a contest between the candidates of two major parties, the Republicans and the Democrats, that these candidates are chosen at nominating conventions, and so on indefinitely (but not infinitely). Furthermore these Intentional states only have their conditions of satisfaction, and the whole Intentional Network only functions, against a Background of what I will, for want of a better term, call nonrepresentational mental capacities. Certain fundamental ways of doing things and certain sorts of know-how about the way things work are presupposed by any such form of Intentionality.

I am really making two claims here, and they need to be distinguished. I am claiming first that Intentional states are in general parts of Networks of Intentional states and only have their conditions of satisfaction relative to their position in the Network. Versions of this view, generally called "holism", are quite common in contemporary philosophy; indeed a certain effortless holism is something of a current philosophical orthodoxy. But I am also making a second, much more controversial claim: in addition to the Network of representations, there is also a Background of nonrepresentational mental capacities; and, in general, representations only function, they only have the conditions of satisfaction that they do, against this nonrepresentational Background. The implications of this second claim are far reaching, but both the argument for it and the exploration of its consequences must wait until Chapter 5. One immediate consequence of both theses is that Intentional states do not neatly individuate. How many beliefs do I have exactly? There is no definite answer to that question. Another consequence is that the conditions of satisfaction of Intentional states are not independently determined, but depend on other states in the Network and on the Background.

5. This account enables us to propose a solution to a traditional problem in the philosophy of mind; the problem can be put in the form of an objection to my account: "We cannot explain Intentionality in terms of representation because in order for there to be a representation there must be some agent who *uses* some entity – a picture or a sentence or some other object – as a representation. Thus if a belief is a representation it must be because some agent *uses* the belief as a representation. But this offers us no account whatever of belief because we are not told what the agent *does* in order to use his belief as a representation, and furthermore the theory requires a mysterious homunculus with its own Intentionality in order that it can use the beliefs as representations; and if we follow this through it will require an infinite regress of homunculi, since each homunculus has to have further Intentional states in order to use the original Intentional states as representations or indeed in order to do anything." Dennett, who thinks this is a genuine problem, calls this "Hume's problem" and believes that the solution is to postulate whole armies of progressively stupider homunculi![9] I do not think it is a

9 D. Dennett, *Brainstorms* (Montgomery, Vermont: Bradford Books, 1978), pp. 122–5.

genuine problem and the account I have presented so far enables us to see the way to its dissolution. On my account, the Intentional content which determines the conditions of satisfaction is internal to the Intentional state: there is no way the agent can have a belief or a desire without it having its conditions of satisfaction. For example, part of what it is to have the conscious belief that it is raining is to be conscious that the belief is satisfied if it is raining and not satisfied if it isn't. But that the belief has those conditions of satisfaction is not something imposed on the belief by its being *used* in one way rather than another, for the belief is not in that sense *used* at all. A belief is intrinsically a representation in this sense: it simply consists in an Intentional content and a psychological mode. The content determines its conditions of satisfaction, and that mode determines that those conditions of satisfaction are represented with a certain direction of fit. It does not require some outside Intentionality in order to become a representation, because if it is a belief it already intrinsically is a representation. Nor does it require some nonintentional entity, some formal or syntactical object, associated with the belief which the agent uses to produce the belief. The false premise in the argument in short is the one that says that in order for there to be a representation there must be some agent who *uses* some entity as a representation. This is true of pictures and sentences, i.e., of derived Intentionality, but not of Intentional states. We might wish to restrict the term "representation" to those cases such as pictures and sentences where we can make a distinction between the entity and its representative content, but this is not a distinction we can make for beliefs and desires *qua* beliefs and desires because the representative content of the belief or the desire isn't in that way separable from the belief or desire. To say that the agent is conscious of the conditions of satisfaction of his conscious beliefs and desires is not to say that he has to have second order Intentional states about his first order states of belief and desire. If it were, we would indeed get an infinite regress. Rather, the consciousness of the conditions of satisfaction is part of the conscious belief or the desire, since the Intentional content is internal to the states in question.

6. This account of Intentionality suggests a very simple account of the relationship between Intentionality-with-a-t and intensionality-with-an-s. Intensionality-with-an-s is a property of a

certain class of sentences, statements, and other linguistic entities. A sentence is said to be intensional-with-an-s if it fails to satisfy certain tests for extensionality, tests such as substitutability of identicals and existential generalization. A sentence such as "John believes that King Arthur slew Sir Lancelot" is usually said to be intensional-with-an-s because it has at least one interpretation where it can be used to make a statement which does not permit existential generalization over the referring expressions following "believes", and does not permit substitutability of expressions with the same reference, *salva veritate*. Traditionally the puzzles about such sentences have concerned how it can be the case that their use to make a statement does not permit the standard logical operations if, as seems to be the case, the words contained in the sentences have the meanings they normally have and if the logical properties of a sentence are a function of its meaning, and its meaning in turn is a function of the meaning of its component words. The answer suggested by the foregoing account, an answer which I will develop in Chapter 7, is simply that since the sentence "John believes that King Arthur slew Sir Lancelot" is used to make a statement about an Intentional state, namely John's belief, and since an Intentional state is a representation, then the statement is a representation of a representation; and therefore, the truth conditions of the statement will depend on the features of the representation being represented, in this case the features of John's belief, and not on the features of the objects or state of affairs represented by John's belief. That is, since the statement is a representation of a representation, its truth conditions do not, in general, include the truth conditions of the representation being represented. John's belief can only be true if there was such a person as King Arthur and such a person as Sir Lancelot, and if the former slew the latter; but my statement that John believes that King Arthur slew Sir Lancelot has an interpretation where it can be true if none of these truth conditions holds. Its truth requires only that John has a belief and that the words following "believes" in the sentence accurately express the representative content of his belief. In that sense, my statement about his belief is not so much a *representation* of a representation, as a *presentation* of a representation, since in reporting his belief I present its content without committing myself to its truth conditions.

One of the most pervasive confusions in contemporary philosophy is the mistaken belief that there is some close connection, perhaps even an identity, between intensionality-with-an-s and Intentionality-with-a-t. Nothing could be further from the truth. They are not even remotely similar. Intentionality-with-a-t is that property of the mind (brain) by which it is able to represent other things; intensionality-with-an-s is the failure of certain sentences, statements, etc., to satisfy certain logical tests for extensionality. The only connection between them is that some sentences about Intentionality-with-a-t are intensional-with-an-s, for the reasons that I have just given.

The belief that there is something inherently intensional-with-an-s about Intentionality-with-a-t derives from a mistake which is apparently endemic to the methods of linguistic philosophy – confusion of features of reports with features of the things reported. Reports of Intentional-with-a-t states are characteristically intensional-with-an-s reports. But it does not follow from this, nor is it in general the case, that Intentional-with-a-t states are themselves intensional-with-an-s. The report that John believes that King Arthur killed Sir Lancelot is indeed an intensional-with-an-s report, but John's belief itself is not intensional. It is completely extensional: It is true iff there is a unique x such that $x =$ King Arthur, and there is a unique y such that $y =$ Sir Lancelot, and x killed y. That is as extensional as anything can get. It is often said, for reasons that are totally confused, that all Intentional entities such as propositions and mental states are somehow intensional-with-an-s. But this is simply a mistake, which derives from confusing properties of reports with properties of the things reported. Some Intentional states are, indeed, intensional-with-an-s, as the next two sections will show, but there is nothing inherently intensional-with-an-s about Intentionality-with-a-t. John's belief is extensional, even though my statement about his belief is intensional.

But what about conditions of satisfaction? Are they intensional or extensional? A great deal of philosophical confusion is contained in this question. If we think of conditions of satisfaction as the features of the world that satisfy or would satisfy an Intentional state then it is strictly senseless to ask if they are intensional or extensional. If I have a true belief that it is raining, then certain features of the world make my belief true, but it makes no sense to ask of those features whether they are intensional or extensional. What the question is trying to ask is: Are the *specifications* of conditions of satisfaction of Intentional states intensional or extensional? And the answer to that question depends on how they are specified. The conditions of satisfaction of John's belief that Caesar crossed the Rubicon are

1. Caesar crossed the Rubicon,

and 1 by itself is extensional. But 1 does not specify the conditions *as* conditions of satisfaction. It, thus, differs from

2. The conditions of satisfaction of John's belief are that Caesar crossed the Rubicon.

2, unlike 1, is intensional and the difference is that 1 states the conditions of satisfaction, while 2 states *that* they are conditions. 1 is a representation simpliciter; 2 is a representation of a representation.

7. We originally introduced the notion of Intentionality-with-a-t in such a way that it applied to mental states and the notion of intensionality-with-an-s in such a way that it applied to sentences and other linguistic entities. But it is now easy to see, given our characterization of Intentionality-with-a-t and its relations to intensionality-with-an-s, how to extend each notion to cover both mental and linguistic entities.

(a) The intensionality-with-an-s of statements about Intentionality-with-a-t states derives from the fact that such statements are representations of representations. But, since Intentional-with-a-t states are representations, there is nothing to prevent there being Intentional-with-a-t states that are also representations of representations, and thus such states would share the feature of intensionality-with-an-s that is possessed by the corresponding sentences and statements. For example, just as my statement that John believes that King Arthur slew Sir Lancelot is intensional-with-an-s because the statement is a representation of John's belief, so my belief that John believes that King Arthur slew Sir Lancelot is an intensional-with-an-s mental state because it is an Intentional state which is a representation of John's belief, and thus its satisfaction conditions depend on features of the representation being represented and not on the things represented by the original representation. But of course from the fact that my belief about John's belief is an intensional-with-an-s belief it does not follow that John's belief is an intensional-with-an-s belief. To repeat, his belief is extensional; my belief about his belief is intensional.

(b) So far I have tried to explain the Intentionality of mental states by appealing to our understanding of speech acts. But of course the feature of speech acts that I have been appealing to is precisely their representative properties, that is to say, their Intentionality-with-a-t. So the notion of Intentionality-with-a-t applies equally well both to mental states and to linguistic entities such as speech acts and sentences, not to mention maps, diagrams, laundry lists, pictures, and a host of other things.

And it is for this reason that the explanation of Intentionality offered in this chapter is not a logical analysis in the sense of giving necessary and sufficient conditions in terms of simpler notions. If we tried to treat the explanation as an analysis it would be hopelessly circular since the feature of speech acts that I have been using to explain the Intentionality of certain mental states is precisely the Intentionality of speech acts. In my view it is not possible to give a logical analysis of the Intentionality of the mental in terms of simpler notions, since Intentionality is, so to speak, a ground floor property of the mind, not a logically complex feature built up by combining simpler elements. There is no neutral standpoint from which we can survey the relations between Intentional states and the world and then describe them in non-Intentionalistic terms. Any explanation of Intentionality, there-fore, takes place within the circle of Intentional concepts. My strategy has been to use our understanding of how speech acts work to explain how the Intentionality of the mental works, but this now raises our next question: What is the relationship between the Intentionality of the mental and the Intentionality of the linguistic?

IV. MEANING

There is one obvious disanalogy between Intentional states and speech acts, which is suggested by the very terminology we have been employing. Mental states are states, and speech acts are acts, i.e., intentional performances. And this difference has an important consequence for the way that the speech act is related to its physical realization. The actual performance in which the speech act is made will involve the production (or use or presentation) of some physical entity, such as noises made through the mouth or marks on paper. Beliefs, fears, hopes, and desires on the other hand are intrinsically Intentional. To characterize them as beliefs, fears, hopes, and desires is already to ascribe Intentionality to them. But speech acts have a physical level of realization, *qua* speech acts, that is not intrinsically Intentional. There is nothing intrinsically Intentional about the products of the utterance act, that is, the noises that come out of my mouth or the marks that I make on paper. Now the problem of meaning in its most general form is the problem of how do we get from the physics to the semantics; that is to say, how do we get (for example) from the sounds that come out of my mouth to the illocutionary act? And the discussion so far in this chapter now gives us, I believe, a new way of seeing that question. From the point of view of this discussion, the problem of meaning can be posed as follows: How does the mind impose Intentionality on entities that are not intrinsically Intentional, on entities such as sounds and marks that are, construed in one way, just physical phenomena in the world like any other? An utterance can have Intentionality, just as a belief has Intentionality, but whereas the Intentionality of the belief is *intrinsic* the Intentionality of the utterance is *derived*. The question then is: How does it derive its Intentionality?

There is a double level of Intentionality in the performance of the speech act. There is first of all the Intentional state expressed, but then secondly there is the intention, in the ordinary and not technical sense of that word, with which the utterance is made. Now it is this second Intentional state, that is the intention with which the act is performed, that bestows the Intentionality on the physical phenomena. Well, how does it work? The development of an answer to that question has to wait until Chapter 6, but in broad outline the answer is this: The mind imposes Intentionality on entities that are not intrinsically Intentional by intentionally conferring the conditions of satisfaction of the expressed psychological state upon the external physical entity. The double level of

Intentionality in the speech act can be described by saying that by intentionally uttering something with a certain set of conditions of satisfaction, those that are specified by the essential condition for that speech act, I have made the utterance Intentional, and thus necessarily expressed the corresponding psychological state. I couldn't make a statement without expressing a belief or make a promise without expressing an intention because the essential condition on the speech act has as conditions of satisfaction the same conditions of satisfaction as the expressed Intentional state. So I impose Intentionality on my utterances by intentionally conferring on them certain conditions of satisfaction which are the conditions of satisfaction of certain psychological states. That also explains the internal connection between the essential condition and the sincerity condition on the speech act. The key to meaning is simply that it can be part of the conditions of satisfaction (in the sense of requirement) of my intention that its conditions of satisfaction (in the sense of things required) should themselves have conditions of satisfaction. Thus the double level.

"Meaning" is a notion that literally applies to sentences and speech acts but not in that sense to Intentional states. It makes good sense to ask, for example, what a sentence or utterance means, but it makes no sense to ask in that sense what a belief or a desire means. But why not, since both linguistic entity and Intentional state are Intentional? Meaning exists only where there is a distinction between Intentional content and the form of its externalization, and to ask for the meaning is to ask for an Intentional content that goes with the form of externalization. Thus it makes good sense to ask for the meaning of the sentence "Es regnet", and it makes good sense to ask for the meaning of John's statement, i.e., to ask what he meant; but it makes no sense to ask for the meaning of the belief that it is raining or for the meaning of the statement that it is raining: in the former case because there is no gulf between belief and Intentional content, and in the latter case because the gulf has already been bridged when we specify the content of the statement.

As usual, the syntactical and semantic features of the corresponding verbs provide us with useful hints as to what is going on. If I say something of the form "John believes that p", that sentence can stand on its own. But if I say "John means that p", that sentence seems to require or at least invite completion in the form "by uttering such-and-such" or "by saying such-and-such John means that *p*". John couldn't mean that *p* unless he was saying or doing something *by way of which* he meant that *p*, whereas John can simply believe that *p* without doing anything. Meaning that *p* isn't an Intentional state that can stand on its own in the way that believing that *p* is. In order to mean that *p*, there must be some overt action. When we come to "John stated that *p*" the overt action is made explicit. Stating is an act, unlike believing and meaning, which are not acts. Stating is an illocutionary act that, at another level of description, is an utterance act. It is the performance of the utterance act with a certain set of intentions that converts the utterance act into an illocutionary act and thus imposes Intentionality on the utterance. More about this in Chapter 6.

V. BELIEF AND DESIRE

Many philosophers think that belief and desire are somehow the basic Intentional states, and in this section I want to explore some of the reasons for and against claiming primacy for these two. I shall construe them very broadly to encompass, in the case of belief: feeling certain, having a hunch, supposing, and many other degrees of conviction; and, in the case of desire: wanting, wishing, lusting and hankering after, and many other degrees of desire. Notice initially that even in these lists there are differences other than mere degrees of intensity. It makes good sense to say of something I believe I have done

I wish I hadn't done it

but it is bad English to say

I want/desire I hadn't done it.

So in construing "desire" broadly we will need to allow for cases of "desire" directed at states of affairs known or believed to have occurred in the past, as when I wish I hadn't done something or am glad I did something else. Recognizing these departures from ordinary English, let us name two broad categories, which we will dub "Bel" and "Des", and see how basic they are. Let us see how far we can go with these categories corresponding roughly to parts of the great traditional categories of Cognition and Volition. Can we reduce other forms of Intentionality to Bel and Des? If so, we could not only simplify the analysis, but also eliminate altogether the forms of Intentionality that have no direction of fit since they would reduce to the two directions of fit of Bel and Des, and we could even eliminate the cases such as love and hate which do not have a whole proposition as Intentional content by showing that they reduce to complexes of Bel and Des.

In order to test this hypothesis we need first to establish that cases of Des, i.e., desiring, wanting, wishing, etc., have whole propositions as Intentional contents. This feature is concealed from us by the fact that in the surface structure of English we have sentences such as "I want your house" which appear to be analogous to "I like your house". But a simple syntactical argument will show that surface structure is misleading and that wanting is indeed a propositional attitude. Consider the sentence

I want your house next summer.

What does "next summer" modify? It can't be "want" for the sentence does not mean

I next – summer – want your house

since it is perfectly consistent to say

I now want your house next summer though by next summer I won't want your house.

What the sentence must mean is

I want (I *have* your house next summer)

and we can say that the adverbial phrase modifies the deep structure verb "have" or if we are reluctant to postulate such deep syntactic structures we can simply say that the semantic content of the sentence "I want your house" is: I want that I have your house. Since any occurrence of a sentence of the form "$S\left\{{\text{desires} \atop \text{wants}}\right\} X$" can take such modifiers we can conclude that all cases of Des are propositional attitudes, i.e., they all have whole propositions as Intentional contents.

Now back to our question, can we reduce all (some, many) Intentional states to Bel and Des? If we allow ourselves an apparatus of logical constants, modal operators, time indicators and implied propositional contents we can go a long way toward making many reductions, perhaps as far as we need to go for most analytical purposes, but I do not believe we can go all the way except in a very few cases. Consider fear. A man who fears that p must believe it is possible that p and he must want it to be the case that not p; thus

Fear $(p) \rightarrow$ Bel $(\diamond p)$ & Des $(\sim p)$

But are these equivalent? Is the following a necessary truth?

Bel $(\diamond p)$ & Des $(\sim p) \leftrightarrow$ Fear (p)

I think not, and a clear illustration is that, even given very strong beliefs and desires, such a combination of belief and desire does not add up to terror. Thus

Terror $(p) \neq$ Bel $(\diamond p)$ and Strong Des $(\sim p)$

I believe, for example, that an atomic war is possible and I very much want it not to occur, but I am not terrified that it will occur. Perhaps I ought to be terrified but I am not. Still, this componential analysis of complex states like fear deepens our understanding of Intentional states and their conditions of satisfaction. In one sense we want to say that the surface phenomenon of fear is satisfied iff the thing I fear comes to pass; but in a deeper sense there isn't any direction of fit to fear other than the belief and the desire, and indeed the desire is what counts because the belief is a presupposition of the fear and not its essence. The main thing about fear is wishing very much that the thing you fear won't happen while believing that it is all too possible that it will. And in this deeper sense my fear is satisfied iff the thing I fear does not happen, for that is what I wish – that it shouldn't happen.

Now let us apply these suggestions to other sorts of Intentional states. Expectation is the simplest case since, in one sense of "expectation", expectations are just beliefs about the future. Thus,

Expect $(p) \leftrightarrow$ Bel (Fut p)

Disappointment is more complicated. If I am disappointed that p I must previously have expected that *not p* and wanted that *not p* and now believe that *p*. Thus,

Disappointment (p) → pres Bel (p) & past Bel (fut ∼ p) & Des ($\sim p$)

Being sorry that p is also relatively simple:

Sorry (p) → Bel (p) & Des ($\sim p$)

Regret places a further restriction on sorrow in that the propositional content must concern things having to do with the person who regrets. I can for example regret not being able to come to your party but I can't regret that it is raining, even though I can be sorry that it is raining.

Regret (p) → Bel (p) & Bel (p is connected to me) & Des ($\sim p$)

Remorse adds the element of responsibility:

Remorse (p) → Bel (p) & Des ($\sim p$) & Bel (I am responsible for p)

Blame is like remorse, only possibly directed at someone else, thus,

Blame X for (p) → Bel (p) & Des ($\sim p$) & Bel (X is responsible for p)

On this account remorse necessarily involves blaming oneself. Pleasure, hope, pride, and shame are also fairly simple:

Being pleased that (p) → Bel (p) & Des (p)

Hope requires uncertainty about whether the hoped for state actually obtains. Thus,

Hope (p) → ∼ Bel (p) & ∼ Bel ($\sim p$) & Bel ($\Diamond p$) & Des (p)

Pride and shame require some connection with the agent, though it need not be as strong as responsibility since one can be proud or ashamed of the size of one's nose or of one's ancestors. Furthermore, shame involves, *ceteris paribus*, a desire to conceal, pride a desire to make known. Thus,

Pride (p) → Bel (p) & Des (p) & Bel (p is connected to me) & Des (others know that p)

Shame (p) → Bel (p) & Des ($\sim p$) & Bel (p is connected to me) & Des (p is concealed from others)

It is also easy to see how these analyses allow for the formal structure of second (third, *n*th) order Intentional states. One can be ashamed of one's desires; one can desire to be ashamed; one can be ashamed of one's desire to be ashamed, etc.

This list could obviously be continued and I leave it as a five finger exercise for the reader to continue it with states of his choice. The method is very simple. Take a specific type of Intentional state with a specific propositional content. Then ask yourself what you must believe and desire in order to have that Intentional state with that content. Even this short list suggests some significant generalizations about the primacy of Bel and Des. First, all of these affective states are more accurately construed as forms of desire, given a belief. That is, it seems a mistake to think of the formal structure of pride, hope, shame, remorse, etc., as simply a conjunction of belief and desire. Rather, all (except expectation) of the cases we have considered, as well as disgust, joy, panic, etc., seem to be more or less strong forms of negative and positive desire given or presupposing a belief. Thus, if I am joyful that I won the race, I have a case of

Strong Des (I won the race)

given

Bel (I won the race)

If I lose the belief, I lose the joy, and what remains is simply disappointment, i.e., a wish that I had won the race imposed on a frustrated belief. Furthermore, in addition to the logical relation of presupposition which is left out by treating the states as conjunctions of Bel and Des, there are also internal causal relations which the conjunction analysis ignores. For example, one sometimes feels ashamed *because* one believes that one has done something bad, even though the belief is also a logical presupposition in the sense that one couldn't have that feeling without that belief. And this leads to a third reason why we can't treat these states simply as conjunctions of Bel and Des. In many of these cases there are conscious feelings that are not captured by an analysis of the state into Bel and Des, which need not be conscious at all. Thus, if I am in panic, joyful, disgusted, or in terror, I must be in some conscious state in addition to having certain beliefs and desires. And to the extent that some of our examples do not require that I be in a conscious state, to that extent we are inclined to feel that the analysis into Bel and Des comes closer to being exhaustive. Thus, if I regret having done something, my regret may simply consist in my believing that I did it and wishing I hadn't done it. When I say that there is a conscious state, I do not mean there is always a 'raw feel' in addition to the belief and desire which we could simply carve off and examine on its own. Sometimes there is, as in those cases of terror where one gets a tight feeling in the pit of one's stomach. The feeling may continue for a time even after the fear has passed. But the conscious state need not be a bodily sensation; and in many cases, lust and disgust for example, the desire will be a part of the conscious state so there is no way to carve off the conscious state leaving only the Intentionality of belief and desire, that is, the conscious states that are parts of lust and disgust are conscious desires.

Perhaps the hardest case of all is intention. If I intend to do A, I must believe it possible for me to do A and I must in some sense want to do A. But we get only a very partial analysis of intention from the following:

Intend (I do A) → Bel ($\diamond$ I do A) & Des (I do A)

The extra element derives from the special causal role of intentions in producing our behavior and we will not be in a position to analyze this until Chapters 3 and 4.

But what about those states that apparently do not require whole propositions as contents, such as love, hate, and admiration. Even these cases involve sets of beliefs and desires, as can be seen from the absurdity of imagining a man who is madly in love but has no beliefs or desires whatever regarding the beloved person, not even a belief that such a person exists. A man in love must believe that the person he loves exists (or has existed, or will exist) and has certain traits, and he must have a complex of desires regarding the beloved, but there is no way to spell out the complex of those beliefs and desires as part of the definition of "love". Different sorts of traits can be the aspects under which someone is loved and lovers notoriously have widely differing sets of desires regarding the beloved. Admiration is less complicated and we can get somewhat further with it than we can with love and hate. If Jones admires Carter then he must believe that there is such a person as

Carter and that Carter has certain traits which Jones is glad that he has and which Jones finds good. But for any real live case of admiration this is hardly likely to be the whole story. Anyone who admires Carter might also wish that more people, perhaps himself included, were like Carter, that Carter will continue to have the traits he admires, etc.

The picture that is now beginning to emerge from this discussion is this. Our original explanation of Intentionality in terms of representation and conditions of satisfaction is not as restricted as might appear on the surface. Many cases which apparently don't have a direction of fit, and thus apparently don't have conditions of satisfaction contain beliefs and desires which have directions of fit and conditions of satisfaction. Joy and sorrow, for example, are feelings that don't reduce to Bel and Des but as far as their Intentionality is concerned, they have no Intentionality in addition to Bel and Des; in each case, their Intentionality is a form of desire, given certain beliefs. In the case of joy one believes one's desire is satisfied; in the case of sorrow one believes that it isn't. And even the nonpropositional cases are feelings, conscious or unconscious, whose Intentionality is in part explainable in terms of Bel and Des. The special *feelings* of love and hate are certainly not equivalent to Bel and Des, but at least a significant part of the Intentionality of love and hate is explainable in terms of Bel and Des.

The hypothesis in short that our brief discussion supports is not that all or even many forms of Intentionality *reduce* to Bel and Des – that is plainly false – but rather that all Intentional states, even those which do not have a direction of fit and those which do not have a whole proposition as content, nonetheless contain a Bel or a Des or both, and that in many cases the Intentionality of the state is explained by the Bel or the Des. If that hypothesis is true then the analysis of Intentionality in terms of representation of conditions of satisfaction under certain aspects and with a certain direction of fit is very general in its application and not simply confined to the central cases. To the extent that the reader finds this hypothesis plausible, he will find it plausible that this book offers the beginnings of a general theory of Intentionality; to the extent that he finds it implausible the account will simply be a special theory dealing with the large number of central cases.

In addition to the reasons for rejecting the conjunction analysis, the greatest limitations on explaining Intentionality in terms of Bel and Des seem to me, first, that the analysis is not fine grained enough to distinguish between Intentional states that are importantly different. For example, being annoyed that p, being sad that p, and being sorry that p are all cases of

$$\text{Bel } (p) \ \& \ \text{Des } (\sim p)$$

but they are clearly not the same states. Furthermore, with some states one cannot get very far with this sort of analysis. For example, if I am amused that the Democrats have lost the election, I must Bel that they have lost the election, but what else? I need have no Des's one way or the other, and I needn't even Bel that the whole situation is *au fond* amusing, even though I personally admit to being amused.

Nonetheless, I believe that the power and scope of an approach to Intentionality in terms of conditions of satisfaction will become more apparent as we turn in the next two chapters to what I take to be the biologically primary forms of Intentionality, perception and action. Their Intentional contents differ from beliefs and desires in a crucial respect: they have Intentional causation in their conditions of satisfaction and this will have consequences we cannot yet clearly state. Beliefs and desires are not the primary forms, rather they are etiolated forms of more primordial experiences in perceiving and doing. Intention, for example, is not a fancy form of desire; it would be more accurate to think of desire as a faded form of intention, intention with the Intentional causation bleached out.

Chapter 2

THE INTENTIONALITY OF PERCEPTION

I

Traditionally the "problem of perception" has been the problem of how our internal perceptual experiences are related to the external world. I believe we ought to be very suspicious of this way of formulating the problem, since the spatial metaphor for internal and external, or inner and outer, resists any clear interpretation. If my body including all of its internal parts is part of the external world, as it surely is, then where is the internal world supposed to be? In what space is it internal relative to the external world? In what sense exactly are my perceptual experiences 'in here' and the world 'out there'? Nonetheless these metaphors are persistent and perhaps even inevitable, and for that reason they reveal certain underlying assumptions we will need to explore.

My aim in this chapter is not, except incidentally, to discuss the traditional problem of perception, but rather to place an account of perceptual experiences within the context of the theory of Intentionality that was outlined in the last chapter. Like most philosophers who talk about perception, I will give examples mostly concerning vision, though the account, if correct, should be general in its application.

When I stand and look at a car, let us say a yellow station wagon, in broad daylight, at point blank range, with no visual impediments, I see the car. How does the seeing work? Well, there is a long story about how it works in physical optics and in neurophysiology, but that is not what I mean. I mean how does it work conceptually; what are the elements that go to make up the truth conditions of sentences of the form "x sees y" where x is a perceiver, human or animal, and y is, for example, a material object? When I see a car, or anything else for that matter, I have a certain sort of visual experience. In the visual perception of the car I don't

37

see the visual experience, I see the car; but in seeing the car I *have* a visual experience, and the visual experience is an experience *of* the car, in a sense of "of" we will need to explain. It is important to emphasize that though the visual perception always has as a component a visual experience, it is not the visual experience that is seen, in any literal sense of "see", for if I close my eyes the visual experience ceases, but the car, the thing I see, does not cease. Furthermore, in general it makes no sense to ascribe to the visual experience the properties of the thing that the visual experience is of, the thing that I see. For example, if the car is yellow and has a certain shape characteristic of a station wagon, then though my visual experience is of a yellow object in the shape of a station wagon it makes no sense to say my visual experience itself is yellow or that it is in the shape of a station wagon. Color and shape are properties accessible to vision, but though my visual experience is a component of any visual perception, the visual experience is not itself a visual object, it is not itself seen. If we try to deny this point we are placed in the absurd situation of identifying two yellow station wagon shaped things in the perceptual situation, the yellow station wagon and the visual experience.

In introducing the notion of a visual experience I am distinguishing between experience and perception in ways that will become clearer in the subsequent discussion. The notion of perception involves the notion of succeeding in a way that the notion of experience does not. Experience has to determine what counts as succeeding, but one can have an experience without succeeding, i.e., without perceiving.

But at this point the classical epistemologist will surely want to object as follows: Suppose there is no car there; suppose the whole thing is a hallucination; what do you see then? And the answer is that if there is no car there, then in the car line of business I see nothing. It may seem to me exactly as if I were seeing a car, but if there is no car I don't see anything. I may see background foliage or a garage or a street, but if I am having a hallucination of a car then I don't see a car or a visual experience or a sense datum or an impression or anything else, though I do indeed *have* the visual experience and the visual experience may be indistinguishable from the visual experience I would have had if I had actually seen a car.

Several philosophers have denied the existence of visual experiences. I think these denials are based on a misunderstanding of the issues involved, and I will discuss this question later. But at this stage, taking for granted that there are visual experiences, I want to argue for a point that has often been ignored in discussions of the philosophy of perception, namely that visual (and other sorts of perceptual) experiences have Intentionality. The visual experience is as much *directed at* or *of* objects and states of affairs in the world as any of the paradigm Intentional states that we discussed in the last chapter, such as belief, fear, or desire. And the argument for this conclusion is simply that the visual experience has conditions of satisfaction in exactly the same sense that beliefs and desires have conditions of satisfaction. I can no more separate this visual experience from the fact that it is an experience *of* a yellow station wagon than I can separate this belief from the fact that it is a belief that it is raining; the "of" of "experience of" is in short the "of" of Intentionality.[1] In both the cases of belief and visual experience I might be wrong about what states of affairs actually exist in the world. Perhaps I am having a hallucination and perhaps it isn't actually raining. But notice that in each case what counts as a mistake, whether a hallucination or a false belief, is already determined by the Intentional state or event in question. In the case of the belief, even if I am in fact mistaken, I know what must be the case in order that I not be mistaken, and to say that is simply to say that the Intentional content of the belief determines its conditions of satisfaction; it determines under what conditions the belief is true or false. Now exactly analogously I want to say that in the case of the visual experience, even if I am having a hallucination, I know what must be the case in order that the experience not be a hallucination, and to say that is simply to say that the Intentional content of the visual experience determines its conditions of satisfaction; it determines what must be the case in order that the experience not be a hallucination in exactly the same sense that the content of the belief determines its conditions of

1 As we noted in Chapter 2 ordinary language is misleading in this regard, for we speak of an experience of pain and an experience of redness, but in the former case the experience just is the pain and the "of" is not the "of" of Intentionality, and in the latter case the experience is not itself red, and the "of" is Intentional.

satisfaction. Suppose we ask ourselves, "What makes the presence or absence of rain even relevant to my belief that it is raining, since after all, the belief is just a mental state?" Now, analogously, we can ask, "What makes the presence or absence of a yellow station wagon even relevant to my visual experience, since, after all, the visual experience is just a mental event?" And the answer in both cases is that the two forms of mental phenomena, belief and visual experience, are intrinsically Intentional. Internal to each phenomenon is an Intentional content that determines its conditions of satisfaction. The argument that visual experiences are intrinsically Intentional, in sum, is that they have conditions of satisfaction which are determined by the content of the experience in exactly the same sense that other Intentional states have conditions of satisfaction which are determined by the content of the states. Now by drawing an analogy between visual experience and belief I do not wish to suggest that they are alike in all respects. Later on I will mention several crucial differences.

If we apply the conceptual apparatus developed in the last chapter we can state several important similarities between the Intentionality of visual perception and, for example, belief.

1. The content of the visual experience, like the content of the belief, is always equivalent to a whole proposition. Visual experience is never simply *of* an object but rather it must always be *that* such and such is the case. Whenever, for example, my visual experience is of a station wagon it must also be an experience, part of whose content is, for example, that there is a station wagon in front of me. When I say that the content of the visual experience is equivalent to a whole proposition I do not mean that it is linguistic but rather that the content requires the existence of a whole state of affairs if it is to be satisfied. It does not just make reference to an object. The linguistic correlate of this fact is that the verbal specification of the conditions of satisfaction of the visual experience takes the form of the verbal expression of a whole proposition and not just a noun phrase, but this does not imply that the visual experience is itself verbal. From the point of view of Intentionality, all seeing is seeing *that*: whenever it is true to say that *x* sees *y* it must be true that *x* sees that such and such is the case. Thus, in our earlier example, the content of the visual perception is not made explicit in the form

I have a visual experience of (a yellow station wagon)[2]

but a first step in making the content explicit would be, for example,

I have a visual experience (that there is a yellow station wagon there).

The fact that visual experiences have propositional Intentional contents is an immediate (and trivial) consequence of the fact that they have conditions of satisfaction, for conditions of satisfaction are always that such and such is the case.

There is an additionl syntactical argument for the same conclusion. Just as verbs of desire take temporal modifiers that require us to postulate an entire proposition as the content of the desire, so the verb "see" takes spatial modifiers that under natural interpretations require us to postulate an entire proposition as the content of the visual experience. When I say, for example, "I see a station wagon *in front of me*", I don't normally just mean that I see a station wagon which *also happens to be* in front of me but rather *I see that* there is a station wagon in front of me. An additional clue that the "see that" form expresses the Intentional content of the visual experience is that this form is intensional-with-an-s with respect to the possibility of substitution whereas third person statements of the form "*x* sees *y*" are (in general) extensional. When in third person reports of seeings we use the "sees that" form we are committed to reporting the content of the perception, how it seemed to the perceiver, in a way that we are not so committed by the use of a simple noun phrase as direct object of "see". Thus, for example,

Jones saw that the bank president was standing in front of the bank

together with the identity statements

---

2 Notice once again that when we are just specifying the Intentional content we cannot use expressions like "see" or "perceive" since they imply success, they imply that the conditions of satisfaction are in fact satisfied. To say I have a visual experience that there is a yellow station wagon there is just to specify the Intentional content. To say I see or perceive that there is a yellow station wagon there implies that the content is satisfied.

The bank president is the tallest man in town

and

The bank is the lowest building in town

do not entail

Jones saw that the tallest man in town was standing in front of the lowest building in town.

But

Jones saw the bank president

together with the identity statement does entail

Jones saw the tallest man in town.

The most obvious explanation of this distinction is that the "see that" form reports the Intentional content of the perception. When in third-person reports we say that an agent saw that p we are committed to reporting the Intentional content of the visual perception, but the "see x" form reports only the Intentional object and does not commit the reporter to the content, to the aspect under which the Intentional object was perceived.

Exactly the same point – the fact that a whole propositional content is the Intentional content of visual perception – is also illustrated by the following distinction:

Jones saw a yellow station wagon, but did not know it was a yellow station wagon

is perfectly consistent; but

Jones saw that there was a yellow station wagon in front of him but did not know that there was a yellow station wagon in front of him

is odd and perhaps even self-contradictory. The "see x" form does not commit the reporter to reporting how it seemed to the agent, but the "see that" form does, and a report of how it seemed to the agent is, in general, a specification of the Intentional content.

2. Visual perception, like belief, and unlike desire and intention, always has the mind-to-world direction of fit. If the conditions of

satisfaction are not in fact fulfilled, as in the case of hallucination, delusion, illusion, etc., it is the visual experience and not the world which is at fault. In such cases we say that "our senses deceive us" and though we do not describe our visual experiences as true or false (because these words are more appropriate when applied to certain sorts of representations, and visual experiences are more than just representations – a point I will come to in a minute) we do feel inclined to describe failure to achieve fit in terms such as "deceive", "mislead", "distort", "illusion", and "delusion"; and various philosophers have introduced the word "veridical" to describe success in achieving fit.

3. Visual experiences, like beliefs and desires, are characteristically identified and described in terms of their Intentional content. There is no way to give a complete description of my belief without saying what it is a belief *that* and similarly there is no way to describe my visual experience without saying what it is an experience *of*. The characteristic philosophical mistake in the case of visual experience has been to suppose that the predicates which specify the conditions of satisfaction of the visual experience are literally true of the experience itself. But, to repeat a point mentioned earlier, it is a category mistake to suppose that when I see a yellow station wagon the visual experience itself is also yellow and in the shape of a station wagon. Just as when I believe that it is raining I do not literally have a wet belief, so when I see something yellow I do not literrally have a yellow visual experience. One might as well say that my visual experience is six cylindered or that it gets twenty-two miles to the gallon as say that it is yellow or in the shape of a station wagon. One is tempted to the mistake of ascribing the latter (rather than the former) predicates to the visual experience, because the Intentional content specified by "yellow" and "in the shape of a station wagon" have greater immediacy to visual experiences than do the other predicates for reasons we will mention in the next section.

There are many things one can say about Intentional states and events which are not specifications of their Intentional contents and where the predicates are literally true of the states and events. One can say of a visual experience that it has a certain temporal duration or that it is pleasant or unpleasant, but these properties of the experience are not to be confused with its Intentional content, even though on occasion these same expressions might specify features of its Intentional content as well.

It is a bit difficult to know how one would argue for the existence of perceptual experiences to someone who denied their existence. It would be a bit like arguing for the existence of pains: if their existence is not obvious already, no philosophical argument could convince one. But I think by way of indirect argument one could show that the reasons philosophers have given for denying the existence of visual experiences can be answered. The first source of reluctance to speak of perceptual experiences is the fear that in recognizing such entities we are admitting sense data or some such, that is, we are admitting entities that somehow get between us and the real world. I have tried to show that a correct description of the Intentionality of visual experience does not have these consequences. The visual experience is not the object of visual perception, and the features which specify the Intentional content are not in general literally features of the experience. A second source of reluctance to concede that there are visual experiences (in, e.g., Merleau-Ponty[3]) is the fact that any attempt to focus our attention on the experience inevitably alters its character. As one proceeds through the active affairs of life one seldom concentrates one's attention on the flow of one's visual experiences, but rather on the things they are experiences of. This tempts us to think that, when we do focus our attention on the experience, we are bringing something into existence which was not there before, that visual experiences only exist as a result of adopting the 'analytic attitude' as when one does philosophy, neurophysiology, or impressionist painting. But this seems to me to misdescribe the situation. One does indeed alter the character (though not, in general, the content) of a visual experience by focussing one's attention on it, but it does not follow from this fact that the visual experience was not there all along. The fact that one shifts one's attention from the conditions of satisfaction of the visual experience to the experience itself does not show that the experience did not really exist prior to the shift in one's attention.

So far in this chapter I have argued for the following main

---

3 M. Merleau-Ponty, *The Phenomenology of Perception* (London: Routledge & Kegan Paul), 1962.

theses. There are perceptual experiences; they have Intentionality; their Intentional content is propositional in form; they have mind-to-world direction of fit; and the properties which are specified by their Intentional content are not in general literally properties of the perceptual experiences.

II

Having so far emphasized the analogies between visual experiences and other forms of Intentionality such as belief, I want in this section to point out several disanalogies. First of all, I said in Chapter 1 that we could justifiably call such Intentional states as beliefs and desires "representations" provided that we recognize that there is no special ontology carried by the notion of representation and that it is just a shorthand for a constellation of independently motivated notions such as conditions of satisfaction, Intentional content, direction of fit, etc. But when we come to visual and other sorts of perceptual experiences we need to say a great deal more in order to characterize their Intentionality. They do indeed have all of the features in terms of which we defined representations, but they have other intrinsic features as well which might make this term misleading. States such as beliefs and desires need not be conscious states. A person can have a belief or desire even when he is not thinking about it and he can be truly said to have such states even when asleep. But visual and other sorts of perceptual experiences are *conscious* mental *events*. The Intentionality of a representation is independent of whether it is realized in consciousness or not, but in general the Intentionality of a perceptual experience is realized in quite specific phenomenal properties of conscious mental events. For this reason the claim that there are visual experiences goes beyond the claim that the perception has Intentionality, since it is an ontological claim about how the Intentionality is realized; it is, in general, realized in conscious mental events.

Not only is the visual experience a conscious mental event but it is related to its conditions of satisfaction in ways which are quite different from beliefs and desires. If, for example, I see a yellow station wagon in front of me, the experience I have is directly of the object. It doesn't just "represent" the object, it provides direct access to it. The experience has a kind of directness, immediacy and involuntariness which is not shared by a belief I might have about the object in its absence. It seems therefore unnatural to describe visual experiences as representations, indeed if we talk that way it is almost bound to lead to the representative theory of perception. Rather, because of the special features of perceptual experiences I propose to call them "presentations". The visual experience I will say does not just represent the state of affairs perceived; rather, when satisfied, it gives us direct access to it, and in that sense it is a presentation of that state of affairs. Strictly speaking, since our account of representations was ontologically neutral, and since presentations have all the defining conditions we laid down for representations (they have Intentional content, conditions of satisfaction, direction of fit, Intentional objects, etc.), presentations are a special subclass of representations. However, as they are a special subclass, involving conscious mental events, I will sometimes oppose "presentation" to "representation" without thereby denying that presentations are representations, as one might oppose "human" to "animal" without thereby denying that humans are animals. Furthermore, when the context warrants it, I will use "Intentional state" broadly to cover both states and events.

The claim that the Intentionality of vision is characteristically realized in visual experiences which are conscious mental events is a genuine empirical ontological claim, and in that respect it contrasts with the claim that beliefs and desires contain propositions as Intentional contents. The claim that there are propositions in the sense previously explained is not an ontological empirical claim, though it is often mistakenly supposed to be so both by its defenders and by its attackers. That is, the claim that there are propositions or other representative contents adds nothing to the claim that there are certain common features of beliefs, hopes, fears, desires, questions, assertions, commands, promises, etc. But the claim that there are visual experiences really adds something to the claim that there are visual perceptions, since it tells us how the content of those perceptions is realized in our conscious life. Someone who claimed that there was a class of beings capable of perceiving optically, that is, beings capable of visual perception but who did not have visual experiences, would be making a genuine empirical claim. But if someone claimed that there was a class of beings who literally had hopes, fears, and beliefs, and who made statements, assertions, and commands, all with their various logical features, but who did not have propositional contents, then such a person doesn't know what he's talking about or else is simply refusing to adopt a notation, for the claim that there are propositional contents isn't in any way an additional empirical claim. It is rather the adoption of a certain notational device for representing common logical features of hopes, fears, beliefs, statements, etc.

Some recent empirical work bears out this crucial distinction between the ontological status of the visual experience as a conscious mental event and that of the propositional content. Weiskrantz, Warrington and their colleagues[4] have studied how certain sorts of brain lesions produce what they call "blind sight". The patient can give correct answers to questions about visual events and objects that he is presented with, but he claims to have no visual awareness of these objects and events. Now, from our point of view the interest of such cases derives from the fact that the optical stimuli the patient is subjected to apparently produce a form of Intentionality. Otherwise, the patient would not be able to report the visual events in question. But the Intentional content produced by their optical stimulation is not realized in the way that our presentational contents are realized. For us to see an object, we have to have visual experiences of a certain sort. But, assuming Weiskrantz's account is correct, the patient can in some sense "see" an object even though he does not have the relevant visual experiences. He simply reports a "feeling" that something is there, or makes a "guess" that it is there. Those who doubt the existence of visual experiences, by the way, might want to ask themselves what it is that we have that such patients seem to lack.

Another distinction between the Intentionality of perception and the Intentionality of belief is that it is part of the conditions of satisfaction (in the sense of requirement) of the visual experience that the visual experience must itself be caused by the rest of the conditions of satisfaction (in the sense of things required) of that

4 L. Weiskrantz et al., 'Visual capacity in the hemianopic field following a restricted occipital ablation', *Brain*, vol. 97 (1974), pp. 709–28.

visual experience. Thus, for example, if I see the yellow station wagon, I have a certain visual experience. But the Intentional content of the visual experience, which requires that there be a yellow station wagon in front of me in order that it be satisfied, also requires that the fact that there is a yellow station wagon in front of me must be the cause of that very visual experience. Thus, the Intentional content of the visual experience requires as part of the conditions of satisfaction that the visual experience be caused by the rest of its conditions of satisfaction, that is, by the state of affairs perceived. The content of the visual experience is therefore self-referential in a sense that I hope to be able to make fairly precise. The Intentional content of the visual experience is entirely specified by stating the conditions of satisfaction of the visual experience, but that statement makes essential reference to the visual experience itself in the conditions of satisfaction. For what the Intentional content requires is not simply that there be a state of affairs in the world, but rather that the state of affairs in the world must cause the very visual experience which is the embodiment or realization of the Intentional content. And the argument for this goes beyond the familiar proof of the "causal theory of perception";[5] the usual argument is that unless the presence and features of the object cause the agent's experience, he does not see the object. But it is essential to my account to show how these facts enter into the Intentional content. The Intentional content of the visual experience therefore has to be made explicit in the following form:

> I have a visual experience (that there is a yellow station wagon there and that there is a yellow station wagon there is causing this visual experience).

This looks puzzling, but I think it is on the right track. The Intentional content of the visual experience determines under what conditions it is satisfied or not satisfied, what must be the case in order that it be, as they say, "veridical". Well, what must be the case in the station wagon scene in order that the experience be a veridical one? At least this much: the world must be as it visually

---

5 See H. P. Grice, 'The causal theory of perception', *Proceedings of the Aristotelian Society*, suppl. vol. 35 (1961), pp. 121–52.

seems to me that it is, and furthermore its being that way must be what causes me to have the visual experience which constitutes its seeming to be that way. And it is this combination that I am trying to capture in the representation of the Intentional content.

The verbal representation that I have just given of the visual Intentional content is not in any sense a *translation*. It is rather a verbal specification of what the Intentional content requires if it is to be satisfied. The sense then in which the visual Intentional content is self-referential is not that it contains a verbal or other representation of itself: it certainly performs no speech act of reference to itself! Rather, the sense in which the visual experience is self-referential is simply that it figures in its own conditions of satisfaction. The visual experience itself does not *say* this but *shows* it; in my verbal representation of the Intentional content of the visual experience I have said it. Furthermore, when I say that the visual experience is causally self-referential I do not mean that the causal relation is seen, much less that the visual experience is seen. Rather, what is seen are objects and states of affairs, and part of the conditions of satisfaction of the visual experience of seeing them is that the experience itself must be caused by what is seen.

On this account perception is an Intentional and causal transaction between mind and the world. The direction of fit is mind-to-world, the direction of causation is world-to-mind; and they are not independent, for fit is achieved only if the fit is caused by the other term of the relation of fitting, namely the state of affairs perceived. We can say either that it is part of the content of the visual experience that if it is to be satisfied it must be caused by its Intentional object; or, more cumbersomely but more accurately, it is part of the content of the visual experience, that if it is to be satisfied it must be caused by the state of affairs that its Intentional object exists and has those features that are presented in the visual experience. And it is in this sense that the Intentional content of the perceptual experience is causally self-referential.

The introduction of the notion of causal self-referentiality of certain sorts of Intentionality – a self-referentiality which is shown but not said – is a crucial addition to the conceptual apparatus of this book. The simple, and I think obvious, observation that perceptual experiences are causally self-referential is the first step in a series of arguments that we will use in attacking several vexing philosophical problems – about the nature of human action, the explanation of behavior, the nature of causation, and the analysis of indexical expressions, to mention just a few. One immediate consequence can be mentioned now: it is quite easy to see how type-identical visual experiences can have different conditions of satisfaction and therefore different Intentional contents. Two 'phenomenologically' identical experiences can have different contents because each experience is self-referential. Thus, for example, suppose two identical twins have type-identical visual experiences while looking at two different but type-identical station wagons at the same time in type-identical lighting conditions and surrounding contexts. Still, the conditions of satisfaction can be different. Twin number one requires a station wagon causing his visual experience and twin number two requires a station wagon causing his numerically different visual experience. Same phenomenology; different contents and therefore different conditions of satisfaction.

Though I think the characterization of causal self-referentiality is correct it does leave us with some difficult questions we are not yet in a position to answer. What is the sense of "cause" in the above formulations, and doesn't this account have the skeptical consequence that we can never be sure our visual experiences are satisfied since there is no neutral position from which we can observe the causal relation to see that the experience really is satisfied? All we can ever have is more of the same sorts of experiences. I will discuss both of these questions later, the first in Chapter 4 and the second at the end of this chapter.

Yet another distinction between the form of Intentionality exemplified by visual perception and other forms of Intentionality such as beliefs and desires has to do with the character of the aspect or the point of view under which an object is seen or otherwise perceived. When I have a representation of an Intentional object in a belief or desire it will always be represented under some aspect or other, but in belief and desire aspect is not constrained in the way that the aspect of visual perception is fixed by the sheer physical features of the situation. For example, I can represent a certain famous planet under its "Morning Star" aspects, or its "Evening Star" aspects. But because the Intentionality of visual perception is realized in a quite specific way the aspect under which we perceive the objects of our perceptions plays a different sort of role than it does in other Intentional states. In visual perception the aspect under which an object is perceived is fixed by the point of view, and the other physical features of the perceptual situation, in which the object is perceived. For example, given a certain position, I can't help but see the left side of the station wagon. To see the car under some other aspect I would have to alter the physical features of the perceptual situation by, for example, walking around the car or moving it.

Furthermore, in the non-perceptual cases, though the Intentional object is always represented by way of some aspect or other, it is nonetheless the object itself that is represented and not just an aspect. That, incidentally, is why there is nothing ontologically fishy about Intentional objects on my account. The aspect under which an object is represented is not something that gets between us and the object. But in at least some cases of visual perception the situation does not seem to be quite so simple. Consider, for example, Wittgenstein's familiar duck/rabbit example.[6]

In this case we are inclined to say that in one sense the Intentional object is the same both in our perception of the duck and in our perception of the rabbit. That is, though we have two visual experiences with two different presentational contents, there is only one picture on the page before us. But in another sense we want to say that the Intentional object of the visual experience is different in the two cases. What is seen is in one case a picture duck and in the other case a picture rabbit. Now Wittgenstein copes, or rather fails to cope, with this difficulty simply by saying that these are different uses of the verb "see". But that doesn't seem to be very much help in clarifying the relation of aspects to Intentional

6 L. Wittgenstein, *Philosophical Investigations* (Oxford: Basil Blackwell, 1953), Part II, section 10.

objects. I think the solution to our puzzle is to point out that just as we can literally see objects, even though whenever we see an object we always see it under an aspect, so we can literally see aspects of objects. I literally see the duck aspect and I literally see the rabbit aspect of the drawing before me. Now on my account that will commit us to the view that we see those aspects under aspects. But why should that bother us? Actually, if we are willing to accept this view, then the parallel with other Intentional states is preserved. As we have already seen when John loves Sally or believes something about Bill, it is always under some aspect that John loves Sally and under some aspect that he believes something about Bill, even though what John's love is directed at or what his belief is about is not an aspect. But furthermore there is nothing to prevent him loving an aspect of Sally or believing something about an aspect of Bill. That is, there is nothing to prevent an aspect from being an Intentional object of a belief or other psychological attitude such as love. And similarly there is nothing to prevent an aspect from being the Intentional object of visual perception. As soon as we recognize that an aspect can be an Intentional object even though all Intentionality including the Intentionality of perception is under an aspect, we can see how the aspect is essential to the Intentional phenomena and yet is not itself the Intentional object.

One way to summarize the foregoing account of the Intentionality of perception is to present a table comparing the formal features of the various kinds of Intentionality discussed. To belief, desire, and visual perception I will add memory of events in one's past, since it shares some features with visual perception (like seeing, it is causally self-referential) and some with belief (like belief, it is a representation rather than a presentation). The verbs "see" and "remember", unlike the verbs "desire" and "believe", imply not only the presence of an Intentional content but also that the content is satisfied. If I really see some state of affairs then there must be more than my visual experience; the state of affairs which is the condition of satisfaction of the visual experience must exist and must cause the visual experience. And if I really remember some event then the event must have occurred and its occurrence must cause my memory of it.

A comparison of some of the formal features of the Intentionality of seeing, believing, desiring, and remembering

	Seeing	Believing	Desiring	Remembering
Nature of the Intentional component	visual experience	belief	desire	memory
Presentation or representation	presentation	represent-ation	represent-ation	represent-ation
Causally self-referential	yes	no	no	yes
Direction of fit	mind-to-world	mind-to-world	world-to-mind	mind-to-world
Direction of causation as determined by Intentional content	world-to-mind	none	none	world-to-mind

III

In my effort to give an account of the Intentionality of visual perception I am anxious not to make it look much simpler than it really is. In this section I want to call attention to some of the complexities, though the cases I mention here are only a few among many puzzles in the philosophy of perception.

We are tempted to think, *á la* Hume, that perceptions come to us pure and unsullied by language, and that we then attach labels by way of ostensive definitions to the results of our perceptual encounters. But that picture is false in a number of ways. First, there is the familiar point that perception is a function of expectation, and the expectations of human beings at least are normally realized linguistically. So language itself affects the perceptual encounter. Over a quarter of a century ago Postman and Bruner[7] did some experiments which showed that the recognition threshold for features varied greatly depending on whether or not the particular feature was expected in that situation.

7 L. Postman, J. Bruner, and R. Walk, 'The perception of error', *British Journal of Psychology*, vol. 42 (1951), pp. 1–10.

If the subject expects that the next color he is going to see is red, he will recognize it much more quickly than if he has no such expectation.

But secondly and more importantly from our point of view, many of our visual experiences aren't even possible without the mastery of certain Background skills and prominent among them are linguistic skills. Consider the following figure:

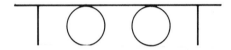

This can be seen as the word "TOOT", as a table with two large balloons underneath, as the numeral 1001 with a line over the top, as a bridge with two pipelines crossing underneath, as the eyes of a man wearing a hat with a string hanging down each side, and so on. In each case, we have a different experience even though the purely physical visual stimuli, the lines on the paper in front of us and the light reflected from them, are constant. But these experiences and the differences between them are dependent on our having mastered a series of linguistically impregnated cultural skills. It is not the failure, for example, of my dog's optical apparatus that prevents him from seeing this figure as the word "TOOT". In such a case one wants to say that a certain conceptual mastery is a precondition of having visual experience; and such cases suggest that the Intentionality of visual perception is tied up in all sorts of complicated ways with other forms of Intentionality such as belief and expectation, and also with our systems of representation, most notably language. Both the Network of Intentional states and the Background of non-representational mental capacities affect perception.

But if the Network and the Background affect perception, how can the conditions of satisfaction be determined by the visual experience? There are at least three sorts of cases we will need to discuss. First, there are cases where the Network of beliefs and the Background actually affect the content of the visual experience. Consider, for example, the difference between looking at the front of a house where one takes it to be the front of a whole house and looking at the front of a house where one takes it to be a mere façade, e.g., as part of a movie set. If one believes one is seeing a whole house, the front of the house actually looks different from the way it looks if one believes one is seeing a false façade of a house, even though the optical stimuli may be identical in the two cases. And this difference in the actual character of the visual experiences is reflected in the differences between the two sets of conditions of satisfaction. It is part of the content of my visual experience when I look at a whole house that I *expect* the rest of the house to be there if, for example, I enter the house or go around to the back. In these sorts of cases the character of the visual experience and its conditions of satisfaction will be affected by the content of the beliefs that one has about the perceptual situation. I am not going beyond the content of my visual experience when I say, "I see a house" instead of "I see the façade of a house", for, though the optical stimuli may be the same, the conditions of satisfaction in the former case are that there should be a whole house there. I do not *infer* from the façade of the house to the presence of the house; I simply see a house.

A second sort of case arises where the content of the beliefs is actually inconsistent with the content of the visual experience. A good example is the appearance of the moon on the horizon. When one sees the moon on the horizon it looks a great deal bigger than it does when it is directly overhead. Yet though the visual experiences are different in the two cases there is no change in the content of one's beliefs. I do not believe the moon has grown on the horizon or shrunk overhead. Now in our first sort of example we saw there was no way we could carve off the content of the visual experience from the beliefs one has about it. The house actually looks different depending on what sort of beliefs we have about it. But in the second sort of case we want to say that the visual experience of the moon's size definitely changes with the moon's position and yet our beliefs remain constant. And what shall we say about the conditions of satisfaction of the visual experiences? Because of the holistic character of the Network of our Intentional states, we are inclined to say that the conditions of satisfaction of the visual experiences remain the same. Since we are not really at all inclined to believe that the moon has changed in size, we suppose that the two visual experiences have the same conditions of satisfaction. But I think in fact that is not the right way to describe the situation. Rather, it seems to me that where the Intentional content of our visual experience is in conflict with our beliefs, and where the beliefs override the visual experience, we nonetheless have the original Intentional content of the visual experience. The visual experiences do indeed have as part of their respective Intentional contents that the moon is smaller overhead than it is on the horizon, and the argument for this is that if we imagine that the visual experiences remained as they are now, but that the beliefs were absent, that we simply had no relevant beliefs, then we really would be inclined to believe that the moon had changed in size. It is only because we believe independently that the moon remains constant in size that we allow the Intentionality of belief to override the Intentionality of our visual experience. In these cases we believe that our eyes deceive us. A similar example is the Müller-Lyer lines:

where the Intentional content of the visual experience is in conflict with and is overridden by the Intentional content of our beliefs. These cases are in sharp contrast to the phenomenon of perceived color constancy under different lighting conditions. In the color constancy case the color looks the same in both light and shadow, even though the light reflected is quite different; and thus the content of the belief and the content of the perceptual experience are consistent, unlike the previous cases.

A third sort of case is where the visual experiences differ but the conditions of satisfaction are the same. Our "TOOT" example is of this type. Another example of this would be seeing a triangle first with one point as apex and then with another point as apex. In these last two examples we are not in the least inclined to think that anything is different in the real world corresponding to the differences in the experiences.

We have then a variety of ways in which the Network and Background of Intentionality are related to the character of the visual experience, and the character of the visual experience is related to its conditions of satisfaction.

1. The house example: Different beliefs cause different visual experiences with different conditions of satisfaction, even given the same optical stimuli.

2. The moon example: The same beliefs coexist with different visual experiences with different conditions of satisfaction even though the content of the experiences is inconsistent with the content of the beliefs and is overridden by the beliefs.

3. The triangle and "TOOT" examples: The same beliefs plus different visual experiences yield the same conditions of satisfaction of the visual experiences.

One feels there ought to be a systematic theoretical account of the relations between these various parameters, but I do not know what it is.

IV

The account of visual perception that I have been arguing for so far is, I guess, a version of 'naive' (direct, common sense) realism and it can be represented diagrammatically as follows:

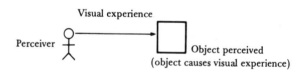

Fig. 1

This visual perception involves at least three elements: the perceiver, the visual experience, and the object (more strictly: the state of affairs) perceived. The fact that an arrow represents the visual perception is meant to indicate that the visual experience has Intentional content, it is directed at the Intentional object, whose existence is part of its conditions of satisfaction (it is not of course meant to suggest that the visual experience exists in the physical space between the perceiver and the object).

In the case of visual hallucination the perceiver has the same visual experience but no Intentional object is present. This case can be represented diagrammatically as in figure 2.

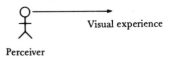

Perceiver

Fig. 2

It is not my aim in this chapter to enter into the traditional disputes concerning the philosophy of perception; however, the thesis I am arguing for concerning the Intentionality of visual experience will perhaps be clearer if we digress a moment to contrast this naive realist view with its great historical rivals, the representative theory and phenomenalism. Both of these theories differ from naive realism in that they both treat the visual experience as itself the object of visual perception and thus they strip it of its Intentionality. According to them what is seen is always, strictly speaking, a visual experience (in various terminologies the visual experience has been called a "sensum" or a "sense datum", or an "impression"). They are thus confronted with a question that does not arise for the naive realist: What is the relationship between the sense data which we do see and the material object which apparently we do not see? This question does not arise for the naive realist because on his account we do not see sense data at all. We see material objects and other objects and states of affairs in the world, at least much of the time; and in the hallucination cases we don't see anything, though we do indeed *have* visual experiences in both cases. Both the phenomenalists and the representative theorists try to drive the line that represents the visual experience in Figure 1 out of the horizontal axis and into the vertical so that the vehicle of the Intentional *content* of our visual perception, the visual experience, becomes itself the *object* of visual perception. The numerous arguments that have been presented for this move, notably the arguments from illusion and the argument from science, have been in my view effectively refuted by other philosophers,[8] and I will not rehearse the arguments here. The

8 See, e.g., J. L. Austin, *Sense and Sensibilia* (Oxford: Oxford University Press, 1962), for a discussion of the argument from illusion.

point for the purposes of the present argument is simply that once one has driven the visual experience line out of the horizontal axis and into the vertical axis in such a way that the visual experience becomes the object of perception one is then confronted with a choice as to how one is to describe the relationship between the sense datum that, according to this theory, one does perceive and the material object that one apparently does not perceive. The two favorite solutions to the problem are that the visual experience or sense datum is in some sense a copy or representation of the material object (this is the representative theory) or that the object somehow just is a collection of sense data (and this, in its various versions, is phenomenalism), each of these theories can be represented diagrammatically as in figures 3 and 4.

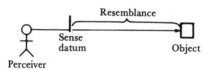

Fig. 3

The representative theory

Fig. 4

Phenomenalism

Even if we ignore the various objections that have been made to the view that all one ever perceives are sense data, it still seems to me that there are other decisive objections against each of these theories. The main difficulty with a representative theory of perception is that the notion of resemblance between the things we perceive, the sense data, and the thing that the sense data represent, the material object, must be unintelligible since the object term is by definition inaccessible to the senses. It is absolutely invisible and otherwise imperceptible. As Berkeley pointed out, it makes no sense to say that the shape and color we see resemble the shape and color of an object which is absolutely invisible or otherwise inaccessible to any of our senses. Furthermore, on this account no literal sense can even be attached to the claim that objects have such sensible qualities as shape, size, color, weight, or the other sensorily accessible qualities, whether 'primary' or 'secondary'. In short, the representative theory is unable to make sense of the notion of resemblance, and therefore it cannot make any sense of the notion of representation, since the form of representation in question requires resemblance.

The decisive objection to the phenomenalist view is simply that it reduces to solipsism. The publicly accessible material objects on the phenomenalist view become sense data, but sense data are always private. Thus, the objects I see are in an important sense my objects since they reduce to sense data and the only sense data to which I have access are my sense data. The world that I perceive is not accessible to anyone else since it consists entirely in my private sense data, and indeed the hypothesis that other people might see the same objects that I see becomes unintelligible, since all I see are my sense data and all they could see would be their sense data. But furthermore the hypothesis that other people even exist and perceive sense data in the sense in which I exist and perceive sense data becomes at best unknowable and at worst unintelligible since my perceptions of other people are always my perceptions of my sense data, that is my perceptions of features of myself.

Once one treats the content of perception as the object of perception, something like the above theories seems inevitable. And indeed the mistake of the sense data theorists seems to me analogous to the mistake of treating the propositional content of the belief as the object of the belief. The belief is no more about or directed at its propositional content than the visual perception is about or directed at its experiential component. However, in rejecting the sense datum hypothesis, it seems to me many 'naive realists' have failed to recognize the role of experiences and the Intentionality of experiences in the perceptual situation. In rejecting the idea that what we see are visual experiences in favor of the idea that what we see are characteristically, for example, material objects in our vicinity, many philosophers, e.g., Austin,[9] have rejected the idea that we have visual experiences at all. I want

9 *Op. cit.*

to argue that the traditional sense data theorists were correct in recognizing that we have experiences, visual and otherwise, but they mislocated the Intentionality of perception in supposing that experiences were the objects of perception, and the naive realists were correct in recognizing that material objects and events are characteristically the objects of perception, but many of them failed to realize that the material object can only be the object of visual perception because the perception has an Intentional content, and the vehicle of the Intentional content is a visual experience.

V

We are now in a position to return to our original question: what are the truth conditions of a sentence of the form

X sees a yellow station wagon.

But from the point of view of a theory of Intentionality this question is ill-formed because the Intentional content of vision is propositional: the correct form is, for example,

X sees that there is a yellow station wagon in front of X.

The truth conditions are:
1. X has a visual experience which has
   a. certain conditions of satisfaction
   b. certain phenomenal properties.
2. The conditions of satisfaction are: that there is a yellow station wagon in front of X and the fact that there is a yellow station wagon in front of X is causing the visual experience.
3. The phenomenal properties are such as to determine that the conditions of satisfaction are as described in 2. That is, those conditions of satisfaction are determined by the experience.
4. The form of the causal relation in the conditions of satisfaction is continuous and regular Intentional causation.
   (This condition is required to block certain sorts of counterexamples involving "deviant causal chains", where the conditions of satisfaction do cause the visual experience but all the same the experience is not satisfied. We will examine these cases and explore the nature of Intentional causation in Chapter 4.)

5. The conditions of satisfaction are in fact satisfied. That is, there actually is a station wagon causing (in the manner described in 4) the visual experience (described in 3) which has the Intentional content (described in 2).

On this account there are, besides the perceiver, two components to visual perception, the visual experience and the scene perceived, and the relation between them is Intentional and causal.

VI

We have now achieved our original objective of assimilating an account of perception to our theory of Intentionality. But a problem immediately arises that we have not yet faced: we have discussed the case where a person sees that a yellow station wagon is in front of him, but what about the case where he sees that a particular, previously identified, yellow station wagon is in front of him. When, for example, I see my own station wagon, the conditions of satisfaction require not merely that there be some station wagon or other satisfying my Intentional content, but rather that it be my very own. Now the question is; how does this particularity get into the Intentional content of the perception? Let us call this "the problem of particularity".[10]

To see that it really is a problem for the theory of Intentionality, imagine a variation of Putnam's twin earth fantasy[11] as follows. Suppose that in a distant galaxy there is the twin of our earth, type identical with our earth down to the last microparticle. Suppose that on our earth Bill Jones sees his wife, Sally, getting out of their yellow station wagon and on twin earth, twin Jones sees twin Sally getting out of their twin station wagon. Now what is it about the *content* of Jones's visual experience that makes the presence of Sally rather than twin Sally part of the conditions of satisfaction of his visual experience, and what makes the presence of twin Sally part of the conditions of satisfaction of twin Jones's experience? By hypothesis both experiences are qualitatively identical, yet it is part of the conditions of satisfaction of each agent's experience that he is not seeing just *any* woman with such and such visual charac-

---

10 I am indebted to Christine Skarda for discussion of this topic.
11 H. Putnam, 'The meaning of meaning', in *Mind, Language, and Reality, Collected Papers*, vol. 2 (Cambridge: Cambridge University Press, 1975), pp. 215–71.

teristics, but that he is seeing his very own wife, Sally, or twin Sally as the case might be. We have already seen (p. 50) how qualitatively identical visual experiences can have different conditions of satisfaction for the general case, but how can qualitatively identical visual experiences have different particular conditions of satisfaction? The point of the fantasy is not epistemic. We are not asking how can Jones tell that it is really his wife and not somebody identical in appearance with his wife. The question we are asking rather is, what is it about Jones's visual experience right here on our earth that makes it the case that it can only be satisfied by one particular previously identified woman and not by some other woman who happens to be type identical with that woman, whether Jones can tell the difference or not? Furthermore, the point of the fantasy is not to suggest that there might actually be a twin earth, rather the point is to remind us that on our very own earth, we have Intentional contents with particular and not general conditions of satisfaction. The question, to repeat, is: How does the particularity get into the Intentional content?

The problem of particularity crops up in a variety of places in the philosophy of mind and in the philosophy of language. And it has a currently fashionable solution which is in fact inadequate. According to this 'solution' the difference between Jones and twin Jones is simply that in Jones's case his experience is actually caused by Sally, and in twin Jones's case his experience is caused by twin Sally. If Jones's visual experience is in fact caused by Sally, then he is seeing Sally, and he would not be seeing her if she did not cause his visual experience. But this alleged solution fails to answer the question as to how this fact gets into the Intentional content. Of course, Jones is only seeing Sally if Sally causes his visual experience and it is part of its Intentional content that it must be caused by Sally if it is to be satisfied, but what is it exactly about his visual experience that requires Sally and not somebody type identical with Sally? The solution is from a third-person point of view. It is a solution of the problem of how we observers can tell which one he is in fact seeing. But the problem as I have posed it is a first-person internal problem. What is it about this experience that requires that it be satisfied by the presence of Sally and not just by any woman with such and such characteristics type identical with Sally's? The problem takes the same form in the theory of reference as in the theory of perception and the causal theory of reference is as inadequate an answer in the one case as the causal theory of perception is in the other. The problem takes the form: "What is it about Jones's Intentionality that makes it the case that when he says 'Sally' he means Sally and not twin Sally?" The third-person causal answer says he refers to Sally rather than twin Sally because the former and not the latter stands in certain causal relations to his utterance. But this answer simply evades the question about his Intentionality. There will indeed be cases where he refers to Sally without knowing it, and cases where he sees Sally without knowing it, cases where true third-person descriptions do not match his Intentionality. But such cases are always dependent on there being first-person Intentionality which sets internal conditions of satisfaction, and no causal answer to our question can ever be adequate until it accounts for how the causation is part of the Intentionality, in such a way as to determine that a particular object is part of the conditions of satisfaction. The question, in short, is not "Under what conditions does he in fact see Sally whether he knows it or not?", but "Under what conditions does he *take himself* to be seeing that Sally is in front of him?" And similarly the question for reference is not "Under what conditions does he refer to Sally whether he knows it or not?", but rather "Under what conditions does he *mean* to refer to Sally by 'Sally'?"

I think one reason, perhaps unconscious, why the causal theorists give no answer to the question about Intentionality and answer a different question is that they despair of getting a first-person Intentional solution to the problem of particularity. If you think of Intentional content solely on the model of Frege's conception of *Sinn*, then it looks like any number of possible objects could satisfy any *Sinn* and nothing in the Intentional content could determine that it could only be satisfied by a *particular* object. Gareth Evans[12] imagines a case where a man knows two identical twins and is in love with one of them. But, says Evans, there is nothing in the man's mind that makes his love directed at one and not the other. He quotes with approval the

12 'The causal theory of names', *Proceedings of the Aristotelian Society*, suppl. vol. 47, pp. 187–208; reprinted in S. P. Schwartz (ed.), *Naming, Necessity and Natural Kinds* (Ithaca and London: Cornell University Press, 1977), pp. 192–215.

claim, attributed to Wittgenstein, that if God looked inside the man He could not tell which twin he had in mind. Since there isn't any answer to the question, "What is it about the man that makes it the case that he means one and not the other?", the solution must be from the third-person or external point of view. As Putnam says, the world takes over. But this solution will not do. Any theory of Intentionality has to account for the fact that one often has Intentional contents directed at particular objects. What one requires is the characterization of Intentional content which shows how it can be satisfied by one and only one previously identified object.

Viewed historically, the two mistakes that have prevented philosophers from finding the solution to this problem are, I believe, first, the assumption that each Intentional content is an isolated unit determining its conditions of satisfaction independently of others and independently of any nonpresentational capacities; and second, the assumption that causation is always a non-Intentional relation, that is, that it is always a natural relation among objects and events in the world. The problem is insoluble given these two assumptions. The causal theorists see correctly that the problem cannot be solved without the notion of causation, but they still keep these two assumptions. They make the usual atomistic assumptions about Intentionality and then in order to give their Humean conception of causality some grip, they adopt the third-person point of view. Phenomenologists such as Husserl, on the other hand, have seen the connectedness of experiences and the importance of a first-person account but have failed to see the relevance of causality, because their conception of the abstract character of Intentional contents has led them to assume tacitly that causation is always a natural, non-Intentional relation.

What then is the solution to the problem of particularity? To assemble the tools necessary to answer this question, we need to remind ourselves of the following: first, the Network and the Background affect the conditions of satisfaction of the Intentional state; second, Intentional causation is always internal to the conditions of satisfaction of Intentional states; and third, agents stand in indexical relations to their own Intentional states, their own Networks, and their own Backgrounds.

Network and Background: On the conception of Intentionality and

Intentional causation advanced in this book, Intentional contents do not determine their conditions of satisfaction in isolation. Rather, Intentional contents in general and experiences in particular are internally related in a holistic way to other Intentional contents (the Network) and to nonrepresentational capacities (the Background). They are internally related in the sense that they could not have the conditions of satisfaction that they do except in relation to the rest of the Network and the Background. This holistic conception involves the denial of the atomistic assumptions mentioned above.

Intentional causation: We have already suggested that causation characteristically figures in determining the conditions of satisfaction of Intentional states when it is Intentional causation, that is, when the causal relation occurs as part of the Intentional content. When we tie this point to the Network and the Background we can see that in order that it be part of the conditions of satisfaction of Jones's Intentional state it must be caused by Sally rather than twin Sally, Jones must have some prior identification of Sally as Sally; and his present experience must make reference to that prior identification in the determination of the causal conditions of satisfaction.

Indexicality: From Jones's point of view, each of his experiences is not just an experience that happens to someone; it is rather *his* experience. The Network of Intentional states that he is aware of is *his* Network and the Background capacities he makes use of have to do with *his* Background. No matter how qualitatively similar Jones's experience is to twin Jones's and no matter how type identical his whole Network of Intentional states is to twin Jones's, from Jones's point of view there is no doubt that these are his experiences, his beliefs, his memories, his propensities; in short, his Network and his Background.

We next need to state explicitly how these features of the system of Intentionality combine to solve the problem of particularity. The problem is to show how the Background and the Network reach inside the Intentional content to determine that the causal conditions of satisfaction are particular rather than general. For the sake of simplicity in exposition, we will consider two cases, first one where we ignore the Background and concentrate on the operation of the Network and then one where we consider the operation of the Background.

Suppose that Jones's entire knowledge of Sally comes from the fact that he has had a sequence of experiences, $x, y, z, \ldots$, visual and otherwise, of Sally in the past. These experiences are past experiences but he still has present memories of them, $a, b, c, \ldots$. The sequence of memories, $a, b, c, \ldots$, is internally related to the experiential sequence, $x, y, z, \ldots$. If, for example, a is a memory of x, then part of the conditions of satisfaction of a is that it must have been caused by x, just as it is part of the conditions of satisfaction of x that if it is a perception of Sally it must have been caused by Sally. By transitivity of Intentional causation it is, therefore, part of the conditions of satisfaction of the memory that it must have been caused by Sally. Furthermore, the sequences must be internally related as sequences because insofar as each of these perceptual experiences is of the same woman and each memory is a memory of an experience of the same woman, then the conditions of satisfaction of some members of the sequence will make reference to other members of the sequence. The conditions of satisfaction of each experience and each memory after the initial encounter with Sally are not just that the experience should be satisfied by a woman satisfying Sally's description in general terms but that it should be caused by the *same* woman who caused Jones's other experiences and memories. This is one of the keys to understanding how Intentionality can be aimed at particular objects: it can be internal to one representation that it makes reference to other representations in the Network.

We are supposing that Jones has an experience whose form is

1. Vis exp (Sally is there and her presence and features are causing this visual experience)

as distinct from

2. Vis exp (a woman with identical Sally-like features is there and her presence and features are causing this visual experience).

The relation of the Network to the present Intentional content from Jones's point of view is

3. I have had in the past a set of experiences $x, y, z, \ldots$ caused by the presence and features of a woman whom I have known as Sally and I have at present a set of memories of

these experiences a, b, c, . . . which are such that my present
visual experience is:

Vis exp (a woman with identical Sally-like features is before
me and her presence and features are causing this visual
experience and that woman is identical with the woman
whose presence and features caused x, y, z, . . . , which in
turn caused a, b, c, . . .).

But from Jones's point of view – and his is the only point of view
that matters for this discussion – the content of 3 is all there is to the
content of 1. In this example, all that Jones has of Sally by way of
Intentionality is a present experience tied to a set of present
memories of past experiences. But that is all he needs to guarantee
that the conditions of satisfaction require Sally and not somebody
type-identical with Sally.

To see the interrelation of members of the Network, ask
yourself what has gone wrong from Jones's point of view if Sally
and twin Sally are switched? Put simply, what has gone wrong is
that the woman he is seeing is not identical with Sally. But from
Jones's point of view, that consists simply in the fact that she fails
to satisfy the last main clause in the specification of the Intentional
content of 3. Suppose that the switch had taken place at birth,
twenty years before Jones had ever seen or heard of Sally, then
Jones's Intentional content is satisfied. From the point of view of
someone else's Intentionality Jones might not be seeing the real
Sally, but from Jones's point of view he is seeing exactly the person
he takes himself to be seeing, i.e., his Intentional content
determines these conditions of satisfaction and is in fact satisfied.

Furthermore, the fact that twin Jones is simultaneously having a
type-identical experience to Jones's is no block to Jones's
experience being directed at Sally and not at twin Sally, because the
elements of his Network are indexically related to him – they are
his experiences and his memories.

Of course, we are not saying that Jones has to be able to spell all
of this out for himself. His way of describing the situation pre-
theoretically might be, "I am now seeing the woman I have always
known as Sally". What we are trying to explain is how both Jones
and twin Jones might simultaneously utter the same sentence, both
have qualitatively identical experiences, and yet mean something
different in each case – each is having an experience which, though

"qualitatively identical" with the other, nonetheless has a different content and different conditions of satisfaction. (Later we will see how this apparatus is relevant to a criticism of the causal theory of names.)

We will next consider a case of the operation of the Background in the determination of particular cases of perceptual recognition. The capacity to recognize people, objects, etc., does not normally require comparison of the object with pre-existing representations, whether images, beliefs, or other sorts of 'mental representations'. One simply recognizes people and things. Now suppose that Bill Jones recognizes a man whom he sees on the street as Bernard Baxter. He need have no recollection, conscious or unconscious, of when or how he met Baxter, and he need have no representation of Baxter with which he is comparing the man who is the object of his present visual inspection. He simply sees Baxter and knows: that is Baxter. Here the Background functions as a non-representational mental capacity; he has the ability to recognize Baxter but that ability itself need not contain or consist in representations.

Since Jones recognizes Baxter and twin Jones recognizes twin Baxter, and both have qualitatively identical experiences, what is it about the one experience that requires Baxter and the other that requires twin Baxter as conditions of satisfaction? Intuitively we feel in this case as we did in the twin Sallys' case that Jones recognizes one man as *his* Baxter and twin Jones recognizes another man as *his* Baxter. But how do we spell out that intuition in a case where there are no prior representations to which the Intentional content can make reference? Each has an experience whose content is

1. Vis exp (a man whom I recognize as Baxter is before me and his presence and features are causing this visual experience)

as distinct from

2. Vis exp (a man with what I recognize as identical Baxter-like features is before me and his presence and features are causing this visual experience).

From Jones's point of view the content of 1. is the same as

3. I have a capacity to recognize a certain man m as Baxter which is such that:

Vis exp (a man with what I recognize as identical Baxter-like features is before me and his presence and features are causing this visual experience and that man is identical with *m*).

Both Jones and twin Jones have qualitatively identical visual experiences. The difference in the two cases is that Jones's experience makes reference to his own Background capacities and twin Jones's to his own Background capacities. Just as the indexicality of the Network solved the twin Sally problem so the indexicality of the Background solves the twin Baxter problem. Normally, the recognitional capacity will be caused by the object of the recognition, but it need not be. It is easy to imagine cases where one might learn to recognize an object without one's capacity being caused by the object.

I have, for the sake of simplicity, considered the operation of the Network and the Background separately, but, of course, in real life they operate together and indeed there is no sharp line between the two.

So far the effort has been to explain how different people with type-identical visual experiences can have different conditions of satisfaction, and even how those conditions of satisfaction can be particular rather than general. But there is a parallel and so far unanswered question about how different people with different experiences can have the same conditions of satisfaction. We might put the question in the form of an objection: "The whole account leads to a kind of solipsism. If the token identity of each visual experience figures in its conditions of satisfaction, then it would be impossible for different people ever to have experiences with the same conditions of satisfaction, but such a thing must be possible since we do see the same things as other people, and what is more we take ourselves to be seeing the same things. Notice that on your account the requisite publicity is not guaranteed by the mere fact that the same state of affairs causes both your visual experience and mine, since the question is: How can that fact be part of the visual experience?"

There is indeed an ineliminable perspectival element in vision and in perception generally. I perceive the world from the location of my body in space and time, and you from yours. But there is nothing mysterious or metaphysical about this. It is simply a consequence of the fact that my brain and the rest of my perceptual apparatus are located in my body and your brain and perceptual apparatus are located in yours. But this does not prevent us from having shared visual and other sorts of experiences. Suppose, for example, that you and I are both looking at the same object, e.g., a painting, and discussing it. Now, from my point of view, I am not just seeing a painting, rather I am seeing it as part of *our* seeing it. And the shared aspect of the experience involves more than just that I believe that you and I are seeing the same thing; but the seeing itself must make reference to that belief, since if the belief is false then something in the content of my experience is unsatisfied: I am not seeing what I took myself to be seeing.

There is a variety of different types of shared experiences, and I am not sure how, or even if, the various complexities can be represented in the notation we have been using so far. One very simple sort of case would be where the content of my visual experience makes reference to the content of a belief about what you are seeing. An example, stated in ordinary English, would be a case in which "I believe there is a particular painting that you are seeing and I am seeing it too". Here the "it" within the scope of "see" is within the scope of the quantifier which in turn is within the scope of the "believe", even though the "see" is not within the scope of the "believe". The sentence doesn't say that I believe I see it, it says I see it. Using square brackets for the scope of the Intentional verbs and round brackets for the quantifiers and allowing the two to cross over we get

Bel [(E! x) (you are seeing x] &
Vis exp [φx and the fact that φx is causing this Vis exp])

The fact that you and I are having a shared visual experience of the object does not require that we see it under the same aspect. Thus, in the above formulation I see it under the aspect φ, I assume you see the same object, but I don't have to assume that you see it under φ.

VII

There is a skeptical argument against the theory of perception presented in this chapter which I promised earlier that I would discuss. Here is the argument: "It looks as if the causal version of naive realism that you have been presenting leads to skepticism about the possibility of ever knowing about the real world on the basis of your perceptions, because there isn't any neutral point of view from which you can examine the relationships between your experiences and their supposed Intentional objects (or conditions of satisfaction) to see if the latter really cause the former. On your account you only really see the car if the car causes your visual experience, but how can you even tell or find out whether the car causes your visual experience? If you try to find out you can only have other experiences, visual and otherwise, and exactly the same problem arises for them. It looks as if the most you could ever get would be some internal coherence to the system of your experiences, but there is no way you can ever break out of the system to find out if there really are objects on the other side of it. The same kind of unknowability of the real world that you accused the representative theory of implying is also implied by your theory, because unless you can know that objects cause your experiences you can't know that you perceive objects; and on your own account you can't know that objects cause experiences because you can't observe the two terms independently to see if there is a causal relation between them. Every time you believe you are observing an object you must presuppose the very causal relation you are trying to ascertain."

In order to see what is wrong with this objection (and what is right about it) we need to set it out as a series of steps.

1. In order that it be really the case that I am seeing the car, my visual experiences must be caused by the car.

2. Therefore, in order for me really to know that there is a car there on the basis of my visual experiences, I must know that the car caused the visual experiences.

3. But the only way I could know such a causal claim is by a causal inference; I infer from the presence and nature of the experiences as effect to the existence and characteristics of the car as cause.

4. But such a causal inference could never be justified, because there is no way to check on the inference since the only access I have to the car is by way of other experiences, of both visual and other sorts. In the way that I can check the causal inference from escaping steam to boiling water in the pot, I cannot check the

inference from visual experience to material object. I therefore can have no justification for accepting the inference.

5. Therefore I can never really know that the car caused my experiences.

6. Therefore, by 2 I can never really know that there is a car there on the basis of my visual experiences.

Using obvious abbreviations, the form of the argument is:

1. See $X \rightarrow X$ caused V.E.
2. Know see X on the basis of V.E. $\rightarrow$ Know X caused V.E.
3. Know X caused V.E. $\rightarrow$ Valid causal inference from V.E. to X
4. Valid causal inference $\rightarrow$ check on the inference, but $\sim$ check on inference, $\therefore \sim$ valid causal inference
5. $\therefore \sim$ know X caused V.E.
6. $\therefore \sim$ know see X, on the basis of V.E.

The steps on which this argument founders are 2 and 3. I do not *infer* (tell, or find out) that the car is causing my visual experience. I simply see the car. From the fact that the visual experience must be caused by the car in order that I see it (step 1) it does not follow that the visual experience is the 'basis' or evidence for my knowledge that I see the car (step 2), nor does it follow that there is any causal inference involved (step 3) from the visual experience as effect to the material object as cause. I no more infer that the car is the cause of my visual experience than I infer that it is yellow. When I see the car I can see that it is yellow and when I see the car I have an experience, part of whose content is that it is caused by the car. The knowledge that the car caused my visual experience derives from the knowledge that I see the car, and not conversely. Since I do not infer that there is a car there but rather simply see it, and since I do not infer that the car caused my visual experience, but rather it is part of the content of the experience that it is caused by the car, it is not correct to say that the visual experience is the 'basis' in the sense of *evidence* or *ground* for knowing that there is a car there. The 'basis' rather is that I see the car, and my seeing the car has no prior basis in that sense. I just do it. One of the components of the event of seeing the car is the visual experience, but one does not make a causal inference from the visual experience to the existence of the car.

On my account of the self-referential causal character of the

Intentional content of perception, Intentional causation cuts across the distinction between the Intentional content and the natural world which contains the objects and states of affairs which satisfy that Intentional content, because the Intentional content both represents and is one term of the causal relation and yet causation is part of the natural world. The distinction between the causation and the other conditions of satisfaction is this: If I have a visual experience of a yellow object and that experience is satisfied, then though that experience is not literally *yellow* it is literally *caused*. Furthermore, it is experienced *as* caused, whether it is satisfied or not; but it is not experienced *as* yellow, rather it is experienced as *of* something yellow.

The skeptical objection would only be valid if I could not directly experience the causal impact of objects on me in my perceptions of them but had to ascertain the presence of the object, as cause, by some further process of inference and validation of the inference. On my account the visual experience does not represent the causal relation as something existing independently of the experience, but rather part of the experience is the experience of being caused. Now the reader might justifiably feel that this notion of causation does not sit comfortably with his Humean theory of causation, and in that he is quite right, the Humean theory is precisely what is being challenged. Furthermore I owe the reader an explanation of my notion of causation, a notion I think is one we in fact all have, and such an explanation will be forthcoming in Chapter 4.

What I believe is entirely correct about the skeptical objection is that once we treat the experience as evidence on the basis of which we infer the existence of the object, then skepticism becomes unavoidable. The inference would lack any justification. And it is at this point that the metaphor of the inner and the outer sets a trap for us, for it inclines us to think we are dealing with two separate phenomena, an 'inner' experience about which we can have a kind of Cartesian certainty, and an 'outer' thing for which the inner must provide the basis, evidence, or ground. What I have been proposing in this chapter is a noninferential, that is, a naive realist, version of the causal theory of perception, according to which we are not dealing with two things one of which is the evidence for the other, but rather we perceive only one thing and in so doing have a perceptual experience.

Of course to say that part of the experience is the experience of being caused is not to say that the experience is in any way self-validating. As the classical skeptic points out, I might be having just this experience and all the same it might not be caused by its Intentional object; it might be, as they say, a hallucination. And thus the classical skeptic would argue that we are in the familiar situation that whatever ground we have for knowledge it is consistent to suppose that the ground could exist and yet the proposition we claimed to know might be false. From the statement that the experience occurs it does not follow that the object exists. But, again, this argument is a conflation of two quite distinct theses.

(1) I could be having an experience 'qualitatively indistinguishable' from this one and yet there might not be a car there.

(2) In order to know in this perceptual situation that there is a car there I have to infer its existence by a causal inference from this experience.

(1) is quite true and indeed it is a trivial consequence of my account of Intentionality. The Intentional state determines what counts as its conditions of satisfaction but it is possible for the state to be unsatisfied. But (2) does not follow from (1) and I have tried to argue that (2) is false.

There is however one further consequence of the analysis that requires special mention: those concepts that mark off real features of the world are causal concepts. Red, for example, is that feature of the world that causes things to look (and otherwise pass the tests for being), systematically and under the appropriate conditions, red. And similarly with the so-called primary qualities. Square things are those which are capable of causing certain sorts of effects on our senses and on our measuring apparatus. And this causal feature is also characteristic of those properties of the world that are not immediately accessible to the senses such as ultraviolet and infrared, for unless they were capable of having some effects – e.g., on our measuring apparatus or on other things which in turn affected our measuring apparatus which in turn affected our senses – we could have no knowledge of their existence. Now this implies that our empirical concepts for describing features of the world are applied relative to our capacity to receive causal inputs from those very features; and this in turn looks as if it leads to a form of skepticism: We can't know how the world really is because we can only know how it is in relation to our own empirical constitution and the forms in which it has a causal impact on our constitution. But this skepticism does not follow; what follows rather is that we can know how the world is, but our very notion of how it is is relative to our constitution and our causal transactions with it.

This form of skepticism is perhaps rather like Kant's skepticism about the possibility of knowledge of things-in-themselves as opposed to the mere appearance of things-in-themselves. I believe that the answer to both is to shift the axis of the question around to the point where one can see that the very notion of how things are themselves is relative to our capacity to receive causal inputs from a world which for the most part exists independently of how we represent it, and yet that this causal relativism is consistent with the most naive of naive realisms. My aim in this section has not been to answer skepticism in general but rather to answer those versions which are directed specifically at causal theories of perception.

VIII

Our account of visual perception, however, appears to lead to a paradoxical result. If the conditions of satisfaction of the visual experience that one has when one sees a building as a whole house are distinct from those that one has when one sees it merely as the façade of a house and if these different conditions of satisfaction are determined by different visual experiences, then it begins to seem as if almost any quality can be the condition of satisfaction of a visual experience. For we say not only "It looks like a house" as distinct from "It looks like the façade of a house", but we also say such things as "He looks drunk" and "She looks intelligent" and in each case the sentence is used quite literally. But how is it possible that the purely visual experience can contain as conditions of satisfaction such features as being intelligent or being drunk? Or to put the problem more generally: If the Intentionality of visual experience has the features that I have claimed, that is, if it involves a causally self-referential presentation, then those very features would appear to place very tight constraints on what can figure as the conditions of satisfaction of visual experiences. For it would seem to have the consequence that only those objects and states of

76

affairs capable of causing certain sorts of visual experiences can be part of the conditions of satisfaction of visual experiences. But on my own account the objects, states of affairs, and features in question must include not only such features as being red or being square but also being a house, being drunk, and being intelligent. And it is hard to see how it is even possible for these features to figure causally in the production of visual experiences. If intelligence is to be the condition of satisfaction of the visual experience, then on my account intelligence must be capable of causing visual experiences. But in any ordinary sense it certainly is not in that way capable of causing visual experiences, and yet we do say such things as "She looks intelligent", and we say these as literally as "It looks red".

I believe the way out of this puzzle is to distinguish between those properties where we ascertain the presence of the property solely or primarily through vision and those where some further tests are required. We do indeed say literally, "She looks intelligent" and "He looks drunk", but we do not find out that she really is intelligent or he really is drunk by mere looking. We have to perform certain other sorts of tests. The relation between "She looks intelligent" and "She is intelligent" is quite different from the relation between "It looks red" and "It is red". For in the case of red the visual conditions of satisfaction are reported in both utterances, but in the case of intelligence the conditions of satisfaction are no longer purely visual. Or to put the point another way, it is possible for somebody to look intelligent to every normal observer in normal conditions and still not be intelligent in a way that it is not possible for something to look red to normal observers in normal conditions and not be red. Looking intelligent is independent of being intelligent in a way that looking red is not independent of being red.

Thus it can be that the conditions of satisfaction of a visual experience are that somebody is intelligent, but it does not follow from this that intelligence has to be capable of causing certain sorts of visual experiences; rather, in such a case the visual features in question are that concatenation of features which constitutes looking intelligent, and looking intelligent is indeed the name of a possible visual feature. More generally, the sentence form "x looks φ" reports the presence of a purely visual feature to the extent that

"x really is φ" can be established by visual inspection. To the extent that "x really is φ" cannot be established by visual inspection, then to that extent φ is not the name of a visual feature. And indeed the sentence form "x looks φ" can itself report a purely visual feature independent of φ.

Chapter 3

INTENTION AND ACTION

I

In the course of our discussion of the Intentionality of mental states such as belief and desire and mental events such as visual experiences, we have developed a fairly extensive conceptual apparatus for analyzing problems of Intentionality, an apparatus that includes the notions of Intentional content, psychological mode, conditions of satisfaction, direction of fit, causal self-referentiality, direction of causation, Network, Background, and the distinction between presentations and other sorts of representations. The explanation of Intentionality in terms of these notions is not intended to be reductive, since each is an Intentional notion. We are not trying to show that Intentionality is really something else, but rather to explain it in terms of a family of notions each of which is explained independently, usually by way of examples. To repeat: there is no nonintentional standpoint from which we can survey the relations between Intentional states and their conditions of satisfaction. Any analysis must take place from within the circle of Intentional concepts.

The aim of this chapter is to explore the relations between intentions and actions, using this apparatus. At first sight intentions and actions seem to fit very neatly into the system. We are inclined to say: Just as my belief is satisfied iff the state of affairs represented by the content of the belief actually obtains, and my desire is satisfied iff the state of affairs represented by the content of the desire comes to pass, so my intention is satisfied iff the *action* represented by the content of the intention is actually performed. If I believe that I will vote for Jones, my belief will be *true* iff I vote for Jones, if I desire to vote for Jones my desire will be *fulfilled* iff I vote for Jones, and if I intend to vote for Jones my intention will be *carried out* iff I vote for Jones. Besides these 'semantic' parallels, there are also syntactical parallels in the sentences reporting

79

Intentional states. Leaving out the problems of tense, the 'deep structure' of the three sentences reporting my belief, desire, and intention is, respectively,

I believe + I vote for Jones
I want + I vote for Jones
I intend + I vote for Jones.

We ought to be deeply impressed by the apparent tightness of fit between the syntax and semantics: each sentence represents an Intentional state; each state represents its conditions of satisfaction and these conditions are represented by the sentence "I vote for Jones", which is exactly the embedded sentence in the sentences representing the Intentional states. The latter two sentences, but not the first, permit an equi NP deletion of the repeated "I" and the insertion of the infinitive in the surface structure, thus:

I want to vote for Jones
I intend to vote for Jones.

Furthermore, the way in which intention and action fit into this general account of Intentionality enables us to give a simple (but provisional) statement of the relations between intentions and intentional actions: an intentional action is simply the conditions of satisfaction of an intention. On this view anything that can be the satisfaction of an intention can be an intentional action. Thus, for example, spilling one's beer is not normally the condition of satisfaction of an intention, because people don't normally spill their beer intentionally; but such a thing can be an intentional action, for it can be the condition of satisfaction of an intention.

As it stands this account won't quite work, because it seems to admit too much. For example, if I intend to weigh 160 pounds by Christmas and I succeed, it won't do to say I performed the intentional action of weighing 160 pounds by Christmas nor will it do to say that weighing 160 pounds by Christmas can be an intentional action. What one wants to say rather is that if I fulfilled my intention to weigh 160 pounds by Christmas, I must have performed certain *actions by means of which* I came to weigh 160 pounds; and that needs to be further explained. Furthermore the account says nothing about general intentions. But, worse yet, this account seems to have very little explanatory power: what we want to know is, what is an intention? What is an action? And what is the character of the relation between them that is described by saying that one is the condition of satisfaction of the other? Still, I believe this provisional account is on the right track and I will come back to it later.

One advantage of it, by the way, is that it ties in with our intuition that there is a close connection between intentional actions and what one can tell people to do. Since, when one gives orders, one orders people to perform intentional actions, one can only order people to do things that they can do intentionally, and indeed it does not make any clear sense to say "I order you to perform A unintentionally". (As opposed to, say, "I order you to put yourself in a situation where you are likely to perform A unintentionally".) A good rough test for whether or not a verb phrase denotes an action type is whether or not it can occur in the imperative. "Walk", "run", and "eat" all take the imperative, but "believe", "intend", and "want" are not names of actions and so do not have a natural imperative mood form. The test is only rough because some verb phrases in the imperative indicate the manner in which actions are to be performed, rather than name actions, e.g., "Be honest!", "Be kind!"

II

So far we seem to be moving quite smoothly in our efforts to assimilate action and intention to a theory of Intentionality. However, now our troubles begin. There are several asymmetries between the relation of intention to action on the one hand, and the relation between the other Intentional states and their conditions of satisfaction on the other, asymmetries which a theory of intention and action ought to be able to explain.

First, it ought to strike us as odd that we have a special name such as "action" and "act" for the conditions of satisfaction of intentions at all. We have, for example, no special names for the conditions of satisfaction of beliefs and desires. Furthermore, the connection between what is named and the Intentional state which it satisfies is much more intimate in the case of intentions than in such other states as beliefs and desires. We saw that my belief will be satisfied iff the state of affairs I believe to obtain really does obtain and my desire will be satisfied iff the state of affairs I desire to obtain does obtain, and, similarly, my intention to do an action will be satisfied iff the action I intend to perform actually is performed. But notice that, whereas there are lots of states of affairs which are not believed to obtain or desired to obtain, there are no actions without intentions. Even where there is an unintentional action such as Oedipus's marrying his mother, that is only because there is an identical event which is an action he performed intentionally, namely, marrying Jocasta. There are many states of affairs without corresponding beliefs and many states of affairs without corresponding desires, but there are in general no actions without corresponding intentions.[1] Why should there be this asymmetry?

Second, even though an event represented in the content of my intention occurs, it isn't necessarily the satisfaction of my intention. As many philosophers have remarked, it has to come about 'in the right way', and this again has no analogue for beliefs and desires. Thus, if I believe it's raining and it is raining, my belief is true no matter how it got to be raining. And if my desire is to be rich and I become rich, that desire is satisfied no matter how I became rich. But a variation on an example of Chisholm's[2] will show that this condition does not hold for actions. Suppose Bill intends to kill his uncle, then it might come about that he kills his uncle and yet the conditions of satisfaction of his intention do not obtain. They may not obtain even in some cases where his intention to kill his uncle actually caused him to kill his uncle. Suppose he is out driving thinking about how he is going to kill his uncle, and suppose his intention to kill his uncle makes him so nervous and excited that he accidentally runs over and kills a pedestrian who happens to be his uncle. Now in this case it is true to say that he killed his uncle and true to say that his intention to kill his uncle was (part of) the cause of his killing his uncle, but not true to say that he carried out his intention to kill his uncle or that

1 On my account such things as snoring, sneezing, sleeping, and many reflex movements are not actions. Whether or not I am right about ordinary usage is less important than whether I can give an account of intention and action that shows such cases to be fundamentally different from those that I count as actions.
2 R. M. Chisholm, 'Freedom and action', in K. Lehrer (ed.), *Freedom and Determinism* (New York: Random House, 1966), p. 37.

his intention was satisfied; because he didn't kill his uncle *intentionally*.

There are several such puzzling examples in the literature. Consider the following from Davidson,[3] which he says illustrates the sources of his

> despair of spelling out . . . the way in which attitudes must cause action if they are to rationalize the action . . . . A climber might want to rid himself of the weight and danger of holding another man on a rope, and he might know that by loosening his hold on the rope he could rid himself of the weight and danger. This belief and want might so unnerve him as to cause him to loosen his hold, and yet it might be the case that he never chose to loosen his hold, nor did he do it intentionally.

And, one could add, he might even form the intention to loosen his hold and his intention might make him so nervous that he loosens his hold unintentionally. In such a case, he intends to loosen his hold, he does loosen his hold, and his intention causes him to loosen his hold, but he does not loosen his hold intentionally nor does he carry out his intention to loosen his hold. Why not?

Another (equally homicidal) example derives from Dan Bennett.[4] A man may try to kill someone by shooting at him. Suppose he misses him, but the shot stampedes a herd of wild pigs which trample the intended victim to death. In this case the man's intention has the death of the victim as part of the conditions of satisfaction and the victim dies as a result, but all the same we are reluctant to say that it was an intentional killing.

III

In this section and the next, I want to develop an account of the relations between intention and action that will show how the relations fit into the general theory of Intentionality sketched in Chapters 1 and 2 and yet account for the paradoxical features of the relation of action and intention discussed in the previous section.

3 D. Davidson, 'Freedom to act', in T. Honderich (ed.), *Essays on Freedom of Action* (London, Henley and Boston: Routledge & Kegan Paul, 1973), pp. 153–4.
4 Cited by D. Davidson in Honderich (ed.), *op. cit.* pp. 152–3.

For the sake of simplicity I will start with very simple actions such as raising one's arm. Later I will consider more complex cases.

We need first to distinguish those intentions that are formed prior to actions and those that are not. The cases we have considered so far are cases where the agent has the intention to perform the action prior to the performance of the action itself, where, for example, he knows what he is going to do because he already has an intention to do that thing. But not all intentions are like that: suppose you ask me, "When you suddenly hit that man, did you first form the intention to hit him?" My answer might be, "No, I just hit him". But even in such a case I hit him intentionally and my action was done with the intention of hitting him. I want to say about such a case that the intention was *in the action* but that there was no *prior intention*. The characteristic linguistic form of expression of a prior intention is "I will do *A*" or "I am going to do *A*". The characteristic form of expression of an intention in action is "I am doing *A*". We say of a prior intention that the agent acts on his intention, or that he carries out his intention, or that he tries to carry it out; but in general we can't say such things of intentions in action, because the intention in action just is the Intentional content of the action; the action and the intention are inseparable in ways that I will shortly try to explain.

There are at least two ways to make the distinction between an intention in action and a prior intention clearer. The first, as our previous example suggests, is to note that many of the actions one performs, one performs quite spontaneously, without forming, consciously or unconsciously, any prior intention to do those things. For example, suppose I am sitting in a chair reflecting on a philosophical problem, and I suddenly get up and start pacing about the room. My getting up and pacing about are clearly intentional actions, but in order to do them I do not need to form an intention to do them prior to doing them. I don't in any sense have to have a plan to get up and pace about. Like many of the things one does, I just do these actions; I just act. A second way to see the same distinction is to note that even in cases where I have a prior intention to do some action there will normally be a whole lot of subsidiary actions which are not represented in the prior intention but which are nonetheless performed intentionally. For example, suppose I have a prior intention to drive to my office, and suppose as I am carrying out this prior intention I shift from second gear to third gear. Now I formed no prior intention to shift from second to third. When I formed my intention to drive to the office I never gave it a thought. Yet my action of shifting gears was intentional. In such a case I had an intention in action to shift gears, but no prior intention to do so.

All intentional actions have intentions in action but not all intentional actions have prior intentions. I can do something intentionally without having formed a prior intention to do it, and I can have a prior intention to do something and yet not act on that intention. Still, in cases where the agent is acting on his prior intention there must be a close connection between the prior intention and the intention in action, and we will also have to explain this connection.

Both prior intentions and intentions in action are causally self-referential in the same sense that perceptual experiences and memories are causally self-referential. That is, like perceptual experiences and memories their conditions of satisfaction require that the Intentional states themselves stand in certain causal relations to the rest of their conditions of satisfaction. We will explore this feature in detail later but it can be illustrated by considering the causal self-referentiality of prior intentions. Suppose I intend to raise my arm. The content of my intention can't be that my arm goes up, for my arm can go up without me raising my arm. Nor can it be simply that my intention causes my arm to go up, for we saw in our discussion of the examples from Chisholm, Davidson, and Bennett that a prior intention can cause a state of affairs represented by the intention without that state of affairs being the action that would satisfy the intention. Nor, oddly enough, can it be

(that I perform the action of raising my arm)

because I might perform the action of raising my arm in ways that had nothing to do with this prior intention. I might forget all about this intention and later raise my arm for some other independent reason. The Intentional content of my intention must be at least

(that I perform the action of raising my arm by way of carrying out *this intention*).

But what is meant by "carrying out" in this formulation? At least this much: If I am carrying out that intention then the intention must play a causal role in the action, and the argument for this is simply that if we break the causal connection between intention and action we no longer have a case of carrying out the intention. Suppose that I forget all about the prior intention to raise my arm in such a way that it plays no causal role, conscious or unconscious, in the subsequent action; in such a case the action is not a case of carrying out that intention. Still, this formulation raises a lot of questions we will have to answer later. What is meant by "action" and what exactly is the role of the causal self-reference?

In the meantime, this causal self-referential character of intentions will seem less mysterious if we compare it to a similar phenomenon in the realm of speech acts (and incidentally it is always a good idea when you get stuck in the theory of Intentionality to go back to speech acts, because the phenomena of speech acts are so much more accessible). Suppose I order you to leave the room. And suppose you respond by saying "I am going to leave the room, but not because you ordered me to, I was just about to leave the room anyhow. But I would not have left the room because you ordered me to." If you then leave the room, have you *obeyed my order?* Well, you certainly didn't *disobey* the order, but there is a sense in which you did not obey it either, because the order did not function as a reason for what you did. We would not, for example, on the basis of a series of such cases describe you as an "obedient" person. But what this illustrates is that the content of my order is not simply that you leave the room, but that you leave the room by way of obeying *this order*; that is, the logical form of the order is not simply

I order you (that you leave the room)

but rather it is causally self-referential in the form

I order you (that you leave the room by way of obeying this order).[5]

---

5 The self-reference does not lead to an infinite regress. When I order you to do *A*, I am indeed creating a reason for your doing *A* such that the order will be obeyed iff you do *A* for that reason, i.e., because I ordered you to do it; but I do not in addition create a reason for it to be a reason, nor do I give a second-level order to you to obey my first-level order.

So far in this section I have argued that we need a distinction between prior intentions and intentions in action, and I have claimed, though not yet fully substantiated, that both are causally self-referential in the same sense as visual experiences and memories. I now want to extend the analogy between perception and action by exploring those experiences that are characteristic of actions. Let us first remind ourselves of the relevant features of perceptions. When you see the table in front of you there are two elements in the perceptual situation: the visual experience and the table, but the two are not independent for the visual experience has the presence and features of the table as conditions of satisfaction. Now how is it with simple actions such as raising your arm? What happens when you perform the intentional action of raising your arm? Just as there are characteristic experiences of seeing a table, so I shall argue there are characteristic experiences of raising your arm. Raising your arm, like seeing the table, characteristically consists of two components: the experience of raising your arm and the physical movement of the arm, but the two are not independent, for just as the visual experience of the table has Intentionality, so the experience of raising your arm has Intentionality; it has conditions of satisfaction. If I have exactly this experience but my arm doesn't go up, I would be in a situation analogous to the situation where I had exactly this experience but there was no table in front of me. I would have an experience with an Intentionality whose content was unsatisfied.

We can probe the parallel between action and perception further by considering Wittgenstein's question: If I raise my arm, what is left over if I subtract the fact that my arm went up?[6] The question seems to me exactly analogous to the question: If I see the table what is left over if I subtract the table? And in each case the answer is that a certain form of presentational Intentionality is left over; what is left over in the case of visual perception is a visual experience; what is left over in the case of action is an experience of acting. When I raise my arm I have a certain experience and, like my visual experience of the table, this arm-raising experience has an Intentional content. If I have this experience and my arm doesn't go up, that content is not satisfied. Furthermore, even if

6 See Chapter 1, p. 16.

my arm goes up, but goes up without this experience, I didn't raise my arm, it just went up. That is, just as the case of seeing the table involves two related components, an Intentional component (the visual experience) and the conditions of satisfaction of that component (the presence and features of the table), so the act of raising my arm involves two components, an Intentional component (the experience of acting) and the conditions of satisfaction of that component (the movement of my arm). As far as Intentionality is concerned, the differences between the visual experience and the experience of acting are in the direction of fit and in the direction of causation: the visual experience stands to the table in the mind-to-world direction of fit. If the table isn't there, we say that I was mistaken, or was having a hallucination, or some such. And the direction of causation is from the object to the visual experience. If the Intentional component is satisfied it must be caused by the presence and features of the object. But in the case of the experience of acting, the Intentional component has the world-to-mind direction of fit. If I have this experience but the event doesn't occur we say such things as that I *failed* to raise my arm, and that I *tried* to raise my arm but did not succeed. And the direction of causation is from the experience of acting to the event. Where the Intentional content is satisfied, that is, where I actually succeed in raising my arm, the experience of acting causes the arm to go up. If it didn't cause the arm to go up, but something else did, I didn't raise my arm: it just went up for some other reason. And just as the visual experience is not a representation of its conditions of satisfaction but a presentation of those conditions, so I want to say, the experience of acting is a presentation of its conditions of satisfaction. On this account, action, like perception, is a causal and Intentional transaction between mind and the world.

Now, just as we don't have a name for that which gives us the Intentional content of our visual perception but have to invent a term of art, "the visual experience", so there is no term for that which gives us the Intentional content of our intentional action, but have to invent a term of art, "the experience of acting". But the term would mislead if it gave the impression that such things were passive experiences or sensations that simply afflict one, or that they were like what some philosophers have called volitions or acts of willing or anything of that sort. They are not acts at all, for we no more *perform* our experience of acting than we *see* our visual experiences.[7] Nor am I claiming that there is any special feeling that belongs to all intentional actions.

The simplest way to *argue* for the presence of the experience of acting as one of the components of such simple actions as raising one's arm is to show how each component may be carved off from the other. Consider first the famous case described by William James[8] in which a patient with an anesthetized arm is ordered to raise it. The patient's eyes are closed and unknown to him his arm is held to prevent it from moving. When he opens his eyes he is surprised to find that he has not raised his arm; that is, he is surprised to discover that there was no arm movement. In such a case he has the experience of acting and that experience plainly has Intentionality; we can say of the patient that his experience is one of *trying* but *failing* to raise his arm. And the conditions of satisfaction are determined by the experience; he knows what he is trying to do and he is surprised to discover that he has not succeeded. Such a case is analogous to the hallucination case in perception because the Intentional component occurs in the absence of the conditions of satisfaction. Now consider cases from Penfield where we have the bodily movements but not the Intentional components.

> When I have caused a conscious patient to move his hand by applying an electrode to the motor cortex of one hemisphere I have often asked him about it. Invariably his response was: "I didn't do that. You did." When I caused him to vocalize, he said, "I didn't make that sound. You pulled it out of me."[9]

In such a case we have a bodily movement but no action; indeed, we have a bodily movement which may be exactly the same as the bodily movement in an intentional action, but the patient is surely

---

7 Prichard's theory of action seems to me to commit the same mistake as sense datum theories of perception. He recognizes the existence of the experience of acting, but he wants to make the experience into the Intentional object in the same way that sense datum theorists want to make the visual experience the object of visual perception (H. A. Prichard, 'Acting, willing, desiring', in A. R. White (ed.) *The Philosophy of Action* (Oxford: Oxford University Press, 1968), pp. 56–69.

8 *The Principles of Psychology*, vol. 2 (New York: Dover Publications, 1950), pp. 489ff.

9 Wilder Penfield, *The Mystery of the Mind* (Princeton: Princeton University Press, 1975), p. 76.

right in denying that he performed any action. If the bodily movements are the same in the two cases, what is missing in the case where the hand moves but there is no action? And how does the patient know with such confidence that in the one case he is moving his hand and in the other case he is not doing anything? As an answer to these questions I am suggesting first there is an obvious phenomenal difference between the case where one moves one's hand and the case where one observes it move independently of one's intentions, the two cases just feel different to the patient; and secondly that this phenomenal difference carries with it a logical difference in the sense that the experience of moving one's hand has certain conditions of satisfaction. Such concepts as "trying", "succeeding", and "failing" apply to it in ways that they do not apply to the experiences the patient has when he simply observes his hand moving. Now this experience with its phenomenal and logical properties I am calling the experience of acting. And I am not claiming that there is a characteristic experience common to every intentional action, but rather that for every conscious intentional action there is the experience of performing that action, and that experience has an Intentional content. One last argument for the same conclusion: we ought to allow ourselves to be struck by the implications of the fact that at any point in a man's conscious life he knows without observation the answer to the question, "What are you now doing?" Many philosophers have noted this fact but none, to my knowledge, have explored its implications for Intentionality. Even in a case where a man is mistaken about what the results of his efforts are he still knows what he is *trying* to do. Now the knowledge of what one is doing in this sense, in the sense in which such knowledge does not guarantee that one knows that one is succeeding, and does not depend on any observations that one makes of oneself, characteristically derives from the fact that a conscious experience of acting involves a consciousness of the conditions of satisfaction of that experience. And again, the parallel with perception holds. Just as at any point in a man's conscious life he knows the answer to the question, "What do you see now?", so he knows the answer to the question, "What are you doing now?" In both cases the knowledge in question is simply knowledge of the conditions of satisfaction of a certain sort of presentation.

	visual perception	intentional action
Intentional component	visual experience	experience of acting
Conditions of satisfaction of the Intentional component	that there be objects, states of affairs, etc., having certain features and certain causal relations to the visual experience	that there be certain bodily movements, states, etc., of the agent, and that these have certain causal relations to the experience of acting
Direction of fit	mind-to-world	world-to-mind
Direction of causation	world-to-mind (i.e., the presence of features of the object cause the experience)	mind-to-world (i.e., the experience causes the movements)
Corresponding features of the world	objects and states of affairs	movements and states of the agent

The parallel between the Intentionality of visual perception and the Intentionality of intentional action can be made explicit in the accompanying table.

IV

So far I have made three claims: first that there is a distinction between prior intentions and intentions in action; second that both are causally self-referential; and third that the action, for example, of raising one's arm, contains two components, the experience of acting (which has a form of Intentionality that is both presentational and causal), and the event of one's arm going up. Next I want to put these conclusions into a general account of the relations of prior intentions, intentions in action, and actions.

The Intentional content of the intention in action and the experience of acting are identical. Indeed, as far as Intentionality is concerned, the experience of acting just is the intention in action. Why then do we need both notions? Because the experience of acting is a conscious experience with an Intentional content, and the intention in action just is the Intentional component, regardless of whether it is contained in any conscious experience of acting. Sometimes one performs intentional actions without any conscious experience of doing so; in such a case the intention in action exists without any experience of acting. The only difference, then, between them is that the experience may have certain phenomenal properties that are not essential to the intention. In exactly the same way, the visual experience has the same Intentionality as its presentational content but the experience has certain phenomenal properties that are not essential to that Intentionality (as the Weiskrantz experiments mentioned in Chapter 2 show).

Our problem now is to lay bare the relations between the following four elements: the prior intention, the intention in action, the bodily movement, and the action. The method is to take a simple example and make fully explicit the Intentional contents of the two intentions. Now why is that the method? Because our aim is to explain the relations between intentions and actions; and since an action is, in some sense at least, the condition of satisfaction of the intention to perform it, any attempt to clarify these relations must make completely explicit how the Intentional content of the intention represents (or presents) the action (or movement) as its conditions of satisfaction. And this method differs somewhat from the standard methods of the philosophy of action because we don't stand back a long way from the action and see which *descriptions* we can make of it, we have to get right up close to it and see what these descriptions are actually describing. The other method incidentally produces such true but superficial results as that an action "can be intentional under one description, but not intentional under another" – one might as well say that a fire-engine can be red under one description but not red under another. What one wants to know is: What facts exactly are these various descriptions describing? What fact about the action makes it "intentional under one description" and what fact about it makes it "not intentional under another"?

Suppose I recently had a prior intention to raise my arm and suppose, acting on that intention, I now raise my arm. How does it work? The representative content of the prior intention can be expressed as follows:

(I perform the action of raising my arm by way of carrying out this intention).

The prior intention thus makes reference to the whole action as a unit, not just the movement, and it is causally self-referential. But the action as we have seen contains two components, the experience of acting and the movement, where the Intentional content of the experience of acting and the intention in action are identical. The next step then is to specify the Intentional content of the intention in action and show the relation of its Intentional content to that of the prior intention. Remember, the method of identifying an Intentional content with a direction of fit is always to ask oneself what must be the case in order that the Intentional content be satisfied: one identifies the Intentionality by its conditions of satisfaction. Using this test the presentational content of the intention in action is

(My arm goes up as a result of this intention in action).

Now at first sight the contents of the prior intention and the intention in action look quite different, because, though both are causally self-referential, the prior intention represents the whole action as the rest of its conditions of satisfaction, but the intention in action presents, but does not *re*present, the physical movement and not the whole action as the rest of its conditions of satisfaction. In the former case the whole action is the 'Intentional object'; in the latter case the movement is the 'Intentional object'. The intention in action, like the prior intention, is self-referential in the sense that its Intentional content determines that it is satisfied only if the event that is its condition of satisfaction is caused by it. Another difference is that in any real-life situation the intention in action will be much more determinate than the prior intention, it will include not only that my arm goes up but that it goes up in a certain way and at a certain speed, etc.[10]

---

10 The relative indeterminacy of prior intentions is most obvious in the case of complex actions. In the earlier example of carrying out my intention to drive to my office, there will be a large number of subsidiary acts that are not represented by the prior intention but are presented by the intentions in action: I intentionally start the engine, shift gears, pass slow-moving vans, stop at red lights, swerve to avoid cyclists, change lanes, and so on with dozens of subsidiary acts that are performed intentionally but need not have been represented by my prior intention. This difference has also been a source of confusion in philosophy. Several philosophers have remarked that not everything I do intentionally is something I have an intention to do. For example, the particular movements of my hand when I brush my teeth are done intentionally, even though I had

Well, if the content of the prior intention and the intention in action are so different, how do they ever – so to speak – get together? In fact the relationship is quite simple as we can see by unpacking the content of the prior intention and making explicit the nature of the causal self-reference of the prior intention. Since the whole action is represented as a unit by the prior intention and since the action consists of two components, the experience of acting and the physical movement, in order to make the content of the prior intention fully explicit we can represent each component separately. Furthermore, since both the self-reference of the prior intention and the self-reference of the intention in action are causal,[11] the prior intention causes the intention in action which causes the movement. By transitivity of Intentional causation we can say that the prior intention causes both the intention in action and the movement, and, since this combination is simply the action, we can say that the prior intention causes the action. The picture that emerges is this:

$$
\underbrace{\text{prior intention} \xrightarrow{\text{causes}} \text{intention in action} \xrightarrow{\text{causes}} \text{bodily movement}}_{\text{action}}
$$

This also enables us to see what was wrong in the Chisholm-style counterexamples I presented earlier. For example, Bill had the prior intention to kill his uncle and his intention caused him to kill his uncle but his prior intention didn't cause an intention in action that presented the killing of his uncle as Intentional object, it just presented his driving his car or some such. (More about this later.) Since, as we have seen, the form of self-reference of the prior intention is causal and since the representation of the action can be

---

no intention to do them. But this view is a mistake that derives from a failure to see the difference between prior intentions and intentions in action. I may have had no prior intention to make just these hand movements but I had an intention in action to make them. G.H. Von Wright, *Explanation and understanding* (Ithaca N.Y.: Cornell University Press), 1971, pp. 89–90.

11 It is perhaps worth emphasizing that this view does not imply determinism. When one acts on one's desires or carries out one's prior intention, the desire and intention function causally, but it is not necessarily the case that one could not have done otherwise, that one simply could not help oneself.

split into two components, the Intentional content of the prior intention can now be expressed as follows:

(This prior intention causes an intention in action which is a presentation of my arm going up, and which causes my arm to go up.)

And thus the prior intention causes the intention in action. By transitivity of Intentional causation, the prior intention represents and causes the entire action, but the intention in action presents and causes only the bodily movement.

I think these points can be made clearer by pursuing our analogy with perception a bit further. Roughly speaking the prior intention to raise my arm is to the action of raising my arm as the memory of seeing a flower is to seeing a flower; or rather the formal relations between the memory, the visual experience of the flower, and the flower are the mirror image of the formal relations between the prior intention, the intention in action and the bodily movement. The seeing consists of two components, the visual experience and the flower, where the presence of (and features of) the flower cause the visual experience and the visual experience has the presence and features of the flower as the rest of its conditions of satisfaction. The content of the visual experience is that there is a flower there and it is self-referential in the sense that, unless the fact that there is a flower there causes this experience, the conditions of satisfaction do not obtain, i.e., I do not actually see that there is a flower there, nor do I see the flower. The memory of seeing the flower represents both the visual experience and the flower and is self-referential in the sense that, unless the memory was caused by the visual experience which in turn was caused by the presence of (and features of) the flower, I didn't really remember seeing the flower. Now similarly the action consists of two components, the experience of acting and the movement, where the experience of acting causes the movement and has the movement (together with its features) as the rest of its conditions of satisfaction. The content of the experience of acting is that there is a movement of my arm, and it is self-referential in the sense that, unless the movement is caused by this experience, the conditions of satisfaction do not obtain, i.e., I do not actually raise my arm. The prior intention to raise my arm represents both the experience of acting and the movement, and is self-referential in the sense that, unless this intention causes the experience of acting which in turn causes the movement, I don't really carry out my prior intention. These relations can be made explicit by expanding our earlier table (p. 91). (Tables are usually boring, but since this one contains a summary of much of the theory of Intentionality, I ask the reader to scrutinize it carefully.)

A few things about this table are worth special mention. First, neither the memory nor the prior intention is essential to the visual perception or the intentional action respectively. I can see a lot of things that I have no memory of seeing and I can perform a lot of intentional actions without any prior intention to perform those actions. Second, the asymmetry of the direction of fit and the direction of causation is too neat to be accidental. Put crudely, the intuitive explanation is this: When I try to make the world be the way I intend it to be, I succeed if the world comes to be the way I intend it to *be* (world-to-mind direction of fit) only if I *make* it be that way (mind-to-world direction of causation). Analogously, I see the world the way it really *is* (mind-to-world direction of fit) only if the way the world is *makes* me see it that way (world-to-mind direction of causation). Third, for the sake of simplicity I have left out of the table the fact that the conditions of satisfaction of the Intentional components will contain various details about what the flower looks like and how the raising of the arm is performed. I have not tried to include everything. Fourth, the formal structure of the chart is not meant to suggest that perception and action function independently of each other. For most complex actions, such as driving a car or eating a meal, I have to be able to perceive what I am doing in order to do it; and similarly there is an intentional element in most complex perceptions, as when I am looking at a painting or feeling the texture of a rug. Fifth, because of the transitivity of causation, I have allowed myself to oscillate between saying the memory of seeing the flower is caused by the event of seeing the flower and the memory of seeing the flower is caused by the visual experience which when satisfied is in turn caused by the presence of the flower. Similarly I oscillate between saying the prior intention causes the action and the prior intention causes the intention in action which causes the movement. Since in each case the complex event contains a

A comparison of the forms of Intentionality involved in seeing a flower and remembering a flower on the one hand, and (prior) intending to raise one's arm and raising one's arm on the other

	visual perception	memory	intentional action	prior intention
How reported	I see the flower	I remember seeing the flower	I am raising my arm	I intend to raise my arm
Nature of the Intentional component	visual experience	memory	intention in action (= experience of acting)	prior intention
Presentation or representation	presentation	representation	presentation	representation
Conditions of satisfaction of the Intentional component	that there be a *state of affairs* that the flower is present and that this state of affairs causes *this visual experience*	that there be an *event of* seeing the flower consisting of two components, the *state of affairs* that the flower is present and the *visual experience*, and the *event* causes *this memory*	that there be an *event* of my arm raising and *this* intention in action causes that *event*	that there be an *action* of raising my arm consisting of two components, the *event* of the arm raising and the *intention in action*, and *this prior intention* causes the *action*
Direction of fit	mind-to-world	mind-to-world	world-to-mind	world-to-mind
Direction of causation	world-to-mind	world-to-mind	mind-to-world	mind-to-world
Nature of the self-reference of the Intentional component	as part of the conditions of satisfaction of the visual experience, it must be caused by the rest of its own conditions of satisfaction	as part of the conditions of satisfaction of the memory, it must be caused by the rest of its own conditions of satisfaction	as part of the conditions of satisfaction of the intention in action it must cause the rest of its own conditions of satisfaction	as part of the conditions of satisfaction of the prior intention it must cause the rest of its own conditions of satisfaction
Corresponding objects and events in the world (Intentional objects)	flower	flower / event of seeing the flower	movement of the arm	movement of the arm / action of raising the arm

component which is both Intentional and causal and since in each case the Intentional component stands in certain causal relations to another Intentional state which represents the whole complex event, it doesn't seem to me to matter which of the two ways of speaking we adopt.

V

We have so far been talking mostly about very simple cases such as raising one's arm and I will now very briefly sketch how this theory could be extended to account for complex intentions and the relations between complex intentions, the accordion effect[12] and basic actions.[13]

Consider Gavrilo Princip and his murder of Archduke Franz Ferdinand in Sarajevo. Of Princip we say that he:

pulled the trigger
fired the gun
shot the Archduke
killed the Archduke
struck a blow against Austria
avenged Serbia

Furthermore, each member of this list is systematically related to those preceding and succeeding it: Princip, for example, fired the gun *by means of* pulling the trigger and he shot the Archduke *by means of* firing the gun. Some but not all of these relations are causal. Pulling the trigger causes the gun to fire; but killing the Archduke doesn't *cause* a blow to be struck against Austria, in the circumstances it just *is* striking a blow against Austria. The members of the list, together with the causal (or other sorts of) relations between them constitute the conditions of satisfaction of a single complex intention in action on the part of Princip. The proof of this is that the specification of any or all of them could have counted as a true answer to the question, "What are you now doing?", where that question asks, "What intentional action are

---

12 The term "accordion effect" is due to J. Feinberg, *Doing and Deserving* (Princeton: Princeton University Press), 1970, p. 34.
13 The term "basic action" is due to A. Danto, 'Basic actions', in White (ed.) *op. cit.* pp. 43–58.

you now performing or trying to perform?" And the test which shows them to be part of the content of the intention in action, to repeat, is: "What counts as succeeding or failing?", i.e., what are the conditions of satisfaction of the Intentional content? There were all sorts of other things going on at the time, many of them known to Princip, which were not part of the conditions of satisfaction and so not part of the complex intention. Complex intentions are those where the conditions of satisfaction include not just a bodily movement a, but some further components of the action, $b, c, d, \ldots$, which we intend to perform by way of (or by means of, or in, or by, etc.) performing $a, b, c, \ldots$, and the representation of both $a, b, c, \ldots$ and the relations among them are included in the content of the complex intention. It is a remarkable and little-noted fact of human and animal evolution that we have the capacity to make intentional bodily movements where the conditions of satisfaction of our intentions go beyond the bodily movements. Princip moved only his finger but his Intentionality covered the Austro-Hungarian Empire. This capacity to have additional conditions of satisfaction beyond our bodily movements is a key to understanding meaning and causation as we will see in subsequent chapters.

Our ability to expand true descriptions of actions in ways exemplified by this list is sometimes called the accordion effect. Starting in the middle we can extend the accordion up or down by earlier or later members of the sequence of intentions. But notice that we can't go on indefinitely. As far as the causal story is concerned there are lots of things that happened up above the top, down below the bottom and off to the side which are not part of the accordion of intentional action. Thus we could add to the list as follows:

He produced neuron firings in his brain
contracted certain muscles in his arm and hand

pulled the trigger
fired the gun
shot the Archduke   moved a lot of
killed the Archduke   air molecules
struck a blow against Austria
avenged Serbia

ruined Lord Grey's summer season
convinced the Emperor Franz Josef that God was punishing the
   family
angered Wilhelm II
started the First World War

But none of these things above, below, or to the side are intentional actions of Princip, and I am inclined to say none of them are actions of his at all. They are just unintended occurrences that happened as a result of his action. As far as *intentional* actions are concerned the boundaries of the accordion are the boundaries of the complex intention; and indeed we have the accordion effect for intentional actions, because we have complex intentions of the sort I have described. But the complex intention does not quite set the boundaries of the *action*, because of the possibility of unintentional actions.

If we are going to have any use for the concept of a basic action at all, we might say that the top member of any such accordion is a basic action, and we might indeed define a basic action type as follows: A is a basic action type for an agent S iff S is able to perform acts of type A and S can intend to do an act of type A without intending to do any other action by means of which he intends to do A. Notice that this definition would make an action basic only relative to an agent and his skills; what is basic for one agent might not be basic for another. But that may be a useful way to describe the facts. For a good skier, making a left turn can be a basic action. He just intends to do it and he does it. For a beginner to make a left turn, he must put his weight on the downhill ski while edging it into the slope, stem the uphill ski, then shift the weight from left to right ski, etc., all of which are reports of the content of his intentions in action. For two agents the physical movements might be indistinguishable even though one was performing a – for him – basic action and the other was performing the same actions by means of performing a basic action. Furthermore, this definition would have the consequence that for any one agent there may be no sharp dividing line between his basic and nonbasic actions. But again, that may be the right way to describe the facts.

In this section I want to tie up a few loose ends before going on to show how this account solves the paradoxes of section II.

Unintentional actions. What do people mean when they say that an action can be "intentional under one description but not intentional under another"? And what is an unintentional action anyhow? An intentional action consists of two components, an Intentional component and an event which is its Intentional object; the intention in action is the Intentional component and it presents the Intentional object as its conditions of satisfaction. But the complex event which constitutes the action will also have all sorts of other features not presented by the Intentional content of the intention in action. Oedipus intended to marry Jocasta but when he married Jocasta he was marrying his mother. "Marrying his mother" was not part of the Intentional content of the intention in action, but it happened anyhow. The action was intentional under the description "marrying Jocasta", it was not intentional under the description "marrying his mother". But all that means is that the total action had elements which were parts of the conditions of satisfaction of the intention in action and other elements which were not. It is misleading to state these facts about actions in terms of descriptions of actions because it suggests that what matters is not the action but the way we describe the action, whereas, according to my account, what matters are the facts that the descriptions describe. This distinction will be clearer if we consider intentional actions performed by animals, and it is no more puzzling, incidentally, to ascribe intentional actions to animals than it is to ascribe visual perceptions to them. Suppose my dog is running around the garden chasing a ball; he is performing the intentional action of chasing the ball and the unintentional action of tearing up the lobelias, but this has nothing to do with anybody's descriptions. The dog certainly can't describe himself, and the facts would remain the same whether or not any human being ever did or could describe them. The sense in which one and the same event or sequence of events can be both an intentional action and an unintentional action has no intrinsic connection with linguistic representation but rather with Intentional presentation.

Some aspects of the event may be conditions of satisfaction of the Intentional content, some other aspects may not; and under the first set of aspects the action is intentional, under the second set, not; even though there need be nothing linguistic about the way an Intentional content presents its conditions of satisfaction.

How do we distinguish between those aspects of the complex event under which it is an unintentional action and those aspects which are so far from the intention that under them it is not an action at all? When Oedipus married his mother he moved a lot of molecules, caused some neurophysiological changes in his brain and altered his spatial relationship to the North Pole. These are all things he did unintentionally and none of them are actions of his. Yet I feel inclined to say that marrying his mother, though it was something he did unintentionally, was still an action, an unintentional action. What is the difference? I do not know of a clear criterion for distinguishing between those aspects of intentional actions under which they are unintentional actions and those aspects of intentional actions under which the event is not an action at all. One possible rough criterion, suggested by Dascal and Gruengard,[14] is that we count an action as unintentional under those aspects which, though not intended, are, so to speak, within the field of possibility of intentional actions of the agent as seen from our point of view. Thus, marrying his mother is in the field of possibility for being an intentional action by Oedipus, but moving molecules is not.

Mental acts and refraining. So far I have discussed only cases where the action involves a bodily movement, but I believe it is easy to extend the account to actions where there is no bodily movement or where only a mental act is performed. If, for example, I am told to hold still and I comply, the relevant content of my intention in action will be

(that this intention in action causes it to be the case that there is no bodily movement).

Thus the absence of bodily movement may be as much a part of the conditions of satisfaction of a causally self-referential intention in

---

14 M. Dascal and O. Gruengard, 'Unintentional action and non-action', *Manuscrito*, vol. 4, no. 2 (April 1981), pp. 103–13.

action as a bodily movement. Similar considerations apply to negative actions. If I am told to stop making so much noise or to refrain from insulting Smith and I comply, the intention in action must cause the absence of a phenomenon if it is to be satisfied.

Mental acts are formally isomorphic to the cases of physical acts we have considered. The only difference is that in the place of a bodily movement as a condition of satisfaction we have a purely mental event. If, for example, I am asked to form a mental image of the Eiffel tower and I comply, the relevant portion of the intention in action will be

(that this intention in action causes me to have a mental image of the Eiffel tower).

Intentions and foreknowledge. A common confusion is to suppose that if someone knows that something will be a consequence of his action then he must intend that consequence. But it is easy to see on my account why this is false. One may know that something will occur as a result of one's action even though its occurrence is not part of the conditions of satisfaction of the intention. If, for example, a dentist knows that a consequence of drilling a patient's tooth will be pain, it does not follow that he intends that consequence, and this is shown by the fact that if no pain occurs he need not say, "I have failed", but rather, "I was mistaken". In my jargon, that amounts to saying that the conditions of satisfaction of his belief were unsatisfied, not those of his intention. A related mistake is to suppose there is some close connection, perhaps even identity, between intention and responsibility. But we hold people responsible for many things they do not intend and we do not hold them responsible for many things they do intend. An example of the former type is the driver who recklessly runs over a child. He did not intend to run over the child but he is held responsible. And an example of the latter is the man who is forced at gunpoint to sign a contract. He intended to sign the contract but is not held responsible.

The reduction of intentions to beliefs and desires. Can we reduce prior intentions to beliefs and desires? I doubt it, and the reason has to do with the special causal self-referentiality of intentions. But it is instructive to see how far we can get. If I have a prior intention to perform an action A, I must believe it is possible to do A and I must have a desire to do A. The desire to do A may be a 'secondary' and not a 'primary' desire, as for example if I want to do A as a means to an end and not 'for its own sake'. Notice further that I do not have to believe that I will actually succeed in doing A, but I must at least believe it is possible for me to succeed. This last condition incidentally explains why a man may consistently have desires which he knows to be inconsistent, but he cannot consistently have intentions which he knows to be inconsistent. Even though I know it is impossible to be in both places at once, I may want to be in Sacramento all day Wednesday and want to be in Berkeley all day Wednesday. But I cannot consistently intend to be in Berkeley all day Wednesday and intend to be in Sacramento all day Wednesday. Since intentions, like desires, are closed under conjunction, the two intentions would imply an intention that I know to be impossible to fulfill.

So far, then, we have

Int (I will do A) → Bel ($\diamond$ I will do A) & Des (I will do A)

To this we need to add the self-referential feature that I desire that the state in question will cause its own conditions of satisfaction and I believe that the state will function causally toward producing its own conditions of satisfaction. As I remarked before, I needn't believe that my intention will succeed, but only that success is possible. Thus the whole state has the following implications:

Int (I will do A)⟶
There is some intentional state x such that x contains
Bel ($\diamond$ I will do A) &
Des (I will do A) &
Bel (x will function causally toward production of:
   I will do A) &
Des (x will cause: I will do A)

Now does all this add up to an intention? I think not. To construct a counterexample we would need only to construct a case where someone satisfied all of these conditions but still hadn't actually formed an intention to do A. Indeed, what the analysis of this chapter and Chapter 2 suggests is that it is a mistake to think of belief and desire as the primary forms of cognition and volition, wrong because they both lack the internal causal self-referentiality which connects cognition and volition to their conditions of satisfaction. Biologically speaking, the primary forms of Intentionality are perception and action, because by their very content they involve the organism in direct causal relations with the environment on which his survival depends. Belief and desire are what is left over if you subtract the causal self-referentiality from the Intentional contents of cognitive and volitive representational Intentional states. Now once you subtract that feature the resulting states are much more flexible. Belief, unlike memory, can be about anything and not just about what could have caused it; desire, unlike intention, can be about anything and not just about what it can cause.

Why are my intentions restricted to propositional contents that make reference to my further actions; why can't I, for example, intend that it will rain? The answer to this question follows immediately from our account: because of the causal self-referentiality of intentions I can only intend what my intention can cause. If I could cause rain as a basic action, as I can, for example, cause my arm to go up, then we could say, for example, "I intend to rain" as we now say "I intend to raise my arm", and we could say "I rained" as we now say "I raised my arm".

Intentions and explanations of action. If intentions really cause actions in the way described, then why is it that we can't normally explain an action by stating its intention. If I am asked, "Why did he raise his arm?", it sounds odd to say, "Because he intended to raise his arm". The reason it sounds odd is because by identifying the action as "raising his arm" we have already identified it in terms of the intention in action. We already reveal an implicit knowledge that the cause of the arm going up was the Intentional component in the action of raising it. But notice it doesn't sound at all odd to specify the intention in action as the cause of the movement: why did his arm go up? He raised it. Nor does it sound odd to give some *further* intention as the cause of the action. Why did he raise his arm? He was voting/waving goodbye/reaching for the book/ exercising/trying to touch the ceiling. This is what people are driving at when they say that we can often explain an action by redescribing it. But if we redescribe it truly there must be some facts we are redescribing which were left out of our first description and these facts are that the action has an Intentional component which was left out of the first description and which causes the other component, e.g., his prior intention to vote by raising his arm causes his intention in action of raising his arm which causes his arm to go up. Remember, on this account all actions consist of an Intentional component and a 'physical' (or other sort of) Intentional object component. We can always explain this non-Intentional component by the Intentional component, and the Intentional component can be as complex as you like. Why is that man wriggling around like that? He's sharpening an axe. But to say he's sharpening an axe is to say his action has at least two components, an axe sharpening intention in action and the series of movements that intention causes. But we can't answer the question, "Why is he sharpening an axe?" by identifying that intention, because we have already identified the axe sharpening intention when we asked the question. But we can say, for example, "He's preparing to chop down a tree".

Further discussion of the explanation of behavior is perhaps a topic for another book, but already implicit in my account is the following constraint on the explanation of behavior: In the Intentional explanation of actions, the propositional content in the explanation must be identical with a propositional content of an Intentional state that functioned causally, via Intentional causation, in the production of the behavior. These states that function causally may be either intentions or they may be antecedent states, such as desires, beliefs, fears, hopes, etc., that cause intentions by way of practical reason. But, in either case, if the explanation really explains, the propositional content in the explanation must be identical with the propositional content of the Intentional state that functions via Intentional causation.

What are you now doing? The content of the intention in action makes reference to itself. That is why it makes perfectly good sense to say, in answer to the question, "What are you now doing?", "I am raising my arm", and not, "I am causing my arm to go up", even though the latter expression articulates the nonself-referential component of the intention in action. But the whole action is an intention in action plus a bodily movement which is caused by the intention in action and which is the rest of the conditions of satisfaction of that intention in action. And so the speaker states the content of the intention quite precisely when he says, "I am raising my arm"; or if he wants to carve off the Intentional content from its satisfaction he can say, "I am trying to raise my arm".

In this section I will try to show how this theory of action explains the paradoxes of section II.

First, the reason there is a more intimate connection between actions and intentions than there is between, say, beliefs and states of affairs is that actions contain intentions in action as one of their components. An action is a composite entity of which one component is an intention in action. If the composite entity also contains elements which constitute the conditions of satisfaction of the Intentional component in the way described earlier, the agent succeeds in the performance of an intentional action. If not, he tries but fails. Thus, to take our overworked example: the action of my raising my arm consists of two components, the intention in action and the movement of the arm. Take away the first and you don't have an action but only a movement, take away the second and you don't have success, but only a failed effort. There are no actions, not even unintentional actions, without intentions, because every action has an intention in action as one of its components.

The sense in which we can say that an intentional action is caused by an intention or simply is the condition of satisfaction of an intention can now be made more precise. Part of the conditions of satisfaction of a prior intention really is the performance of an action, but not all actions are performed as the result of prior intentions. As we have seen, there can be actions without corresponding prior intentions, e.g., when I just haul off and hit somebody without any prior intention to hit him. But there can't be any actions, not even unintentional actions, without intentions in action. Actions thus necessarily contain intentions in action, but are not necessarily caused by prior intentions. But the Intentional content of the intention in action is not that it should cause the action, but rather that it should cause the movement (or state) of the agent which is its condition of satisfaction, and the two together, intention in action and movement, constitute the action. So it wasn't quite right to say that an intentional action just is the condition of satisfaction of an intention; it was wrong for two reasons: actions don't require prior intentions and though they do require intentions in action, the condition of satisfaction of the intention in action is not the action but rather the movement or state of the agent as caused by the intention in action. An action, to repeat, is any composite event or state that contains the occurrence of an intention in action. If that intention in action causes the rest of its conditions of satisfaction, the event or state is a successfully performed intentional action, if not, it is unsuccessful. An unintentional action is an intentional action, whether successful or not, which has aspects which were not intended in it, i.e., were not presented as conditions of satisfaction of the intention in action. However, lots of things I do unintentionally, e.g., sneezing, are not actions at all, for though they are things I cause, they contain no intentions in action.

Second, we now have a very simple explanation of the Chisholm-style counterexamples to the view that actions which are caused by intentions are intentional actions. In the uncle example, the prior intention caused the killing of the uncle but the killing of the uncle was unintentional. Why? In our analysis we saw there are three stages: the prior intention, the intention in action, and the physical movement. The prior intention causes the movement by way of causing the intention in action, which causes and presents the movement as its condition of satisfaction. But in the uncle example this middle stage was left out. We did not have the death of the uncle as the condition of satisfaction of any intention in action, and that is why he was killed unintentionally.

Davidson's example is formally just like Chisholm's: the reason the climber's loosening of his hold is unintentional in the case as described is that he has no intention in action of loosening his hold. There is no moment at which he could say, "I am now loosening my hold", as a way of articulating the content of his intention in action, i.e., as a way of making explicit the conditions of satisfaction of his intention, even though he might say just that as a way of describing what was happening to him. Even if on the basis of his belief and desire he formed a secondary desire to loosen his hold and this desire caused him to loosen his hold it is still not an intentional action if he does not have an intention in action to loosen his hold. In an intentional action, on the other hand, the standard way the sequence of Intentional states would work is as follows:

> I want (I rid myself of weight and danger)
> I believe (the best way to rid myself of weight and danger is to loosen my hold).

And by practical reason this leads to a secondary desire

> I want (I loosen my hold).

And this leads, either with or without a prior intention, to an intention in action: the climber says to himself, "Now!" And the content of his intention in action is

> I am now loosening my hold.

That is,

> This intention in action causes my hand to loosen its hold on the rope.

The whole structure is both Intentional and causal; the sequence of Intentional states causes the bodily movement. Bennett's example is genuinely different from the other two because the would-be killer actually does have an intention in action to kill the victim and it actually does cause the death of the victim. Why then are we at all reluctant to say the intention was satisfied? I think the reason is obvious: we assume that the killer had a complex intention involving a specific series of by-means-of relations. He intended to kill the victim by means of shooting him with a gun, etc., and these conditions were not satisfied. Instead the victim was killed by an unintended stampede of wild pigs.

Some people have thought that the problem in all these cases has to do with the oddity of the causal sequences, but the oddity of the causal sequence only matters if it is part of the Intentional content of the intention in action that it should not be odd. To see this we can vary the above example as follows: The killer's assistant, knowing about the pigs in advance, tells the killer, "Shoot your gun in that direction and you will kill him". The killer does as instructed with the death of the victim as the ultimate result; and in this case the killing is intentional, even though we have the same causally bizarre sequence as in Bennett's original example.

Could we find similar counterexamples where something gets between the intention in action and the event so that, though we could say the intention in action caused the physical event, the action was not intentional? One class of potential counterexamples are cases where some other intention in action intervenes to bring about the event. Thus, suppose that unknown to me my arm is rigged up so that whenever I try to raise it, somebody else causes it to go up, then the action is his not mine, even though I had the intention in action of raising my arm and in some sense that intention caused my arm to go up. (The reader will recognize this as essentially the occasionalist solution to the mind–body problem. God does all of our actions for us.)

But this class of potential counterexamples is eliminated by simply construing the relation of intention in action to its conditions of satisfaction as precluding intervention by other agents or other Intentional states. And that this is the right way to construe intentions in action is at least indicated by the fact that, when my intentions in action make explicit reference to the intentions of other agents, then in general the actions become the actions of those agents. Thus, suppose I know how my arm is rigged up and I want it to go up. My intention in action then is *getting the other agent to raise it*, not *raising it*. *My* action is getting him to raise it, *his* action is raising it.

But as long as there is no intervening Intentionality and as long as its functioning is regular and reliable, it doesn't matter how weird the physical apparatus might be. Even if unknown to me my arm is rigged up to a whole lot of electrical wires that go through Moscow and return via San Diego and when I try to raise my arm it activates this whole apparatus so that my arm goes up, all the same, I raise my arm. And indeed for some complex action types we even allow that one can perform an action by getting others to perform it. We say, for example, "Louis XIV built Versailles", even though the actual construction was not done by him.

The counterexamples we have so far discussed then are easily accounted for by a theory of the Intentionality of intention and action, and especially by an account of intentions in action. However, this account is still incomplete because there is a class of possible counterexamples I have not yet discussed, cases where the prior intention causes something else which causes the intention in action. Suppose, for example, Bill's intention to kill his uncle causes him to have a stomachache and his stomachache makes him so angry that he forgets all about his original intention but in his rage he kills the first man he sees whom he recognizes as his uncle. The elimination of these counterexamples, along with some other counterexamples concerning the Intentionality of perceptual experiences, will have to wait until we can give an account of Intentional causation in Chapter 4.

Chapter 4

INTENTIONAL CAUSATION

I

In the philosophy of mind there is an uneasy relation between Intentionality and causality. Causality is generally regarded as a natural relation between events in the world; Intentionality is regarded in a variety of ways but not generally as a natural phenomenon, as much a part of the natural order as any other biological phenomenon. Intentionality is often regarded as something transcendental, something that stands over or beyond, but is not a part of the natural world. But what then of the relation between Intentionality and causality? Can Intentional states act causally? And what causes them? I have several aims in this chapter, but a primary one is to take a step toward Intentionalizing causality and, therefore, toward naturalizing Intentionality. I begin this enterprise by examining some of the roots of the modern ideology of causation.

In the overworked philosophical example (and the recurrence of these same examples in philosophy ought to arouse our suspicions) billiard ball *A* makes its inevitable way across the green table, where it strikes billiard ball *B*, at which point *B* starts to move and *A* ceases to move. This little scene, endlessly re-enacted, is the paradigm of causality: the event of *A*'s striking *B* caused the event of *B*'s moving. And, according to the traditional view, when we witness this scene we don't actually see, or otherwise observe, any causal connections between the first event and the second. What we actually observe is one event followed by another event. We can, however, observe the repetition of similar pairs of events and this constant repetition gives us the right to say that the two members of the pairs are causally related even though we cannot observe any causal relation.

There is a metaphysical theory deeply embedded in this brief account, and even though theories of causation vary a great deal from one philosopher to the next, certain formal properties are so widely accepted as features of the causal relation as to constitute the core of the theory; its main principles are worth a separate statement.

1. The causal nexus is not itself observable. One can observe causal regularities; that is, one can observe certain sorts of regular sequences of events in which events of a certain type are followed by events of another type; but in addition to regularities one cannot observe a relation of causation between events. In the way that I can literally see that the cat is on the mat, or that one event followed another event, I cannot literally see that one event caused another event. In the billiard ball example I see events which are in fact causally related, but I don't see any causal relation in addition to regularity.

2. Whenever there is a pair of events related as cause and effect, that pair must instantiate some universal regularity. For every individual case where one event causes another event there must be some description of the first event and some description of the second event such that there is a causal law correlating events fitting the first description with those fitting the second.

The idea that every particular causal relation instantiates some universal regularity is, I believe, the heart of the modern regularity theory of causation. In stating it, it is important to distinguish between its metaphysical and its linguistic versions. In the metaphysical version every particular causal relation is in fact an instance of a universal regularity. In the linguistic version it is part of the *concept* of causation that every singular causal *statement* entails that there is a causal *law*[1] correlating events of the two types under some description or other. The linguistic claim is stronger than the metaphysical claim in the sense that it entails the metaphysical claim but is not entailed by it.

Contemporary versions of the regularity thesis do not state that a singular causal statement entails any *particular* law, but simply

---

1 In some versions it has also been claimed that to know that *A* caused *B* one must *know* that there is a law. Thus Davidson writes "In any case, in order to know that a singular causal statement is true, it is not necessary to know the truth of a law; *it is necessary only to know that some law covering the events at hand exists*" (italics mine), 'Actions, reasons, and causes', reprinted in A. R. White (ed.), *The Philosophy of Action* (Oxford: Oxford University Press, 1968), p. 94.

that there is a law. And, of course, the law need not be stated in the same terms in which the singular statement was couched. Thus, for example, the statement, "The thing that Sally did caused the phenomenon that John saw", might be true even though there is no causal law concerning what Sally does and what John sees under these descriptions. Thus, suppose that Sally turned the stove on under the kettle full of water and John saw the water boil. The original causal statement can be true and can instantiate a causal law or laws, even though the law is stated in terms of the kinetic energy of water molecules in the atmosphere and not in terms of Sally's doings or John's seeings.[2]

Furthermore, on some versions of this regularity theory of causation the causal laws are required to justify the counterfactual claims that we normally take to be associated with causal statements. The claim that in a particular instance, if the cause had not occurred, the effect would not have occurred, other things being equal, has to be justified by a universal correlation between events of the first type with events of the second type under some description or other.

3. Causal regularities are distinct from logical regularities. There are many regularities that are not even possible candidates for being causal regularities because the phenomena in question are logically related. Thus, for example, being a triangle is always associated with being three-sided, but something's being a triangle could never cause it to be three-sided since the correlation is by logical necessity. The aspects under which one event causes another event must be logically independent aspects. Again, this metaphysical thesis has a linguistic correlate in the formal mode. The causal law must state regularities under logically independent descriptions, and therefore must state a contingent truth.[3]

This account of causation is subject to numerous objections, some of them notorious. Here are several such. First, the account flies in the face of our common-sense conviction that we do perceive causal relations all the time. The experience of perceiving

---

2 Cf. Davidson, *op. cit.*

3 In objecting to this view Davidson claims that whether or not events are logically related depends only on how they are described (Davidson, *op. cit.*). I will subsequently argue that both views are defective.

one event following another event is really quite different from the experience of perceiving the second event as caused by the first, and the researches of Michotte[4] and Piaget[5] would seem to support our common-sense view. Second, it is hard to see how this account can distinguish causal regularities from other kinds of contingent regularities. Why, to take a famous example, don't we say that night causes day? Third, it is difficult to square this account with the apparent fact that in performing human actions we seem to be aware of causally affecting our environment. Some philosophers have been so impressed by the peculiarities of human action that they have postulated a special kind of causation that goes with agents. According to them there are really two different kinds of causation, one for agents and one for the rest of the universe; thus they distinguish between "agent" causation and "event" causation or "immanent" and "transeunt" causation.[6] Fourth, this account is ambiguous about what must be the crucial question: are causes really out there in the world or not? Surely, one wants to say, just as event tokens can really be related to each other in space and time so they can be related as cause and effect in addition to being related by the regular co-occurrence of other tokens of the types they exemplify. But it is hard to see how there can be any such relations in addition to regularities on the traditional theory. Hume, who more or less invented that theory, had the consistency to see that one could not accept it and still be a realist about causation. In addition to priority, contiguity, and constant conjunction there isn't anything else to causation in the real world, only an illusion in the mind. Kant thought that the question didn't even make sense, since the causal principles form necessary categories of the understanding, without which experience and knowledge of the world would be impossible altogether. Many philosophers have thought that we could get the notion of causation by observing human actions, but even for them there is still a serious problem about how we can then generalize that notion to things that aren't human actions and how we can

---

4 A. Michotte, *La Perception de la causalité* (Louvain: Publications Universitaires de Louvain, 1954).
5 J. Piaget, *Understanding Causality* (New York: W. W. Norton & Co., 1974).
6 See R. M. Chisholm, 'Freedom and action', in K. Lehrer (ed.), *Freedom and Determinism* (New York: Random House, 1966), pp. 11–44.

conceive of causation as a real relation in the world independent of our actions. Von Wright, for example, who thinks that we get the idea of causal necessity "from observations we make when we interfere and abstain from interfering with nature" addresses this problem as follows:

> One could say that on both Hume's view and on the view taken here, causal necessity is not to be found "in nature." In nature there are only regular sequences.[7]

He goes on to claim that this does not render our talk of causation purely "subjective" because there really are certain features of nature that correspond to our causal talk, namely the regular recurrence of discrete instantiations of generic states of affairs, but von Wright's account, like Hume's, ends up by denying the common-sense view that causal relations are really 'out there' in nature in addition to regularities.

Fifth, this account fails to distinguish between *causings*, where, for example, some event causes another event or change, and other sorts of *causal relations*, which may exist between permanent states of affairs and features of objects. Billiard ball *A*'s striking billiard ball *B* and thus causing it to move is an instance of a *causing*. But not all causal relations are causings. For example, if the billiard balls remain motionless on the green table, causal forces are acting on them all the time, e.g., gravity. All statements of causings are statements of causal relations, but not all statements of causal relations are statements of causings. "Event *x* caused event *y*" is a characteristic form of a statement of a causing, but by no means the only form of statement of a causal relation. "The billiard ball is gravitationally attracted to the center of the earth" states a causal relation, but it is not a relation between events and the statement describes no causings. I believe it is because they confuse causal relations with causings that adherents of the standard view are inclined to treat causal relations as holding only between events, but causal relations exist between things which are not events, e.g., billiard balls and planets.

Furthermore, though it is common to distinguish between those

---

7 G. H. von Wright, *Casuality and Determinism* (New York and London: Columbia University Press, 1974), pp. 53ff.

statements of the form "*x* caused *y*" which constitute causal *explanations* and those which do not, it has not – to my knowledge – been adequately emphasized that the explanatory power of a statement of the form *x* caused *y* depends on the extent to which the specifications of *x* and *y* describe them under *causally relevant aspects*. In our earlier example the thing that Sally did caused the phenomenon that John saw, but being done by Sally and being seen by John are not aspects under which the two events are causally related. Some relevant causal aspects in this case are that the water was heated and that it boiled. There is little explanatory power in saying that the thing that Sally did caused the phenomenon that John saw because being done by Sally is not a causal aspect that is responsible for the event to be explained, and being seen by John is not an aspect of the event under which it is explained by the causal aspects of the event which caused it.

Since Føllesdal's article[8] on the subject, it has been widely accepted that certain forms of causal statements are intensional. For example, whereas statements of the form "*x* caused *y*" are extensional, those of the form "*x* causally explains *y*" are intensional. I believe that the explanation for this linguistic fact is that only certain features of events are causally relevant aspects; and therefore, since the statement claims explanatory power, truth is not preserved under substitution of other expressions which do not specify *x* and *y* under causally relevant aspects. For example, if Jones's eating the poisoned fish causally explains his death and the event of Jones's eating the poisoned fish is identical with the event of his eating rainbow trout with sauce béarnaise for the first time in his life, it does not follow that his eating rainbow trout with sauce béarnaise for the first time in his life causally explains his death. The notion of a causally relevant aspect and its relation to causal explanation are crucial to the argument of the rest of this chapter.

II

I now want to call attention to the fact that there are certain sorts of very ordinary causal *explanations* having to do with human mental

8 D. Føllesdal, 'Quantification into causal contexts', in L. Linsky (ed.), *Reference and Modality* (Oxford: Oxford University Press, 1971), pp. 53–62.

states, experiences, and actions that do not sit very comfortably with the orthodox account of causation. For example, suppose I am thirsty and I take a drink of water. If someone asks me why I took a drink of water, I know the answer without any further observation: I was thirsty. Furthermore, in this sort of case it seems that I know the truth of the counterfactual without any further observations or any appeal to general laws. I know that if I hadn't been thirsty right then and there I would not have taken that very drink of water. Now when I claim to know the truth of a causal explanation and a causal counterfactual of this sort, is it because I know that there is a universal law correlating 'events' of the first type, my being thirsty, with events of the second type, my drinking, under some description or other? And when I said that my being thirsty caused me to drink the water, was it part of what I meant that there is a universal law? Am I *committed* to the existence of a law in virtue of the very meaning of the words I uttered? Part of my difficulty in giving affirmative answers to these questions is that I am much more confident of the truth of my original causal statement and the corresponding causal counterfactual than I am about the existence of any universal regularities that would cover the case. It seems to me quite unlikely that there are any relevant purely psychological laws: suppose all the psychological factors were repeated exactly (whatever that means); suppose I have the same degree of thirst, water has the same degree of known availability, etc. Does my original claim commit me to the view that in an exactly similar situation I would behave similarly? I doubt it. The second time around I might or might not take a drink of water. It's up to me. Perhaps there are physical laws at the neurophysiological or even molecular level that would describe the case, but I certainly do not know for a fact that there are such laws, much less what they might be, and I do not in making my original causal claim commit myself to the view that there are such laws. As a child of the modern era I believe that there are all sorts of physical laws, both known and unknown, but that is not what I meant or part of what I meant when I said that I took a drink of water because I was thirsty. Well, what did I mean?

Let us consider some other examples. In the cases of perceptions and actions there are two sorts of causal relations between Intentional states and their Intentional objects. In the case of perception, my visual experience is typically caused by an encounter with some object in the world, and, for example, if someone asked me "What caused you to have the visual experience of the flower?", the natural answer would surely be "I saw the flower". And in the case of action my Intentional state causes some movement of my body. So that, for example, if I am asked "What caused your arm to go up?", the natural answer would be "I raised it". And notice that both of these rather ordinary causal explanations seem to share the puzzling features of the example of drinking the water, if we try to assimilate them to the official theory. I know without further observation the answer to the questions, "What caused your arm to move and what caused you to have a visual experience of the flower?", and I know without further observation the truth of the corresponding counter-factuals, and furthermore the truth of the causal statement and the counterfactuals does not seem to depend on there being universal covering laws. And though I do indeed believe that there probably are some universal laws of perception and intentional action, it is not at all obvious that in making these singular causal claims I am committed to the existence of such universal laws, that it is part of the meaning of the claims themselves that there are such laws.

A slightly more complex case might be of the following sort. I am walking along when suddenly a man coming the other way accidentally stumbles into me, pushing me into the gutter. Now, again, barring hallucinations and the like, I know without any further observation the answer to the question "What caused you to go into the gutter?" The man bumped into me and pushed me into the gutter. In this case, one wants to say "I know all of this because I *felt* myself being pushed into the gutter, and I *saw* the man doing it to me".

All of these four cases involve Intentionality in one form or another, and all of the explanations in question seem to depart from the standard theory of what causal explanation is supposed to be like. Let us call these cases, and others like them, cases of *Intentional causation*, and explore how, exactly, the form of explanation in Intentional causation differs from that prescribed by the standard regularity theory of causation.

First, in each case I know both the answer to the causal question and the truth of the corresponding counterfactual without any further observations other than the experience of the event in question. When I say I know the answer to the causal question without further observations, I don't mean that such knowledge claims are incorrigible. I might be having a hallucination when I say that this visual experience was caused by seeing a flower, but the justification for the original claim does not depend on further observations.

Second, these causal claims do not commit me to the existence of any relevant causal laws. I might additionally, and as a matter of fact I do indeed, believe that there probably are causal laws corresponding to these four types of events but that is not what I *meant* in each case when I gave the answer to the causal question. The claim that there are causal laws corresponding to these events is not a logical consequence of these singular causal statements. And the argument for this independence is that it is logically consistent to insist on the truth of these causal explanations and yet deny a belief in corresponding causal laws. I know, for example, what made me take the drink of water: I was thirsty; but when I say that, I am not *committed* to the existence of any causal law, even if *in fact* I believe there are such laws. Furthermore, in each case my knowledge of the truth of the counterfactuals does not derive from my knowledge of any corresponding laws or even from the knowledge that there are such laws.

If you think about it for a moment, it seems that the traditional view, at least in its linguistic version, makes an extraordinarily strong and unsupported claim, viz., that any statement such as

My thirst caused my drinking

entails a statement of the form

There is some law L such that there is some description φ of my thirst and some description ψ of my drinking, and L asserts a universal correlation of events of type φ and events of type ψ.

This is certainly not intuitively plausible, so what is the argument for it supposed to be? The only argument I have ever seen is the Humean argument that since there isn't anything to causation except regularity, then for every true causal statement there must be a regularity. If we deny causal realism then there isn't anything for a causal statement to be about except regularities. But if we are causal realists, if we believe as I do that "cause" names a real relation in the real world, then the statement that that relation exists in a particular instance does not by itself entail a universal correlation of similar instances.

Third, in every case there seems to be a logical or internal connection between cause and effect. And I do not mean just that there is a logical relation between the *description* of the cause and the *description* of the effect, though that was also true in our examples; but rather that the cause itself quite independently of any description is logically related to the effect itself quite independently of any description. How is such a thing possible? In each case the cause was either a presentation or representation of the effect or the effect was a presentation or representation of the cause. Going through the examples: thirst, regardless of how described, contains a desire to drink, and that desire has as conditions of satisfaction, that one drinks; an intention in action to raise one's arm, regardless of how described, has as part of its conditions of satisfaction, that one's arm go up; a visual experience of a flower, regardless of how described, has as conditions of satisfaction that there be a flower there; tactile and visual experiences of being pushed by a man, regardless of how described, have as part of their conditions of satisfaction, that one is pushed by a man. The reason that there is a logical or internal relation between the description of the cause and the description of the effect in our examples is that in every case there is a logical or internal relation between the cause and effect themselves, since in every case there is an Intentional content that is causally related to its conditions of satisfaction. The specification of cause and effect under those causally relevant aspects involving Intentionality and the conditions of satisfaction of that Intentionality will give us logically related descriptions of cause and effect precisely because the cause and effect themselves are logically related; not logically related by entailment, but rather by Intentional content and conditions of satisfaction. I believe it reveals a fundamental confusion if we suppose that events can only be logically related under a description, for the events themselves may have intentional contents which relate them logically regardless of how they are described.

What is the notion of causation according to which these rather ordinary forms of explanation are even possible? Since these forms do not seem to comply with the standard Humean requirements for what a causal explanation is supposed to look like, we must answer the question how such forms of explanation are even possible. The formal structure of the phenomenon of Intentional causation for the simple cases of perception and action is as follows. In each case there is a self-referential Intentional state or event, and the form of the self-reference (in the case of action) is that it is part of the content of the Intentional state or event that its conditions of satisfaction (in the sense of requirement) require that it cause the rest of its conditions of satisfaction (in the sense of thing required) or (in the case of perception) that the rest of its conditions of satisfaction cause the state or event itself. If I raise my arm, then my intention in action has as its conditions of satisfaction that that very intention must cause my arm to go up; and if I see that there is a flower there, then the fact that there is a flower there must cause the very visual experience whose conditions of satisfaction are that there is a flower there. In each case, cause and effect are related as Intentional presentation and conditions of satisfaction. Direction of fit and direction of causation are asymmetrical. Where the direction of causation is world-to-mind, as in the case of perception, the direction of fit is mind-to-world; and where the direction of causation is mind-to-world, as in the case of action, the direction of fit is world-to-mind. As we saw in Chapter 3, analogous remarks apply to the representational cases of causal self-reference in prior intentions and memories of events. However, not all cases of Intentional causation involve self-referential Intentional contents: for example, a desire to perform an action may cause an action even though it is not part of the Intentional content of the desire that it should cause the action. But in every case of Intentional causation, at least one term is an Intentional state or event and that state or event either causes or is caused by its conditions of satisfaction.

More precisely, if x causes y, then x and y stand in a relation of Intentional causation iff

1. Either (a) x is an Intentional state or event and y is (or is part of) the conditions of satisfaction of x
2. or (b) y is an Intentional state or event and x is (or is part of) the conditions of satisfaction of y

3. if (a), the Intentional content of x is a causally relevant aspect under which it causes y

if (b), the Intentional content of y is a causally relevant aspect under which it is caused by x.

Because of the functioning of the Intentional content as a causally relevant aspect, statements of Intentional causation will be, in general, intensional.

The foregoing definition still leaves us with the notion of cause as an unexplained concept. What is "cause" supposed to mean when I say that in Intentional causation an Intentional state causes its conditions of satisfaction or that the conditions of satisfaction cause the state? The basic notion of causation, the notion which occurs in statements of causings and on which all the other various uses of "cause" depend, is the notion of making something happen: in the most primitive sense, when C causes E, C makes E happen. Now the peculiarity of Intentional causation is that we directly experience this relationship in many cases where we make something happen or something else makes something happen to us. When, for example, I raise my arm, part of the content of my experience is that this experience is what makes my arm go up, and when I see a flower, part of the content of the experience is that this experience is caused by the fact that there is a flower there. In such cases we directly experience the causal relation, the relation of one thing making something else happen. I don't need a covering law to tell me that when I raised my arm I caused my arm to go up, because when I raised my arm I directly experienced the causing: I did not *observe* two events, the experience of acting and the movement of the arm, rather part of the Intentional content of the experience of acting was that that very experience was making my arm go up. Just as I can directly experience a red object by seeing it, so I can directly experience the relation of one thing making another thing happen either by making something happen as in the case of action or by something making something happen to me as in the case of perception.

We might put one difference between the standard theory and the one I am urging by saying that according to the standard theory one never has an experience of causation and according to me it is not only the case that one often has an experience of causation, but indeed every experience of perceiving or acting is precisely an experience of causation. Now this statement would be misleading if it suggested that causation is the Intentional object of these experiences, rather the underlying idea behind this way of expressing the point is that whenever we perceive the world or act on the world we have self-referential Intentional states of the sort I have described and the relationship of causation is part of the *content*, not the object, of these experiences. If the relationship of causation is a relationship of making something happen, then it is a relationship we all experience whenever we perceive or act, i.e., more or less all of the time.[9]

On my account the Humeans were looking in the wrong place. They sought causation (force, power, efficacy, etc.) as the object of perceptual experience and failed to find it. I am suggesting that it was there all along as part of the content of both perceptual experiences and experiences of acting. When I see a red object or raise my arm I don't see causation or raise causation, I just see the flower and raise my arm. Neither flower nor movement is part of the *content* of the experience, rather each is an *object* of the relevant experience. But in each case causation is part of the content of the experience of that object.

I believe this view will be clearer if I compare it to the view of several philosophers, from Reid to von Wright, that the notion of causation is one that is derived from the observations we make of ourselves when we perform intentional actions. My view differs from this in at least three respects. First, it is not in the *observation* of actions that we become aware of causation, it is in the *performance* of actions, for part of the Intentional content of the experience of acting when I perform intentional actions is that this experience causes the bodily movement. Notice that I am arguing here not

---

9 Many philosophers are prepared to agree with me that causation is part of the experience of acting or of tactile bodily perceptions, but they do not concede that the same thing could hold for vision. They do not think causation is part of visual experiences. Perhaps the following thought experiment will help to remove some of these doubts. Suppose we had the capacity to form visual images as vivid as our present visual experiences. Now imagine the difference between forming such an image of the front of one's house as a voluntary action, and actually seeing the front of the house. In each case the purely visual content is equally vivid, so what would account for the difference? The voluntarily formed images we would experience as caused by us, the visual experience of the house we would experience as caused by something independent of us. The difference in the two cases is a difference in the causal content of the two experiences.

merely that the concept of causation enters into the description of the action, but rather that part of the actual phenomena of the action is the experience of causation. In these cases there isn't any problem about how we get from the experience to causation, the experience itself does the causing; where successful, it causes what it is directed at. And this is not to say that the experience is infallible, I might have the experience and think that it was what caused my arm to go up and still be mistaken – a point I will return to shortly.

Second, on my account we are as much directly aware of causation in perception as we are in action. There is nothing privileged about action, as far as the experience of causation is concerned. In action our experiences cause bodily movements and other physical events; in perception, physical events and states cause our experiences. But in each case we are directly aware of the causal nexus because in each case part of the content of the experience is that it is the experience of something causing or being caused.

Hume's question was how can the content of our experiences tell us that there is a cause and effect relation out there, and his answer was, it can't. But if part of an experience is that it itself causes something or is caused by something then there can't be any question as to how an experience can give us an awareness *of* causation since such an awareness is already part of the experience. The causal nexus is internal to the experience and not its object.

Third, my view differs from the views of Reid and von Wright in that they do not tell us exactly how observation of action gives us knowledge of causation, and in fact it is hard to see how they could, for if the actions in question are events, and if I get the knowledge of causation by observing these events, then it looks like all of the Humean arguments against the possibility of an experience of necessary connection would be in force, for all I could observe would be two events: my action and whatever events were prior or subsequent to it. On my account one does not observe a "necessary connection" between events, rather, one event, e.g., my experience of acting, is a causal Intentional presentation of the other event, e.g., the movement of my arm, and the two together make up the composite event, my raising my arm.

On at least one interpretation of the principles of the traditional theory with which I began this chapter I have challenged all three principles. For, in the case of Intentional causation:

1. In both perception and action one experiences the causal relationship. It is not inferred from regularity.

2. It is not the case that every singular causal statement entails that there is a corresponding universal causal law. For example, the statement that my thirst caused me to drink does not entail that there is a universal law correlating events of the relevant types under some description or other. Furthermore, one often knows that a singular causal statement is true without knowing that there is any corresponding law; and finally, one often knows the truth of the corresponding counterfactual without basing one's knowledge on any such law.

3. There is a logical relation of a sort (much weaker than the entailment relation between statements) between cause and effect in the cases of Intentional causation, because, for example, in the case of prior intention and intention in action the cause contains a representation or presentation of the effect in its conditions of satisfaction and in perception and memory the effect contains a representation or presentation of the cause in its conditions of satisfaction. In every case of Intentional causation, where the Intentional content is satisfied, there is an internal relation between cause and effect under causally relevant aspects. And, to repeat, I am not saying simply that the *description* of the cause is internally related to the description of the effect, but rather that the causes and effects themselves are in this way internally related, since the one is a presentation or representation of the other.

III

Even assuming I am right so far, there are several serious questions about and objections to the foregoing. First, how on my account can we ever be justified in supposing entities other than our experiences can be causes and effects? Second, doesn't my account have the absurd result that the agent's experience of causation is somehow self-verifying? Third, what role does regularity play on my account? After all, in some sense, which I haven't so far explained, it seems that regularity must be an essential part of our notion of causation. I will now develop the first two of these objections and attempt to answer them; I will discuss the third objection in the next section.

First objection: Let us grant for the sake of argument that we can become aware of causal relations as part of the contents of our experiences; this would still only give us knowledge of causal relations where one of the terms is an experience, but most of the interesting cases of causation are cases where neither term is an experience. And how does my account even allow for the bare possibility of knowledge of that sort of relation or even of its existence? How, for example, on my account is it possible to know that the event of billiard ball *A*'s striking billiard ball *B* caused the event of billiard ball *B*'s moving; and indeed, how on my account is it possible that there is anything to this relation other than the regular recurrence of resembling instances? To put it crudely, haven't I still left causation as a property of feelings in the mind and not as a feature of the real world outside the mind?

This seems to be a powerful objection and the account must now be extended to meet it. But first a disclaimer. In what follows I will frequently talk in ontogenetic terms, but what follows is not intended as an empirical hypothesis about how causal concepts are acquired. I think they probably are acquired in this way, but it is perfectly consistent with my account to suppose they are not, and, indeed, for all I know they may be innate ideas. The point is not how we come by the belief that cause is a real relation in the real world, but how we might be *justified* in holding that belief, how we as empiricists might rationally believe that causation is a feature of the real world in addition to regular recurrence. We have seen that we can be rationally justified in believing that we as agents act causally and as perceivers are acted upon causally; but now the question is, how can we be justified in supposing that something devoid of Intentionality can stand in the same relations that our Intentional states and events stand in?

One of the theses that Piaget's experiments seem to substantiate is that the child acquires a knowledge of the by-means-of relation (what Piaget calls "transitivity")[10] very early on. Even small infants discover that by means of pushing a suspended object with their hands they can move the object back and forth. Now what is it

10 In *Understanding Causality.*

exactly that such a child has discovered from the point of view of Intentionality? Let us take a slightly more complex case. Suppose a somewhat older child discovers, as so many do, that by hitting a vase with a stone he can smash it. The child has discovered that this intention in action results in this movement of the hand and arm, which results in this movement of the stone which results in this smashing of the vase. And here the regularities come into play, for on the basis of *repeated* occasions the child can discover that by means of this movement he can move the stone, and by means of the movement of the stone he can smash the vase. And each of these various steps in the by-means-of relation becomes part of the conditions of satisfaction of the intention in action. The intention is to smash the vase by means of doing these other things. But we have already seen that causation is part of the content of the intention in action, for if the intention in action does not cause the rest of the conditions of satisfaction, the intention is not satisfied. The causality of the intention in action can carry through to the final step, the smashing of the vase, because it goes through each of the intervening steps of the by-means-of relation. Each step is a causal step, and the transitivity of the by-means-of relation enables the intention in action to encompass all of them. It is part of the content of the child's intention in action that this intention cause this movement of the arm, but also that this movement of the stone cause this smashing of the vase, because that is what the child is trying to do: cause the smashing of the vase by hitting it with the stone. The child's intention is not just to move his arm and then watch and see what happens; that is a different sort of case altogether. That the movement of the stone causes the smashing of the vase is then part of the child's experience when he does the smashing, because the causality of the intention in action extends to each step of the by-means-of relation. It is often said that causality is closely connected to the notion of manipulation; and this is correct, but manipulation stands in need of analysis. Manipulating things is precisely exploiting the by-means-of relation.

One of the points at which the regularity account of causation and the Intentional account of causation come together is in manipulation. It is a fact about the world that it contains discoverable causal regularities. The regularity of these causal relations enables us to discover them, for by trial and error the child discovers how it works with the stones and the vases; but that they are manipulable enables us to discover that they are causal, for what the child discovers in his trials and errors with stones and vases is a way of making things happen.

Once a child has acquired the capacity to encompass the causal by-means-of relation as part of the content of his intention in action he has acquired the capacity to discover and not merely project causal relations in a natural world that is largely independent of himself, indeed, he already has discovered instances of the causal relation in the world. For what exactly has the child discovered when he has discovered that he can, for example, smash a vase by hitting it with a hard object? Well, part of what he has discovered is that a hard object hitting a vase will cause it to break, but that relationship remains the same whether or not he is hitting the vase with the hard object or, for example, the hard object is falling on the vase. Where we have a sequence of causal by-means-of relations the initial term of which is an experience of acting, the Intentional content can include each of the various steps – the intention can be, for example, to break the vase by means of hitting it with a hard object, by means of moving the hard object, by means of moving the hand holding the hard object. But the steps beyond the movement of the hand are all causal steps, and the same causation which is part of the *content* of the experience in manipulation can be *observed* in cases where there is no manipulation. The relation that the agent observes when he sees the stone smash the vase by falling on it is – as far as causation is concerned – the same relation which he experiences when he smashes the vase with the stone. In the cases where he observes the causation of events independent of his will, he does not experience the causal nexus in the same way as he experiences the causal nexus in the experience of acting or perceiving, and in that respect the Humeans are right in claiming that causation between events independent of us is not observable in the way that the events themselves are observable. But the agent does observe the events *as* causally related, and not just *as* a sequence of events, and he is justified or can be justified in ascribing causality to such a sequence of events, for what he ascribes in the case of observation is something he has experienced in the case of manipulation.

The problem of how there can be causes in the world independent of our experiences is a problem of the same form as the problem of how there can be square objects in the world independent of our looking at them, and the problem of how we can see events *as causally related* is a problem of the same form as the problem of how we can see a house *as a whole house* and not just as a façade, even though only one face of the house is visible to us. I do not say that there is no problem about either of these phenomena — the existence of features of the world at times when they are unobserved and the ability to see things as something in addition to what is optically presented — but I do say that realism about causation, the view that causes are real relations in the real world, does not pose any special problems. There is no special skeptical problem about the existence of causal relations which are not experienced, beyond the general problem of the existence of features of the world at times when they are unobserved.

Second objection: The experience of acting or the experience of perceiving cannot contain the experience of causation because, for example, it is always possible that something else might actually be causing the bodily movement we think the experience is causing. It is always possible that I might think I am raising my arm when in fact some other cause is raising it. So there is nothing in the experience of acting that actually guarantees that it is causally effective. The answer to this is that it is true but irrelevant. I get a direct experience of causation from the fact that part of the Intentional content of my experience of acting is that it causes the bodily movement, i.e., it is satisfied only if the bodily movement is caused by it; and I get a direct experience of causation from the fact that part of the Intentional content of my experience of perceiving is caused by the object perceived, i.e., it is satisfied only if it is caused by the presence and features of the object. Now, what counts as the conditions of satisfaction of my Intentional event is indeed determined by the Intentional event, but that the Intentional event is in fact satisfied is not itself part of the content. Actions and perceptions on my account are causal and Intentional transactions between mind and the world, but that the transactions are actually taking place is not up to the mind. And indeed this fact is a consequence of the fact that there is nothing subjective about causation. It is really there. The objection that I might have the experience and yet the relation not in fact be causal is of exactly the same form as the objection to the view that I get the idea of red from seeing red things that I might, in any case of seeing a red thing, be having a hallucination: true but irrelevant. That a red object is causing me to have a visual experience is part of the conditions of satisfaction of the experience, and that is sufficient to give me an experience of something red. Whether or not in any given instance there actually is a red object in front of me is a separate problem, one which is independent of the question how it is possible for me to acquire the concept red on the basis of my experiences. An exactly analogous argument is that I get the idea of causation from experiencing causation as part of my experience of acting or perceiving. But whether or not my experience in any given case is deceiving me, whether or not I am actually standing in the causal relation to the Intentional object of the Intentional content of my experience, is simply irrelevant.

Still, though this objection is invalid it does point up a crucial asymmetry between causation and other perceptual contents. Redness is not a feature of my visual experience but part of the conditions of satisfaction; the experience is *of* something red, but is not itself a red experience. But causation is part of the content of my experience. The experience is satisfied only if it itself causes (in the case of action) the rest of its conditions of satisfaction or is caused by (in the case of perception) the rest of its conditions of satisfaction. The experience of something red, when satisfied, is not literally *red*, but it is literally *caused*. And the paradoxical aspect of the asymmetry is this: on my account the concept of reality is a causal concept. Part of our notion of the way the world really is, is that its being the way it is causes us to perceive it as being that way. Causes are part of reality and yet the concept of reality is itself a causal concept.

There is a variation on this objection which can be stated as follows. If experience is anything like what either the empiricist or intellectualist tradition tells us it is, then it is hard to see how experiences could have the features I am claiming. If experience is a sequence of impressions "all on the same footing" as Hume says, then it seems nobody could experience an impression as causal as part of the content of the impression. But if Kant and the intellectualists are right in thinking that experiences already come to us as causal, it is only because we have the concept of causation already as an *a priori* concept. It will be obvious to the reader who has followed the argument so far that I am rejecting both accounts of experience. Both accounts fail to describe the Intentionality of our experiences of acting and perceiving. They both fail to account for the fact that the conditions of satisfaction are determined by the experience and that part of the conditions of satisfaction is that the experience is one of making its Intentional object happen or one of its Intentional object making it happen. For this reason we can experience causation, but we don't have to have an *a priori* concept of cause to do it, any more than we have to have an *a priori* concept of red to experience redness.

IV

We now have at least two elements in our account of causality: the primitive experience of causation in perception and action and the existence of regularities in the world, some of which are causal, some not. We can extend the primitive experience of causation beyond the boundaries of our bodies by discovering manipulable causal regularities in the world. What we discover when we discover such a manipulable regularity is what we experience in the primitive experience of causality, the relation of one event making another event happen. It is a consequence of this account that a being incapable of action or perception could not have our experience of causality.

But the puzzle we are still left with, our third objection, is this: What exactly is the relation between the primitive experience of causation and regularities in the world? The statement that one thing caused another thing, i.e., made it happen, and the statement that one has experienced such makings happen in action and perception, do not by themselves entail the existence of any regularities. A world in which somebody makes something happen but where the event sequence does not instantiate any general co-occurrence relation is a logically possible world. Yet, at the same time we feel that there must be some important connection between the existence of regularities and our experience of causation. What is it? One temptation is to suppose that in addition to the actual experience of causes and effects we hold a *hypothesis* of general regularity in the world. And along this line we are inclined to think that this hypothesis is challenged by those parts of physics that deny general determinism. According to this view we hold a *theory* that causal relations instantiate general laws, and this theory is presumably an empirical theory like any other.

This conception has a long history in philosophy and it underlies some attempts, e.g., Mill's, to state a general principle of regularity that would 'justify induction'. It seems to me to misdescribe the way that the presumption of regularity plays a role in our use of the causal vocabulary and in our activities of action and perception. Consider the following example. Suppose as I raise my arm I discover to my amazement that the window across the room is going up. And suppose as I lower my arm the window goes down. In such a case I will wonder if my raising and lowering my arm is making the window go up and down. In order to find out I will try again. Suppose it works a second time. My Intentional content will be altered on subsequent occasions. I am no longer just raising my arm; but I am *trying to* raise and lower the window by raising and lowering my arm. A causal relation between the movement of the arm and the movement of the window is now part of the Intentional content of the intention in action. But the only way I can tell if that Intentional content is really satisfied, that is, the only way I can tell whether or not my arm movement really has an effect on the window, is by trial and error. But the trial and error only has its point against a Background presumption of general regularities. I don't hold a *hypothesis* that the world is such that causal relations manifest general regularities, but rather a condition of the possibility of my applying the notion of making something happen is my ability to make some distinction between cases where something really made something happen and cases where it only seemed to make something happen; and a condition of the possibility of that distinction is at least the presumption of some degree of regularity. In investigating the distinction between apparent and real cases of causal relations, as in any investigation, I adopt a certain stance. Having that stance will not consist solely in a set of beliefs: the stance is in part a matter of Background capacities. In investigating how the world. actually works with causes and effects the presumption of regularities is part of the Background.

A similar point emerges if we examine cases where there appears to be an element of randomness. When I try to shoot baskets from the free-throw line sometimes I succeed, sometimes not, even though I try as hard as I can to do the same thing each time. Now for such cases it is more than just a hypothesis that different effects proceed from different causes, for if it were merely a hypothesis then the evidence would suggest that it is false. As far as I can tell, I do the same thing but with different results on different occasions. The presumption of regularity underlies or grounds my attempt to shoot the basket and is not a hypothesis invoked to explain the success or failure of that attempt. I simply cannot apply the idea of making something happen – as opposed to its merely seeming to be the case that I make something happen – without my Background capacities manifesting a presumption of at least some degree of regularity. Notice in the present example that if the ball moves completely at random then I have literally lost control of it and we would not say that my intention in action had caused it to go into the basket even if I had the intention to make it go in the basket and it did go in the basket.

To see these points a little more clearly we need to distinguish between the belief in particular causal laws and the presumption of some general degree of causal regularity in the world. I have many beliefs concerning particular causal regularities, e.g., concerning the liquid properties of water, the behavior of cars and typewriters, and the tendency of skis to turn when edged. But in addition to beliefs in specific regularities I don't have or need to have a general hypothesis of regularity. Similarly, the tribe that stores food for the winter doesn't have to have a theory of induction, but it does need certain general conceptions of the conditions of nourishment and some idea of the cycle of the seasons.

The answer, then, that I am proposing to the question "What is the relation between the primitive experience of causation in action and perception and the existence of regularities in the world?" is this: Neither statements asserting the existence of the experience of causation nor the existence of instances of causation entails that there are general causal laws. Nonetheless, causal laws do exist, and a condition of the possibility of applying the notion of causation in specific cases is a general presumption of regularity in the world. Unless I presume some level of regularity – it need not be universal regularity – I cannot begin to make the distinction between its seeming to be the case that my experiences stand in causal relations as part of their conditions of satisfaction and its really being the case that they stand in such relations. I can only apply the notion of something making something else happen, as opposed to its seeming to be the case that it makes it happen, against a presumption of causal regularities, for it is only by the failure or success of the regularities that I can assess the individual case.

After three centuries of failure in attempting to analyze the concept of causation in terms of regularities, we ought to be able to say why such attempts failed. The short answer is that the notion of making something happen is different from the notion of a regularity, so any attempt to analyze the former in terms of the latter is doomed to failure. And even if we agree that regularity is necessary for the applicability of the concept of causation, still the only regularities that matter are causal regularities, and any attempt to analyze causation in terms of regularities previously identified as causal is doomed to circularity.

A further upshot of our discussion of the relation between Intentional causation and regularity is this: there are not two kinds of causation, regularity causation and Intentional causation. There is just one kind of causation and that is efficient causation; causation is a matter of some things making other things happen. However, in one special subclass of efficient causation, the causal relations involve Intentional states, and these cases of Intentional causation are special in several respects: we can be directly aware of the causal nexus in some of these cases, there is a 'logical' connection between cause and effect, and these cases are the primitive forms of causation as far as our experiences are concerned. Singular causal statements do not entail that there is a universal causal regularity which they instantiate, but the concept of efficient causation, whether Intentional or not, only has applicability in a universe where a high degree of causal regularity is presupposed.

V

Our discussion of Intentional causation has now prepared the way for an examination of the so-called deviant causal chains in action and perception, an examination we began but did not complete in Chapter 3. No matter how tight we make the constraints between the different stages in the Intentional analysis of perception and action, it seems nonetheless that we will still be able to produce counterexamples which involve "deviant causal chains". In each of these cases, the formal requirements of Intentional causal self-reference appear to be satisfied, and yet we would not say, or at least we would be reluctant to say, that the Intentional state is satisfied. In the case of perception, there are examples where, though the visual experience is caused by the object, nonetheless the agent does not literally "see" the object; and in the case of action, though there are cases where the prior intention causes the intention in action and cases where the intention in action causes the movement, we would not say that the prior intention was carried out or that the action was intentional. Let us consider some examples of each.

Example 1.[11] Suppose a man is unable to raise his arm because the nerves have been cut. Try as he might, he is unable to lift the arm away from his side. He keeps trying and trying without success; however, on one occasion he tries so hard that his effort makes him fall into a switch which activates a magnet in the ceiling which attracts the metal in the watch on his wrist which raises his arm. Now in such a case his intention in action caused his arm to go up, but it didn't cause it 'in the right way'. In such a case we are reluctant to say that he raised his arm intentionally or even that he raised his arm.

Example 2. Bill intends to kill his uncle. This prior intention makes him so upset that it gives him a stomachache and he forgets all about the intention, but the stomachache makes him angry and because of his anger, he kills the next man he sees, who happens to be, and whom he recognizes as, his uncle. In this case, the prior intention caused the intention in action by way of causing the stomachache which caused the anger, and the intention in action caused its own conditions of satisfaction. Nonetheless, though it was an intentional killing, it was not a case of carrying out the prior intention.

Example 3. Suppose a man looks at a table, and suppose that

---

11 I owe this example to Steve White.

unknown to him he does not actually see the table. But suppose that the table gives off a certain odor, and this odor causes him to have a visual hallucination which is qualitatively indistinguishable from the visual experience that he would have had if he had actually seen the table. In such a case, the table causes the visual experience, and the conditions of satisfaction presented in the visual experience are in fact satisfied, viz., there really is a table there, but all the same the man does not see the table.

All of these examples, like other examples I have seen of deviant causation, exhibit certain common features: either they involve some failure of the Intentional content to be the causal aspect, or they involve some *lack of plannable regularity* in the causal relations of the Intentional state. The way to eliminate these examples is to see that Intentional causation must function under Intentional aspects, and that in order for it to do so there must be plannable regularities. Consider example 1. Suppose the man knows about the magnet and he knows that he can raise his arm simply by activating the magnet by pushing the button. If he did this on a regular basis and knew what was going on, we would have no hesitation in saying that he raised his arm intentionally, though it could not be a basic action. His intention in action would be to move the switch and that would be part of the intended by-means-of relation that resulted in the arm going up. Furthermore, suppose in another variation on this example that we wired the man up so that unknown to him whenever he tried to raise his arm it activated overhead magnets and his arm went up. In such a case we would simply say that he raised his arm, though the form of the causal sequence is quite different from the standard case. Indeed, in this case raising his arm would be a basic action. The feature of the original case which troubles us is its accidental and inadvertent character: when his arm goes up things are not going according to plan. In the example, it is just accidental that the man's arm went up on that particular occasion. But if we have some form of consistent Intentional efficacy, then we have no hesitation in saying that the Intentional state was satisfied.

Now consider example 2. It was essential to that example that the man forgot completely about his original intention. It was his anger and not his prior intention that caused him to kill his uncle. If we did not have the feature of the intention being forgotten, but if he still remembered the intention and acted on it, even if he acted on it only because he was so angry, it would still be a case of carrying out that intention. What is absent in this example is the causal operation of the Intentional state under its intentional aspect. The prior intention does not function causally up to the point of the production of the intention in action, and in consequence, when the agent acts, he does not act by way of carrying out his prior intention. A necessary condition for satisfying the Intentional content of a prior intention is that the Intentional content must function causally as the causal aspect in the production of its conditions of satisfaction and in this case that feature was lost. The original Intentional content produced only a stomachache.

Now consider example 3. Like example 1 it is a case of an accidental rather than a plannable, regular causal sequence, and that is why it is not a case of really seeing the table. This point becomes clear if we alter the example so that it manifests a plannable regularity. Suppose that the man's 'hallucination' of the table is not a one-time event, but suppose that he can consistently get the same type of visual experiences of tables, chairs, mountains, rainbows, etc., from his olfactory nerve endings that we get from our visual apparatus. Then in such a case we would simply say that the man saw everything we saw but did not see in the normal way. What is wrong with the original example, in short, is the lack of plannable consistency.

We can now state the conditions necessary to amend the account so as to eliminate all the deviant causal chains we have considered. A first condition is that there should be continuous efficacy of Intentional content under its Intentional aspects. This eliminates all cases of intervening or intermittent Intentionality. A second condition is that there should be at least a reasonable degree of plannable consistency or regularity. When I use expressions like "consistency" and "regularity" I do not mean them in any statistical sense. For example, in the ordinary nondeviant examples, we do not always have *statistical* consistency. When I try to shoot free throws from the free-throw line I am only occasionally successful. But the point is that, when I do succeed, *things go according to plan*. If the ball were carried in by an occasional gust of wind, unplanned and unforeseen, we would not attribute my successes to my intentions.

Now in both example 1 and example 3 as originally stated things are not going according to plan, and in both cases it is because of some accidental or inadvertent feature that stands outside the agent's Network and Background of expectations. As soon as we revise these features so that the bizarre feature is under control to the extent that it can become part of the plan, i.e., can become represented by our Network of how things work when we perceive or act, the cases are no longer counterexamples. This suggests what I think is in fact the case: there is no such thing as a deviant causal chain *per se*. A causal chain is only deviant relative to our expectations and relative to our Network and Background of Intentionality generally.

Though these two conditions – that Intentional causation must be under Intentional aspects and that it must manifest plannable regularities – are sufficient to eliminate the counterexamples we have considered, I am still not entirely satisfied. The conditions are still vaguely stated and my instinct is to think we may still be able to think up other sorts of counterexamples. Something may still be eluding us. But I believe we can appreciate the force of the answer I have given so far if we ask Peacocke's question:[12] Why does it matter to us how the causal chain works? If we get the right sort of bodily movement or the right sort of visual experience, why do we care whether or not it was caused "in the right way"? I am suggesting that the beginnings of an answer to that question have to be along the following lines. Our most fundamental ways of coping with the world are through action and perception, and these ways essentially involve Intentional causation. Now when it comes to forming concepts for describing these basic Intentional relations, concepts such as *seeing an object*, or *carrying out an intention*, or *trying* and *succeeding*, we require more for the application of the concept than just that there be a correct match between Intentional content and the state of affairs that it causes or that causes it. We make the further requirement which philosophers have expressed by saying the match must come about "in the right way". But why do we make this requirement and what is it exactly? We make the requirement because we want our concepts to express the condition that the Intentionality in action and perception must

<hr>

12 C. Peacocke, 'Deviant causal chains', *Midwest Studies in Philosophy*, vol. 4 (1979), pp. 123–55.

really work; thus we insist that the Intentionality must not be epiphenomenal. And we insist that the Intentionality must work with enough regularity and consistency to fit into our overall plans and expectations. I have expressed these two conditions as a way of explaining the meaning of "in the right way" by saying that the Intentional content must be a causally relevant aspect and it must exemplify a plannable regularity.

Chapter 5

THE BACKGROUND

Intentional states with a direction of fit have contents which determine their conditions of satisfaction. But they do not function in an independent or atomistic fashion, for each Intentional state has its content and determines its conditions of satisfaction only in relation to numerous other Intentional states.[1] We saw this in the case of the man who forms the intention to run for the Presidency of the United States. He would normally believe, for example, that the United States is a republic, that it has periodic elections, that in these elections the candidates of two major parties vie for the Presidency, and so on. And he would normally desire that he receive the nomination of his party, that people work for his candidacy, that voters cast votes for him, and so on. Perhaps no one of these is essential to the man's intention, and certainly the existence of none of them is entailed by the statement that the man has the intention to run for the Presidency of the United States. Nonetheless, without some such Network of Intentional states the man could not have formed what we would call "the intention to run for the Presidency of the United States". We might say that his intention 'refers' to these other Intentional states in the sense that it can only have the conditions of satisfaction that it does, and thus can only be the intention that it is, because it is located in a Network of other beliefs and desires. Furthermore, in any real life situation, the beliefs and desires are only part of a larger complex of still other psychological states; there will be subsidiary intentions as well as hopes and fears, anxieties and anticipations, feelings of frustration and satisfaction. For short, I have been calling this entire holistic network, simply, the "Network".

---

1 I am discussing human Intentional states such as perceptions, beliefs, desires, and intentions. Perhaps there might be more biologically primitive Intentional states which do not require a Network, or perhaps not even a Background.

We understand completely what it is for a man to intend to become President, but we have no clear idea at all what it would be for a man to intend to become a coffee cup or a mountain, because – among other reasons – we don't know how to fit such an intention into the Network. But now suppose, taking the hypothesis of the Network seriously, we begin to try to follow out the various threads that connect one Intentional state with another; suppose we try to get rid of those "and so ons" in the previous paragraph by actually spelling out each of the Intentional states in the Network. We would soon find the task impossible for a number of reasons. First, because much, perhaps most, of the Network is submerged in the unconscious and we don't quite know how to dredge it up. Second, because the states in the Network do not individuate; we don't know, for example, how to count beliefs. But third, if we actually tried to carry out the task we would soon find ourselves formulating a set of propositions which would look fishy if we added them to our list of beliefs in the Network; "fishy" because they are in a sense too fundamental to qualify as *beliefs*, even as unconscious beliefs. Consider the following propositions: elections are held at or near the surface of the earth; the things people walk on are generally solid; people only vote when awake; objects offer resistance to touch and pressure. As contents of beliefs, these propositions do not sit comfortably with such beliefs as that the U.S. has presidential elections every four years or that larger states have more electoral votes than smaller states. A man might indeed believe unconsciously (and in this case that just means he never thinks about his belief) that larger states have more electoral votes than smaller states, but it seems wrong to say that I now, in that sense, also believe that the table that I am working on will offer resistance to touch. I would certainly be surprised if it didn't, and that at least suggests that we have something like conditions of satisfaction. Furthermore, a man certainly *could* have the belief that tables offer resistance to touch, but in the course of this chapter I will argue that that isn't the correct way to describe the stance that I, for example, now take towards this table and other solid objects. For me, the hardness of tables manifests itself in the fact that I know how to sit at a table, I can write on a table, I put stacks of books on tables, I use a table as a work bench, and so on. And as I do each of these things I do not in addition think unconsciously to myself, "it offers resistance to touch".

I believe that anyone who tries seriously to follow out the threads in the Network will eventually reach a bedrock of mental capacities that do not themselves consist in Intentional states (representations), but nonetheless form the preconditions for the functioning of Intentional states. The Background is "preintentional" in the sense that though not a form or forms of Intentionality, it is nonetheless a precondition or set of preconditions of Intentionality. I do not know how to demonstrate this hypothesis conclusively, though in this chapter I will explore it and try to present some arguments in favor of it.

I. WHAT EXACTLY IS MEANT BY "THE BACKGROUND"?

The Background is a set of nonrepresentational mental capacities that enable all representing to take place. Intentional states only have the conditions of satisfaction that they do, and thus only are the states that they are, against a Background of abilities that are not themselves Intentional states. In order that I can now have the Intentional states that I do I must have certain kinds of know-how: I must know how things are and I must know how to do things, but the kinds of "know-how" in question are not, in these cases, forms of "knowing that".

To illustrate this point consider another example. Think of what is necessary, what must be the case, in order that I can now form the intention to go to the refrigerator and get a bottle of cold beer to drink. The biological and cultural resources that I must bring to bear on this task, even to form the intention to perform the task, are (considered in a certain light) truly staggering. But without these resources I could not form the intention at all: standing, walking, opening and closing doors, manipulating bottles, glass, refrigerators, opening, pouring and drinking. The activation of these capacities would normally involve presentations and representations, e.g., I have to see the door in order to open the door, but the ability to recognize the door and the ability to open the door are not themselves further representations. It is such nonrepresentational capacities that constitute the Background.

A minimal geography of the Background would include at least the following: we need to distinguish what we might call the "deep Background", which would include at least all of those Background capacities that are common to all normal human beings in virtue of their biological makeup – capacities such as walking, eating, grasping, perceiving, recognizing, and the pre-intentional stance that takes account of the solidity of things, and the independent existence of objects and other people – from what we might call the "local Background" or "local cultural prac-tices", which would include such things as opening doors, drinking beer from bottles, and the preintentional stance that we take toward such things as cars, refrigerators, money and cocktail parties.

Now within both the deep and the local Background we need to distinguish those aspects which have to do with "how things are" from those aspects that have to do with "how to do things", although it is important to emphasize that there is no sharp dividing line between "how things are for me" and "how I do things". It is, for example, part of my preintentional stance toward the world that I recognize degrees of the hardness of things as part of "how things are" and that I have numerous physical skills as part of "how to do things". But I cannot activate my preinten-tional skill of, say, peeling oranges independently of my preinten-tional stance toward the hardness of things. I can, for example, intend to peel an orange, but I cannot in that way intend to peel a rock or a car; and that is not because I have an unconscious belief, "you can peel an orange but you cannot peel a rock or a car" but rather because the preintentional stance I take toward oranges (how things are) allows for a completely different range of possibilities (how to do things) from that which I take toward rocks or cars.

II. WHAT ARE THE ARGUMENTS FOR THE HYPOTHESIS OF THE BACKGROUND?

Let the "hypothesis of the Background" be the claim that Intentional states are underlain by nonrepresentational, preinten-tional capacities in the manner I have sketched above. How would one show that such a claim is true? And what empirical difference would such a claim make anyway? I know of no demonstrative arguments that would prove the existence of the Background. Perhaps the best way to argue for the hypothesis of the Background is to explain to the reader how I became convinced of it myself. This conviction was the result of a series of more or less independent investigations, the cumulative effect of which was to produce a belief in the hypothesis of the Background.

(i) The understanding of literal meaning

The understanding of the literal meaning of sentences, from the simplest sentences, such as "The cat is on the mat", to the most complex sentences of the physical sciences, requires a preintentional Background. For example, the sentence "The cat is on the mat" only determines a definite set of truth conditions against a Background of preintentional assumptions that are not part of the literal meaning of the sentence. This is shown by the fact that, if we alter the preintentional Background, the same sentence with the same literal meaning will determine different truth conditions, different conditions of satisfaction, even though there is no change in the literal meaning of the sentence. This has the consequence that the notion of the literal meaning of a sentence is not a context-free notion; it only has application relative to a set of preintentional Background assumptions and practices.[2]

Perhaps the best way to argue this point is to show how the same literal meaning will determine different truth conditions given different Backgrounds, and, given some Backgrounds, sentences which are semantically impeccable from the classical point of view are simply incomprehensible, they determine no clear set of truth conditions. Consider the occurrence of the verb "open" in the following five English sentences, each of which is a substitution instance of the open sentence "X opened Y":

Tom opened the door
Sally opened her eyes
The carpenters opened the wall
Sam opened his book to page 37
The surgeon opened the wound.

It seems clear to me that the word "open" has the same literal meaning in all five of these occurrences. Anyone who denied this

2 For a detailed discussion of examples, see 'Literal meaning', in J. R. Searle, *Expression and Meaning* (Cambridge: Cambridge University Press, 1979).

would soon be forced to hold the view that the word "open" is indefinitely or perhaps even infinitely ambiguous since we can continue these examples; and indefinite ambiguity seems an absurd result. Furthermore, these examples contrast with other occurrences of "open" where it is at least arguable that the word has a different sense or meaning. Consider the following examples:

The chairman opened the meeting
The artillery opened fire
Bill opened a restaurant.

Now the point I want to make is: though the semantic content contributed by the word "open" is the same in each member of the first set, the way that semantic content is understood is quite different in each case. In each case the truth conditions marked by the word "open" are different, even though the semantic content is the same. What constitutes opening a wound is quite different from what constitutes opening a book, and understanding these sentences literally requires understanding each differently, even though "open" has the same literal meaning in each case. You can see that the interpretations are different by imagining how one would carry out literal directives containing the word "open". Suppose in response to the order "Open the door" I begin making incisions in it with a surgical scalpel; have I opened the door, that is, have I literally 'obeyed' the literal order, "Open the door"? I think not. The literal utterance of the sentence "Open the door" requires for its understanding more than the semantic content of the component expressions and the rules for their combination into sentences. Furthermore, the 'right' interpretation is not forced by the semantic content of the expressions we substitute for "x" and "y", since it would be easy to imagine Background practices where these words kept their same meanings but we understood the sentences quite differently: if eyelids evolved into doors on brass hinges with big iron padlocks we would understand the sentence "Sally opened her eyes" quite differently from the way we now understand it.

I have tried so far to show that there is more to understanding than grasping meanings because, to put it crudely, what one understands goes beyond meaning. Another way to make the same point is to show that it is possible to grasp all the component meanings and still not understand the sentence. Consider the following three sentences also containing the verb "open":

Bill opened the mountain
Sally opened the grass
Sam opened the sun.

There is nothing grammatically wrong with any of these sentences. They are all perfectly good sentences and we easily understand each of the words in the sentences. But we have no clear idea at all of how to interpret these sentences. We know, for example, what "open" means and we know what "mountain" means, but we don't know what "open the mountain" means. If somebody orders me to open the mountain, I haven't the faintest idea what I am supposed to do. I could of course invent an interpretation for each of these, but to do that I would have to contribute more to understanding than is contributed by literal meaning.

We need then to explain two sets of facts: first that we understand the *same* literal meaning *differently* in each instance of the first set of examples, and second that in the latter set we don't understand the sentences at all even though we have no difficulty grasping their component literal meanings.

The explanation, I believe, is simple and obvious, but it has far-reaching consequences for the classical theory of meaning and understanding. Each of the sentences in the first group is understood within a Network of Intentional states and against a Background of capacities and social practices. We know how to open doors, books, eyes, wounds and walls; and the differences in the Network and in the Background of practices produce different understandings of the same verb. Furthermore, we simply have no common practices of opening mountains, grass or suns. It would be easy to invent a Background, i.e., to imagine a practice, that would give a clear sense to the idea of opening mountains, grass and suns, but we have no such common Background at present.

About the relation of the Background and literal meaning I want to consider two further connected questions. First, even if the relevant portions of the Background are not already parts of semantic content, why can't they by fiat be made part of semantic content? Second, if the Background is a precondition of representation, whether linguistic or other forms of representation, why can't the Background also itself consist of Intentional states such as unconscious beliefs?

In answer to the first: If we try to spell out the relevant parts of the Background as a set of sentences expressing further semantic contents, that would simply require yet further Backgrounds for their comprehension. Suppose, for example, we write down all the facts about doors and about opening that we think would fix the correct understanding of "Open the door". Those facts will be stated in a set of sentences, each with its own semantic content. But now those sentences themselves have to be understood and that understanding will require yet more Background. If we try to spell out the Background as part of the semantic content, we would never know when to stop, and each semantic content we produce will require yet more Background for its comprehension. About the second question: If representation presupposes a Background, then the Background cannot itself consist in representations without generating an infinite regress. We know that the infinite regress is empirically impossible because human intellectual capacities are finite. The sequence of cognitive steps in linguistic understanding comes to an end. On the conception presented here, it does not come to an end with the grasp of semantic content in isolation or even with semantic content together with a set of presupposed beliefs, but rather the semantic content only functions against a Background that consists of cultural and biological know-how, and it is this Background know-how which enables us to understand literal meanings.

(ii) The understanding of metaphor

It is tempting to think that there must be some definite set of rules or principles that enables users of a language to produce and understand metaphorical utterances and that these rules and principles must have something like an algorithmic character, such that given a strict application of the rules one would get the right interpretation of any metaphor. However, as soon as one tries to state these principles of interpretation one discovers some interesting facts. The rules that one can reasonably adduce are by no means algorithmic. There are indeed discoverable principles that enable users of the language to figure out that when a speaker says metaphorically that X is Y he means X is like Y with respect to certain features F. But such rules do not function in a mechanical fashion: there is no algorithm for discovering when an utterance is intended metaphorically, and no algorithm for calculating the values of F, even after the hearer has figured out that the utterance is intended metaphorically. Furthermore, and perhaps more interestingly for the present case, there are many metaphors whose interpretation does not rely on any perception of literal similarity between the extension of the Y term and the referent of the X term. Consider, for example, taste metaphors for personality traits or temperature metaphors for emotional states. Thus, for example, we speak of a "sweet person", a "sour disposition" and a "bitter personality". We also speak of a "warm welcome", a "cool reception", a "lukewarm friendship", a "heated argument", a "hot love affair" and "sexual frigidity". But in neither the case of the taste metaphors nor the case of the temperature metaphors are there any literal similarities between the extension of the Y term and the referent of the X term which are sufficient to account for the metaphorical utterance meaning. For example, the metaphorical utterance meaning of the expression "a lukewarm reception", is not based on any literal similarity between lukewarm things and the character of the reception so described. There are indeed principles of similarity on which certain metaphors function; but the point of the present examples is that there are also certain metaphors, and indeed whole classes of metaphors, that function without any underlying principles of similarity. It just seems to be a fact about our mental capacities that we are able to interpret certain sorts of metaphor without the application of any underlying 'rules' or 'principles' other than the sheer ability to make certain associations. I don't know any better way to describe these abilities than to say that they are non-representational mental capacities.

Both the nonalgorithmic character of the rules and the fact that some of the associations are not determined by rules at all suggest that there are nonrepresentational capacities involved, but that claim would be misleading if it is taken to imply that a complete and algorithmic set of rules for metaphor would show that there is no such Background; for even such rules would require a Background for their application as we shall see.

The Background

(iii) Physical skills

Consider what it is like to learn how to ski. The beginning skier is given a set of verbal instructions as to what he is supposed to do: "lean foward", "bend the ankles", "keep the weight on the downhill ski", etc. Each of these is an explicit representation, and, to the extent that the skier is seriously trying to learn, each will function causally as part of the Intentional content determining the behavior. The skier tries to keep the weight on the downhill ski by way of obeying the instructions to keep the weight on the downhill ski. Here we have a perfectly standard case of Intentional causation: the instructions have world-to-word direction of fit and word-to-world direction of causation. Skiing is one of those skills which is learned with the aid of explicit representations. But after a while the skier gets better; he no longer needs to remind himself of the instructions, he just goes out and skis. According to the traditional cognitivist view, the instructions have become internalized and now function unconsciously but still as representations. Indeed, according to some authors, e.g., Polanyi,[3] it is essential to their functioning that these Intentional contents should function unconsciously, because if one thinks about them or tries to bring them into consciousness, they get in the way, and one is no longer able to ski as well. Rather like the proverbial centipede who thinks about which leg he is supposed to move next and becomes paralyzed, the skier will become paralyzed, or at any rate impeded, if he tries to remember the instructor's rules; he is better off letting them function unconsciously.

I find this account of what happens when the skier gets better implausible, and I want to suggest an alternative hypothesis. As the skier gets better he does not internalize the rules better, but rather the rules become progressively irrelevant. The rules do not become 'wired in' as unconscious Intentional contents, but the repeated experiences create physical capacities, presumably realized as neural pathways, that make the rules simply irrelevant. "Practice makes perfect" not because practice results in a perfect memorization of the rules, but because repeated practice enables the body to take over and the rules to recede into the Background.

3 M. Polanyi, *Personal Knowledge: Toward a Post-Critical Philosophy* (Chicago: University of Chicago Press, 1958).

We are able to account for the data with a more economical explanatory apparatus if we do not have to suppose that each physical skill is underlain by a large number of unconscious mental representations, but rather that repeated practice and training in a variety of situations eventually makes the causal functioning of representation unnecessary in the exercise of the skill. The advanced skier doesn't follow the rules better, rather he skis in a different sort of way altogether. His movements are flowing and harmonious, whereas the beginning skier, consciously or unconsciously concentrating on the rules, makes movements which are jerky, abrupt, and inept. The expert skier is flexible and responds differently to different conditions of terrain and snow; the beginning skier is inflexible, and when different and unusual situations come up he tends simply to fall down. A downhill racer on the course moves very rapidly, over 60 miles an hour, over a terrain that is rough and uneven. His body makes thousands of very rapid adjustments to variations in the terrain. Now which is more plausible: when his body makes these adjustments, it is only because he is making a very rapid series of unconscious calculations applying unconscious rules; or is it rather that the racer's body is so trained that these variations in the terrain are dealt with automatically? On my view, the body takes over and the skier's Intentionality is concentrated on winning the race. This is not to deny that there are forms of Intentionality involved in the exercise of skills, nor is it to deny that some of this Intentionality is unconscious.

None of these three sets of considerations is in any way decisive and certainly no formal argument has been presented to demonstrate the hypothesis of the Background. Nonetheless, a certain picture is beginning to emerge: we do have Intentional states, some conscious, many unconscious; they form a complex Network. The Network shades off into a Background of capacities (including various skills, abilities, preintentional assumptions and presuppositions, stances, and nonrepresentational attitudes). The Background is not on the *periphery* of Intentionality but *permeates* the entire Network of Intentional states; since without the Background the states could not function, they could not determine conditions of satisfaction. Without the Background there could be no perception, action, memory, i.e., there could be no such Intentional states. Given this picture as a working hypothesis, evidence for the Background piles up everywhere one looks. For example, the rules for performing speech acts or the rules for interpreting indirect speech acts, have an application as dependent on a Background as the 'rules' of metaphor.

Ultimately, these considerations suggest a more traditional sounding argument for the Background (though I must confess I find the "considerations" more convincing than the "argument"): Suppose that the converse of the hypothesis of the Background were true, that is, suppose that all Intentionalistic mental life and all cognitive capacities could be entirely reduced to representations: beliefs, desires, internalized rules, knowledge that such and such is the case, etc. Each of these representations would be expressible as an explicit semantic content (even though, of course, many of them are unconscious and thus unavailable to the introspection of the agent), and mental processes would consist in going from one such semantic content to another. But there are certain difficulties with this picture. The semantic contents with which the conception provides us are not self-applying. Even given the semantic contents we still have to know what to *do* with them, how to apply them, and that knowledge cannot consist in further semantic contents without infinite regress. Suppose, for example, that my ability to walk really did consist in my having internalized a set of rules for walking. What could such rules be like? Well, as a start, suppose that we try this as a rule of walking: "First, move the left foot forward, then the right foot, then the left foot, and continue on in this manner." But as we have already seen, any semantic content of the sort we have just expressed is subject to a variety of interpretations. What exactly is to count as a "foot", as "movement", as "forward", what counts as "continuing on in this manner"? Given different Background assumptions, we could interpret this rule in an indefinite number of ways, though as things stand we all know the 'correct' interpretation. Now that knowledge cannot be represented as a further semantic content, because then the same problem would arise all over again for it: we would need another rule for the correct interpretation of the interpretation rule for the walking rule. The way out of the paradox is to see that we don't need the walking rule in the first place; we just walk.[4] And in the cases where we do in fact act according to a rule, where we follow a rule, as in the rules of speech acts, we just act on the rule, we don't need any further rules for interpreting the rules. There are indeed representations, some of which function causally in the production of our behavior, but eventually in the sequence of representations we reach a bedrock of capacities. As Wittgenstein suggests, we just act.

Suppose you wrote down on a huge roll of paper all of the things you believed. Suppose you included all of those beliefs which are, in effect, axioms that enable you to generate further beliefs, and you wrote down any "principles of inference" you might need to enable you to derive further beliefs from your prior beliefs. Thus, you needn't write down that "$7 + 1 = 8$" and "$8 + 1 = 9$"; a statement of the principles of arithmetic *á la* Peano would account for the infinite generative capacity of your arithmetical beliefs. Now suppose in this fashion you wrote down every one of your beliefs. About this list I want to say, if all we have is a verbal expression of the content of your beliefs, then so far we have no Intentionality at all. And this is not because what you have written down are 'lifeless' marks, without significance, but because even if we construe them as expressing Fregean semantic entities, i.e., as propositional contents, the propositions are not self-applying. You still have to know what to do with the semantic elements before they can function; you have to be able to apply the semantic contents in order that they determine conditions of satisfaction. Now it is this capacity for applying or interpreting Intentional contents which I am saying is a characteristic function of the Background.

III. IN WHAT SENSE IS THE BACKGROUND MENTAL?

One could argue, and I have seen it argued, that what I have been calling the Background is really social, a product of social interaction, or that it is primarily biological, or even that it consists of actual objects in the world such as chairs and tables, hammers

---

.[4] Cf. L. Wittgenstein, *Philosophical Investigations* (Oxford: Basil Blackwell, 1953), paras 198–202.

and nails – "the referential totality of ready-to-hand equipment", in a Heideggerian vein. I want to say there is at least an element of truth in all these conceptions but that does not detract from the crucial sense in which the Background consists of mental phenomena.

Each of us is a biological and social being in a world of other biological and social beings, surrounded by artifacts and natural objects. Now, what I have been calling the Background is indeed derived from the entire congeries of relations which each biological–social being has to the world around itself. Without my biological constitution, and without the set of social relations in which I am embedded, I could not have the Background that I have. But all of these relations, biological, social, physical, all this embeddedness, is only relevant to the production of the Background because of the effects that it has on me, specifically the effects that it has on my mind-brain. The world is relevant to my Background only because of my interaction with the world; and we can appeal to the usual "brain-in-the-vat" fable to illustrate this point. Even if I am a brain in a vat – that is, even if all of my perceptions and actions in the world are hallucinations, and the conditions of satisfaction of all of my externally referring Intentional states are, in fact, unsatisfied – nonetheless, I do have the Intentional content that I have, and thus I necessarily have exactly the same Background that I would have if I were not a brain in a vat and had that particular Intentional content. *That* I have a certain set of Intentional states and *that* I have a Background do not logically require that I be in fact in certain relations to the world around me, even though I could not, as a matter of empirical fact, have the Background that I do have without a specific biological history and a specific set of social relations to other people and physical relations to natural objects and artifacts. The Background, therefore, is not a set of things nor a set of mysterious relations between ourselves and things, rather it is simply a set of skills, stances, preintentional assumptions and presuppositions, practices, and habits. And all of these, as far as we know, are realized in human brains and bodies. There is nothing whatever that is "transcendental" or "metaphysical" about the Background, as I am using that term.

IV. HOW CAN WE BEST STUDY THE BACKGROUND?

I find that it is most useful to study the Background in cases of breakdown, cases where Intentional states fail to achieve their conditions of satisfaction because of some failure in the set of preintentional Background conditions on Intentionality. Consider two sorts of examples. Suppose as I go into my office, I suddenly discover a huge chasm on the other side of the door. My efforts to enter my office would certainly be frustrated and that is a failure to achieve the conditions of satisfaction of an Intentional state. But the reason for the failure has to do with a breakdown in my Background presuppositions. It is not that I have always had a belief – conscious or unconscious – that there would be no chasms on the other side of my door, or even that I always believed that my floor was 'normal'; rather, the set of habits, practices, and preintentional assumptions that I make about my office when I intentionally attempt to enter it have failed in this case, and for that reason my intention is frustrated. A second sort of case concerns the exercise of physical skills. Suppose that when I attempt to swim I suddenly find that I am unable to. Having always been able to swim since childhood, I suddenly find that I am unable to make a single stroke. In this case one might say that two Intentional states have been frustrated. First, my intention to swim has been frustrated, and second, my belief that I am able to swim is falsified. But the actual capacity to swim is neither an intention nor a belief. The actual capacity to swim, my ability to carry out certain physical movements, in this case has simply failed me. What we have in the first case, one might say, is a failure in "how things are", and what we have in the second case is a failure in "how to do things". In both cases we have a breakdown, and the breakdown manifests itself in the failure to achieve the conditions of satisfaction of some Intentional state; but the reason for the failure in each case is not a further failure of Intentionality, but rather a breakdown in the functioning of the preintentional capacities that underlie the intentional states in question.

V. WHY ARE WE HAVING SO MUCH TROUBLE DESCRIBING THE BACKGROUND OR EVEN IN GETTING A NEUTRAL TERMINOLOGY FOR DESCRIBING IT? AND WHY, INDEED, DOES OUR TERMINOLOGY ALWAYS LOOK 'REPRESENTATIONAL'?

The reader by now will have noticed that there is a real difficulty in finding ordinary language terms to describe the Background: one speaks vaguely of "practices", "capacities", and "stances" or one speaks suggestively but misleadingly of "assumptions" and "presuppositions". These latter terms must be literally wrong, because they imply the apparatus of representation with its propositional contents, logical relations, truth values, directions of fit, etc.; and that is why I normally preface "assumption" and "presumption" with the apparently oxymoronic "preintentional", since the sense of "assumption" and "presupposition" in question is not representational. My preferred expressions are "capacities" and "practices", since these can succeed or fail, but only in their exercise; and they can succeed or fail without being themselves representations. However, even they are inadequate since they fail to convey an appropriate implication that the phenomena are explicitly mental. The fact that we have no natural vocabulary for discussing the phenomena in question and the fact that we tend to lapse into an Intentionalistic vocabulary ought to arouse our interest. Why is it so?

The main function of the mind is, in our special sense of that word, to represent; and, not surprisingly, languages such as English provide us with a rather rich vocabulary for describing these representations, a vocabulary of memory and intention, belief and desire, perception and action. But just as language is not well designed to talk about itself, so the mind is not well designed to reflect on itself: we are most at home with first-order Intentional states and most at home with a first-order vocabulary for those states, e.g., we *believe* that it has stopped raining, *wish* we had a cold beer and are *sorry* that interest rates have declined. When the time does come to make second-order investigations of our first-order states, we have no vocabulary at hand except the first-order vocabulary. Our second-order investigations into the first-order phenomena quite naturally use the first-order vocabulary, so we can be said quite naturally to *reflect* about reflection or have *beliefs* about believing or even to *presuppose* presupposing. But when it comes to examining the conditions of the possibility of the functioning of the mind, we simply have very little vocabulary to hand except the vocabulary of first-order Intentional states. There simply is no first-order vocabulary for the Background, because the Background has no Intentionality. As the precondition of Intentionality, the Background is as invisible to Intentionality as the eye which sees is invisible to itself.

Furthermore, since the only vocabulary we have available is the vocabulary of first-order mental states, when we do reflect on the Background, the temptation is to represent its elements on the model of other mental phenomena, to think that our representations are of representations. What else could they be? Eating lunch in a restaurant, I am surprised when I lift my mug of beer by its near weightlessness. Inspection reveals that the thick mug is not glass but plastic. We would naturally say I *believed* that the mug was made of glass, and I *expected* it to be heavy. But that is wrong. In the sense in which I really do believe without ever having explicitly thought about it that interest rates will go down and I really do expect a break in the current heat wave, I had no such expectations and beliefs about the mug; I simply acted. Ordinary usage invites us to, and we can and do, treat elements of the Background as if they were representations, but it does not follow from that, nor is it the case that, when these elements are functioning they function as representations. The price we pay for deliberately going against ordinary language is metaphor, oxymoron, and outright neologism.

VI. HOW DOES THE BACKGROUND WORK?

The Background provides a set of enabling conditions that make it possible for particular forms of Intentionality to function. Just as the Constitution of the United States enables a certain potential candidate to form the intention to become President, and just as the rules of a game enable certain moves to be made in the game, so the Background enables us to have particular forms of Intentionality. These analogies, however, go lame when we reflect that the rules of the game and the Constitution are both sets of representations, specifically they are sets of constitutive rules. The Background, to repeat, is not a set of representations, but like the structure of the game or of the Constitution it nonetheless provides a set of enabling conditions. The Background functions causally, but the causation in question is not determining. In traditional terms, the Background provides necessary but not sufficient conditions for understanding, believing, desiring, intending, etc., and in that sense it is enabling and not determining. Nothing forces me to the right understanding of the semantic content of "Open the door", but without the Background the understanding that I have would not be possible, and any understanding at all requires some Background or other. It would, therefore, be incorrect to think of the Background as forming a bridge between Intentional content and the determination of conditions of satisfaction, as if the Intentional content itself could not reach up to the conditions of satisfaction. It would be even more incorrect to think of the Background as a set of functions that take Intentional contents as arguments and determine conditions of satisfaction as values. Both of these conceptions construe the Background as some further Intentional content that latches on to the primary Intentional content. On the conception I am presenting, the Background is rather the set of practices, skills, habits, and stances that enable Intentional contents to work in the various ways that they do, and it is in that sense that the Background functions causally by providing a set of enabling conditions for the operation of Intentional states.

Many philosophical problems arise from the failure to understand the nature and operation of the Background. I will mention only one source of these: as I remarked earlier, it is always possible to take an element of the Background and treat it as a representation, but from the fact that it is possible to treat an element of the Background as a representation, it does not follow that, when it is functioning, it is functioning as a representation. A good illustration of this is the current and recurring philosophical dispute concerning something called "realism". Realism, I want to say, is not a hypothesis, belief, or philosophical thesis; Realism is part of the Background in the following sense. My commitment to "realism" is exhibited by the fact that I live the way that I do, I drive my car, drink my beer, write my articles, give my lectures, and ski my mountains. Now in addition to all of these activities, each a manifestation of my Intentionality, there isn't a further 'hypothesis' that the real world exists. My commitment to the existence of the real world is manifested whenever I do pretty much anything. It is a mistake to treat that commitment as if it were a hypothesis, as if in addition to skiing, drinking, eating, etc., I held a belief – there is a real world independent of my representations of it. Once we misconstrue the functioning of the Background in this way, that is once we treat that which is preintentional as if it were a sort of Intentionality, it immediately becomes problematic. It seems I could never show or demonstrate that there existed a real world independent of my representations of it. But of course I could never show or demonstrate that, since any *showing* or *demonstrating* presupposes the Background, and the Background is the embodiment of my commitment to realism. Contemporary discussions of realism are, for the most part, strictly senseless, because the very posing of the question, or indeed of any question at all, presupposes the preintentional realism of the Background. There can't be a fully meaningful question "Is there a real world independent of my representations of it?" because the very having of representations can only exist against a Background which gives representations the character of "representing something". This is not to say that realism is a true hypothesis, rather it is to say that it is not a hypothesis at all, but the precondition of having hypotheses.

Chapter 6

MEANING

The approach taken to Intentionality in this book is resolutely naturalistic, I think of Intentional states, processes, and events as part of our biological life history in the way that digestion, growth, and the secretion of bile are part of our biological life history. From an evolutionary point of view, just as there is an order of priority in the development of other biological processes, so there is an order of priority in the development of Intentional phenomena. In this development, language and meaning, at least in the sense in which humans have language and meaning, comes very late. Many species other than humans have sensory perception and intentional action, and several species, certainly the primates, have beliefs, desires, and intentions, but very few species, perhaps only humans, have the peculiar but also biologically based form of Intentionality we associate with language and meaning.

Intentionality differs from other sorts of biological phenomena in that it has a logical structure, and just as there are evolutionary priorities, so there are logical priorities. A natural consequence of the biological approach advocated in this book is to regard meaning, in the sense in which speakers mean something by their utterances, as a special development of more primitive forms of Intentionality. So construed, speakers' meaning should be entirely definable in terms of more primitive forms of Intentionality. And the definition is nontrivial in this sense: we define speakers' meaning in terms of forms of Intentionality that are not intrinsically linguistic. If, for example, we can define meaning in terms of intentions we will have defined a linguistic notion in terms of a nonlinguistic notion even though many, perhaps most, human intentions are in fact linguistically realized.

On this approach the philosophy of language is a branch of the philosophy of mind. In its most general form it amounts to the view that certain fundamental semantic notions such as meaning are analyzable in terms of even more fundamental psychological notions such as belief, desire, and intention. Such views are fairly common in philosophy, but there is considerable disagreement among adherents of the view that language is dependent on mind as to what the analysis of semantic notions should look like. One of the most influential versions of this view (deriving from Grice)[1] is that for a speaker to mean something by an utterance is for him to have a certain set of intentions directed at an actual or possible audience: for a speaker to mean something by an utterance is for him to make that utterance with the intention of producing certain effects on his audience. Characteristically, the adherents of this view have taken the notions of intention and action, as well as other mental notions such as belief and desire, as unanalyzed.

In this chapter, I want to resume the discussion of the analysis of meaning in terms of speakers' intentions. The approach I will adopt differs from that of the tradition, my own earlier work included, in two important respects. First, I will use the account of actions and Intentional states provided in previous chapters in order to ground the notions of meaning and speech acts in a more general theory of the mind and action. Meaning is one kind of Intentionality; what distinguishes it from other kinds? Speech acts are kinds of acts; what distinguishes them from other kinds? Second, I will reject the idea that the intentions that matter for meaning are the intentions to produce *effects* on audiences. The primary question I will address is simply this: What are the features of speakers' intentions in meaningful utterances that make it the case that the speaker means something by his utterance? When a speaker makes an utterance he produces some physical event; to put the question crudely: What does his intention add to that physical event that makes that physical event a case of the speaker's meaning something by it? How, so to speak, do we get from the physics to the semantics?

This question, "What are the characteristics of speakers' intentions that make them meaning conferring?", has to be distinguished from several other questions in the philosophy of language that are, I believe, quite irrelevant to it. For example, the

1 H. P. Grice, 'Meaning', *The Philosophical Review*, vol. 66 (1957), no. 3, pp 377–88.

problem of how speakers are able to produce and understand a potentially infinite number of sentences is an important problem, but it has no special connection with the problem of meaning. The problem of meaning, at least in the form I am posing it, would remain exactly the same for a speaker of a language that allowed only a finite number of sentences.

Another related question is: What knowledge must a speaker have in order to be said to know a language, such as French or English? What does a speaker know when he knows French for example? This is also an interesting question but it has no special connection with the problem of meaning, at least as I am construing that problem. The problem of meaning would arise even for people who were communicating with each other without using a common language. It sometimes happens to me in a foreign country, for example, that I attempt to communicate with people who share no common language with me. In such a situation the problem of meaning arises in an acute form, and my question is: What is it about my intentions in such a situation that makes them specifically meaning intentions? In such a situation I mean something by my gestures, whereas in another situation, by making the very same gestures, I might not mean anything. How does it work in the meaningful cases?

In our discussion of the structure of action in Chapter 3 we analyzed simple actions such as raising one's arm into their related components: a successfully performed intentional action consists of an intention-in-action and a bodily movement. The intention-in-action both causes and presents the bodily movement. The bodily movement, as caused by it, is its condition of satisfaction. In a sequence involving a prior intention and an action which consists in carrying out that intention, the prior intention represents the whole action, it causes the intention-in-action which in turn causes the bodily movement and by transitivity of causation we can say that the prior intention causes the whole action.

In real life, however, very few intentions and actions are this simple. One type of complex intention involves a causal by-means-of relation. Thus, for example, as we saw in Chapter 3, section v, a man might intend to squeeze the trigger of a gun in order to fire the gun in order to shoot his enemy. Each step in the sequence – squeezing the trigger, firing the gun, shooting his enemy – is a causal step and the intention-in-action encompasses all three. The killer intends to shoot his enemy by means of firing the gun and he intends to fire the gun by means of squeezing the trigger. But not all complex intentions are causal in this way. If a man were ordered to raise his arm he might raise his arm with the intention of obeying the order. He thus has a complex intention: the intention to raise his arm in order to obey the order. But the relationship between raising his arm and obeying the order is not a causal relation in the way that squeezing the trigger and firing the gun is a causal relation. In such a case there are conditions of satisfaction related to the bodily movement which are not intended to be caused by or to cause the bodily movement: he intends to raise his arm by way of obeying the order, but he does not intend that his arm going up will cause some further phenomenon of his obeying the order. In that context, raising his arm just is obeying the order and is intended as such. Such non-causal additional conditions of satisfaction are also characteristic of meaning intentions, as we will shortly see.

In order to get clear about meaning intentions, we must understand these various notions: the distinction between prior intentions and intentions in action, the causal and self-referential character of both, and the presence of both causal and non-causal conditions in complex intentions, whether prior intentions or intentions in action.

II. THE STRUCTURE OF MEANING INTENTIONS

With this apparatus in hand let us turn to the main question of this chapter; what is the structure of meaning intentions? The problem is what are the conditions of satisfaction of the intentions in action of utterances that give them semantic properties? I make a noise through my mouth or I make some marks on paper. What is the nature of the complex intention in action that makes the production of those marks or sounds something more than just the production of marks or sounds? The short answer is that I intend their production as the performance of a speech act. The longer answer is to characterize the structure of that intention.

Before I attack that question head on, I want to mention some other peculiar features we need to explain. I want to specify some further conditions of adequacy on the analysis.

I said earlier that there is a double level of Intentionality in the performance of illocutionary acts, a level of the Intentional state expressed in the performance of the act and a level of the intention to perform the act. When, for example, I make the statement that it is raining, I both express the *belief* that it is raining and perform an *intentional act* of stating that it is raining. Furthermore, the conditions of satisfaction of the mental state expressed in the performance of the speech act are identical with the conditions of satisfaction of the speech act itself. A statement will be true iff the expressed belief is true, an order will be obeyed iff the expressed desire is fulfilled, a promise will be kept iff the expressed intention is carried out. These parallels are not accidental and any theory of meaning has to explain them. But, at the same time, we have to keep in mind the distinction between making a statement and making a true statement, between giving an order and giving an order which is obeyed, between making a promise and making a promise which is kept. In each case the meaning intention is an intention only to perform the first half – making a statement, giving an order, making a promise – and yet in some sense, that intention already has some 'internal' relation to the second half, since the intention to make a particular statement has to determine what counts as the truth of the statement, the intention to issue an order has to determine what counts as obedience to the order, etc. The fact that the conditions of satisfaction of the expressed Intentional state and the conditions of satisfaction of the speech act are identical suggests that the key to the problem of meaning is to see that in the performance of the speech act the mind intentionally imposes the same conditions of satisfaction on the physical expression of the expressed mental state, as the mental state has itself. The mind imposes Intentionality on the production of sounds, marks, etc., by imposing the conditions of satisfaction of the mental state on the production of the physical phenomena.

At least the following are conditions of adequacy on our analysis:

1. There is a double level of Intentionality in the performance of the speech act, a level of the psychological state expressed in the performance of the act and a level of the intention with which the act is performed which makes it the act that it is. Let us call these respectively the "sincerity condition" and the "meaning intention". In its most general form, our task is to characterize the

meaning intention, and a condition of adequacy on that characterization is that it should explain this double level of Intentionality.

2. The conditions of satisfaction of the speech act and the conditions of satisfaction of the sincerity condition are identical. Now our account of the meaning intention must show how this comes about even though the conditions of satisfaction of the meaning intention are different from both the conditions of satisfaction of the speech act and of the sincerity conditions. The intention to make a statement, for example, is different from the intention to make a true statement, and yet the intention to make a statement must already commit the speaker to making a true statement and to expressing the belief in the truth of the statement he is making. In short, our second condition of adequacy is that our account of the meaning intention must explain how it comes about that, though the conditions of satisfaction of the meaning intention are not the same as the conditions of satisfaction of the speech act or of the expressed psychological state, nonetheless the content of the meaning intention must determine both that the speech act and the sincerity conditions have the conditions of satisfaction that they do and that they have identical conditions of satisfaction. Why is it, for example, that my intention to state that it is raining, which can be satisfied even if it is not raining, nonetheless determines that my speech act will be satisfied iff it is raining and will be an expression of a belief which will be satisfied iff it is raining?

3. We need to have a clear distinction between representation and communication. Characteristically a man who makes a statement both intends to represent some fact or state of affairs and intends to communicate this representation to his hearers. But his representing intention is not the same as his communication intention. Communicating is a matter of producing certain effects on one's hearers, but one can intend to represent something without caring at all about the effects on one's hearers. One can make a statement without intending to produce conviction or belief in one's hearers or without intending to get them to believe that the speaker believes what he says or indeed without even intending to get them to understand it at all. There are, therefore, two aspects to meaning intentions, the intention to represent and

the intention to communicate. The traditional discussion of these problems, my own work included, suffers from a failure to distinguish between them and from the assumption that the whole account of meaning can be given in terms of communication intentions. On the present account, representation is prior to communication and representing intentions are prior to communication intentions. Part of what one communicates is the content of one's representations, but one can intend to represent something without intending to communicate. And for speech acts with a propositional content and direction of fit the converse is not the case. One can intend to represent without intending to communicate, but one cannot intend to communicate without intending to represent. I cannot, for example, intend to inform you that it is raining without intending that my utterance represent, truly or falsely, the state of affairs of the weather.[2]

4. I have argued elsewhere[3] that there are five and only five basic categories of illocutionary acts: assertives, where we tell our hearers (truly or falsely) how things are; directives, where we try to get them to do things; commissives, where we commit ourselves to doing things; declarations, where we bring about changes in the world with our utterances; and expressives, where we express our feelings and attitudes. Now I find these five types of illocutionary points, so to speak, 'empirically'. The speech acts one performs and encounters just exhibit these five types. But if these really are the five basic types, there must be some deeper reason for that. If the way that language represents the world is an extension and realization of the way the mind represents the world, then these five must derive from some fundamental features of the mind.

The Intentionality of the mind not only creates the possibility of meaning, but it limits its forms. Why is it, for example, that we have performative utterances for apologizing, stating, ordering, thanking, and congratulating – all cases where we can perform an act by saying that we are performing it, i.e., by representing

---

2 For further discussion of this point, see J. R. Searle, 'Meaning, communication, and representation', in Grandy (ed.), A Festschrift for H. P. Grice (forthcoming).
3 See 'A taxonomy of illocutionary acts', in *Expression and Meaning* (Cambridge: Cambridge University Press, 1979), pp. 1–29.

ourselves as performing it – but we do not and could not have a performative for, for example, frying an egg? If one says "I apologize" one can thereby apologize, but if one says "I fry an egg" no egg is so far fried. Perhaps God could fry an egg simply by uttering such a performative sentence, but we can't. Why not? Another aim, then, of the analysis of meaning is to show how the possibilities and limitations of meaning derive from the Intentionality of the mind.

We need an example to work with, so let us take a case where a man performs a speech act by performing some simple basic action such as raising his arm. Suppose that you and I have arranged in advance that if I raise my arm that act is to count as a signal that such and such is the case. Suppose, in a military context, I signal to you on one hill while I am standing on another hill that the enemy has retreated, and by prearrangement I signal this by raising my arm. How does it work? The complex intention in action has the following content, as far as representation is concerned:

> (My arm goes up as a result of this intention in action and my arm going up has as conditions of satisfaction with the mind(or utterance)-to-world direction of fit that the enemy is retreating).

This sounds somewhat odd, but I think it is on the right track. The problem of meaning is how does the mind impose Intentionality on entities that are not intrinsically Intentional? How is it possible that mere things can represent? And the answer I am proposing is that the utterance act is performed with the intention that the utterance itself has conditions of satisfaction. The conditions of satisfaction of the belief that the enemy is retreating are transferred to the utterance by an Intentional act. The reason, then, that the performance of the speech act, that is, in this case the raising of the arm, would count as an expression of belief that the enemy is retreating is that it is performed with the intention that its conditions of satisfaction are precisely those of the belief. Indeed what makes it a meaningful action in the linguistic sense of a meaningful action is that it has those conditions of satisfaction intentionally imposed upon it. The key element in the analysis of meaning intentions is simply this: For most types of speech acts, meaning intentions are at least in part intentions to represent, and an intention to represent is an intention that *the physical events which constitute part of the conditions of satisfaction (in the sense of things required) of the intention should themselves have conditions of satisfaction (in the sense of requirement).* In the example, the conditions of satisfaction of my intention are that my arm should go up, and that its going up has conditions of satisfaction, in this case truth conditions. The first set of conditions of satisfaction are causally related to the intention: the intention has to cause my arm to go up. In this assertive case the second set of conditions of satisfaction – that the enemy has retreated – are not causally related to the intention. The utterance is intended to have the mind(or utterance)-to-world direction of fit.

Now, if I am on the right track so far, the move from the representation intention to the communication intention is fairly simple. The communication intention consists simply in the intention that the hearer should recognize that the act was performed with the representation intention. Thus, my intention when I signal you by raising my hand is to get you to recognize that I am signalling that the enemy has retreated. And in the jargon so far used that amounts to the following:

> (This intention in action causes my arm to go up, and my arm going up has as conditions of satisfaction with the mind(or utterance)-to-world direction of fit that the enemy is retreating, and my audience recognizes both that my arm is going up and that its going up has those conditions of satisfaction).

Notice that this account makes a clear separation between that part of meaning that has to do with representation, which, as I said, I believe is the core of meaning, and that part which has to do with communication. Second, it does not have the defect that we confuse the intention to make a statement with the intention to make a true statement, or the intention to make a statement with the intention to produce certain effects such as belief or conviction on our audience. Characteristically, when we do make a statement we intend to make a true statement and we do intend to produce certain beliefs in our audience, but the intention to make a statement is nonetheless different from the intention to produce conviction or the intention to speak the truth. Any account of language must allow for the fact that is is possible to lie, and it is possible to perform a statement while lying. And any account of language must allow for the fact that one can completely succeed in making a statement, while failing to make a true statement. Furthermore, any account of language must allow for the fact that a person can make a statement and be quite indifferent about whether or not his audience believes him or even whether or not his audience understands him. The present account allows for these conditions because on this account the essence of statement making is representing something as being the case, not communicating one's representations to one's hearers. One can represent something as being the case even when one believes that it isn't the case (a lie); even when one believes that it is the case, but it isn't (a mistake); and even if one is not interested in convincing anybody that it is the case or indeed in getting them to recognize that one is representing it as being the case. The representing intention is independent of the communication intention and the representing intention is a matter of imposing the conditions of satisfaction of an Intentional state on an overt act, and thereby expressing that Intentional state.

Another way to approach the same point is to ask what is the difference between saying something and meaning it and saying it without meaning it? Wittgenstein frequently asks us this sort of question to remind us that "meaning" is not the name of an introspective process; nonetheless there is a difference between saying something and meaning it and saying it without meaning it. What is it exactly? At least this much: When I say something and mean it, my utterance has conditions of satisfaction in a way that it does not have any such conditions if I say it without meaning it. If I say "Es regnet" as a way of practicing German pronunciation, then the fact that the sun is shining when I utter this sentence is irrelevant. But if I say "Es regnet" and mean it, then the fact that the sun is shining is relevant, and it becomes relevant because saying something and meaning it is a matter of saying it with the conditions of satisfaction intentionally imposed on the utterance.

I believe we will deepen our understanding of these points if we show how they apply to other sorts of speech acts. When we turn to directives and commissives we find that, unlike statements, they have the world-to-word direction of fit and their analysis is further complicated by the fact that they have an additional form of causal self-reference. In the case of an order, the order is obeyed only if the act that the hearer is ordered to perform is carried out by way of obeying the order; and in the case of a promise, the promise is kept only if the action promised is done by way of fulfilling the promise. This can be illustrated with the sort of example we considered in Chapter 3 (derived from Wittgenstein). Suppose you order me to leave the room. I might say, "Well, I was going to leave the room anyhow, but I wouldn't do it because you ordered me to". Have I obeyed the order if I then leave the room? I certainly haven't disobeyed it; but in the full sense, we couldn't say I had obeyed it either. We would not, for example, on the basis of a series of such examples describe our hearer as an "obedient" person. Analogous remarks apply to promising. What such examples are designed to show, for the present discussion, is that, in addition to the self-referential character of all intentions, the intention to make a promise or an order must impose an additional self-referential condition of satisfaction on the utterance. Promises and orders are self-referential because their conditions of satisfaction make reference to the promises and orders themselves. In the full sense one only *keeps* a promise or *obeys* an order if one does what one does *by way of* keeping the promise or obeying the order.

Another way to see this same feature is to note that both promises and orders create *reasons* for the conditions of satisfaction in a way which is quite unlike statements. Thus, making a statement by itself does not create evidence for the truth of the statement. But making a promise does create a reason for doing the thing promised, and asking someone to do something creates a reason for his doing it.

What, then, is the structure of the meaning intention in issuing an order? Suppose in our earlier situation I raise my arm by way of signalling to you that you are to retreat, that is, by way of *ordering* you to retreat. If I intend the raising of the arm as a directive then I intend at least this much:

> (My arm goes up as a result of this intention in action, and my arm going up has as conditions of satisfaction, with the world-to-mind(or utterance) direction of fit, that you retreat and that you retreat because my arm going up has those conditions of satisfaction).

What I order is your obedience, but to *obey* my order you have to do the thing I order you to do, and my order has to be a reason for your doing it. My order is obeyed only if you do the act *by way of obeying the order.*

The communication intention is simply the intention that this representation intention should be recognized by the hearer. That is, all that the communication intention adds to what has been stated so far is:

> (The audience recognizes my arm going up and that its going up has these conditions of satisfaction).

The formal structure of the intention in making a commissive is quite similar, the main difference being that the speaker is the subject of the conditions of satisfaction of a commissive and the hearer is the subject of the directive.

Thus, to take a similar example, suppose by raising my arm I signal to you my commitment to advance on the enemy. The representing intention has the following conditions of satisfaction:

> (My arm goes up as a result of this intention in action, and my arm going up has as conditions of satisfaction with the world-to-mind(or utterance) direction of fit that I advance on the enemy and that I do so, at least in part, because my arm going up has those conditions of satisfaction).

What I promise is the fulfillment of my promise, but to fulfill my promise I have to do the thing I promised and my having promised to do it has to function as a reason for doing it. And again, all that the communication intention adds is

> (the audience recognizes my arm going up and that its going up has these conditions of satisfaction).

Declarations, such as declaring war, pronouncing some couple man and wife, adjourning the meeting, or resigning, have two special features not common to other types of speech acts. First, since the illocutionary point of the declaration is to bring about some new state of affairs solely in virtue of the utterance, declarations have both directions of fit. One brings it about that p by way of representing it as being the case that p. Thus, "I now pronounce you man and wife", makes it the case that you are man and wife (world-to-word direction of fit) by way of representing it as being the case that you are man and wife (word-to-world direction of fit). For this to work the speech act must be performed within some extra-linguistic institution where the speaker is appropriately empowered to bring about new institutional facts solely by the appropriate performance of speech acts. With the exception of supernatural declarations, all declarations bring about institutional facts, facts which exist only within systems of constitutive rules, and which are, therefore, facts by virtue of human agreement.

Suppose, then, that we have some extra-linguistic institution, such that, by the authority vested in me in the institution, by raising my arm I can perform a declaration. Suppose, for example, by raising my arm I can adjourn the meeting. Then given this institutional authority the structure of the intention in action is:

(This intention in action causes my arm to go up and my arm going up has as conditions of satisfaction with the world-to-mind direction of fit that the meeting is adjourned, which state of affairs is caused by the fact that my arm going up has as conditions of satisfaction with the mind-to-world direction of fit that the meeting is adjourned).

This is rather a hefty mouthful but the underlying idea is very simple: In general, we can get at the content of an intention by asking, "What is the agent trying to do?" Well, what is he trying to do when he makes a declaration? *He is trying to cause something to be the case by representing it as being the case.* More precisely, he is trying to cause a change in the world so that a propositional content achieves world-to-mind direction of fit, by representing the world as having been so changed, that is, by expressing the same propositional content with mind-to-world direction of fit. He performs not two speech acts with two independent directions of fit, but one with double directions of fit, since if he succeeds he will have changed the world by representing it has having been so changed, and thus satisfied both directions of fit with one speech act.

This analysis has the consequence that a declaration expresses both a belief and a desire. A man who sincerely declares the meeting adjourned must want to adjourn the meeting and must believe that the meeting is thereby adjourned. As in other sorts of speech acts the communication intention is simply:

(The audience recognizes my arm going up and that my arm going up has these conditions of satisfaction).

In the analysis of assertives, directives, commissives and declarations I have used the notion of direction of fit as an unanalyzed primitive. I think this is justifiable because the notion of direction of fit is not reducible to something else. Nonetheless, different directions of fit have different consequences concerning causation. In the case of assertives (self-reference cases excepted), the assertive is supposed to match an *independently existing* reality, so an assertive would not be satisfied if it caused the state of affairs it represents. But in the case of directives, commissives, and declarations, the utterance, if satisfied, will in various ways function causally in the production of the state of affairs it represents. This asymmetry is a consequence of the difference in direction of fit. In an earlier version of this analysis[4] I used these causal differences instead of treating direction of fit as a primitive feature of the *analysans*.

The illocutionary point of expressives such as apologizing, thanking, and congratulating, is simply to express an Intentional state, the sincerity condition of the speech act, about some state of affairs which is presupposed to obtain. When, for example, I apologize for stepping on your toe, I express my remorse for having stepped on your toe. Now we saw in Chapter 1 that my remorse contains the beliefs that I stepped on your toe, that I am responsible for stepping on your toe, and the wish that I had not stepped on your toe. But the point of the speech act is not to express my beliefs and desire, it is to express my remorse, presupposing the truth of my beliefs. Though the beliefs have conditions of satisfaction with a direction of fit (truth conditions) and the desire has conditions of satisfaction with a direction of fit (fulfillment conditions), the speech act, as far as its illocutionary point is concerned, has no direction of fit. I am neither trying to claim that your toe has been stepped on, nor am I trying to get it stepped on. Though the presuppositions have truth conditions, the speech act as such has no direction of fit and no additional conditions of satisfaction imposed on it. But now, how shall we analyze the presupposition? There are a large number of treatments of presupposition in the philosophical and linguistic literature and I am really not satisfied with any of those I have seen. Perhaps presupposition just is a psychological primitive and

4 'Meaning, communication and representation', forthcoming, in Grandy, *op. cit.*

cannot be analyzed away either as a felicity condition on the performance of speech acts, or as a kind of logical relation similar to but not the same as entailment. In any case, for the purpose of this discussion I will simply treat it as a primitive notion.

Since there is, in general, no direction of fit in expressives, there are no conditions of satisfaction other than that the utterance should be an expression of the relevant psychological state. If I intend my utterance as an expression of such and such a state, then it will be an expression of that state, though of course I may not succeed in communicating that expression, that is, my hearer may or may not recognize my intentions.

Suppose that the speaker and hearer have an agreed convention that when the speaker raises his arm that is to count as an expressive, e.g., as an apology for some state of affairs p. Then the conditions of satisfaction on the meaning intention are simply and tautologically:

(This intention in action causes my arm to go up and my arm going up is an expression of remorse, presupposing that p).

The communication intention, again, is simply that this meaning intention should be recognized by the hearer on the model of our earlier cases, except that in this case there is no intention to represent, and hence no question of the hearer recognizing additional conditions of satisfaction imposed on the utterance.

We can now state, briefly, how this account meets our four conditions of adequacy.

1. and 2. In each of the first four types of cases, where we have a distinction between the sincerity condition on the speech act and the intention with which the act is performed, the characterization of the meaning intention is such as to determine that the utterance itself will have conditions of satisfaction. But in each case the conditions of satisfaction of the utterance imposed by the meaning intention are identical with the conditions of satisfaction of the expressed sincerity conditions. In the case of assertives, for example, a man performs an intentional act of uttering and he also intends that utterance to have certain conditions of satisfaction. But those conditions of satisfaction are identical to the conditions of satisfaction of the corresponding belief. Thus, he has performed an action which commits him to having a certain belief. There is no

way he can produce that utterance with those conditions of satisfaction without expressing a belief because the commitment of the utterance is exactly the same as the commitment of an expression of belief. Similar remarks apply to directives, commissives and declarations. In the case of expressives, his meaning intention is simply to express the Intentional state, so there is no problem of explaining how his utterance is an expression of its sincerity conditions. In each of the five cases the meaning intention differs from the sincerity condition (thus the double level of Intentionality), yet, where there is a direction of fit, the meaning intention determines the conditions of satisfaction of the speech act and that those conditions of satisfaction are identical with the conditions of satisfaction of the sincerity condition.

3. In every case we have explicitly isolated the primary meaning intention from the communication intention.

4. Since linguistic meaning is a form of derived Intentionality, its possibilities and limitations are set by the possibilities and limitations of Intentionality. The main function which language derives from Intentionality is, obviously, its capacity to represent. Entities which are not intrinsically Intentional can be made Intentional by, so to speak, intentionally decreeing them to be so. But the limitations on language are precisely the limitations that come from Intentionality. Wittgenstein often talks as if one could invent a new language game at will, but if you actually try it you will find your new language games are expressions of pre-existent forms of Intentionality. And the taxonomy is fundamentally a reflection of the various ways in which representations can have directions of fit. The mind-to-world direction of fit corresponds to assertives, and since this direction of fit is pre-eminently assessable as true or false, it is a defining characteristic of assertives that they admit of truth values. Corresponding to the world-to-word direction of fit are directives and commissives. Dividing utterances which have this direction of fit into two speech act categories is motivated by the pre-eminence of speaker and hearer as *dramatis personae* in the performance of speech acts. In commissives the speaker is responsible for achieving fit; in directives the hearer is responsible. Both also involve derived Intentional causation; that is, it is part of the conditions of satisfaction of both commissives and directives, that they should function causally in bringing about

the rest of their own conditions of satisfaction. Their derived Intentionality is similar in structure to certain forms of intrinsic Intentionality in that they share the feature of causal self-reference. Furthermore, just as there are Intentional states with no direction of fit, so there are nonrepresentational speech acts, the category of expressives. Indeed, the simplest form of speech act is one whose illocutionary point is simply to express an Intentional state. There are some expressives which are expressions of states with a direction of fit, e.g., expressions of desire as in "If only John would come", but even in these cases it is not the illocutionary point of the speech act to achieve fit, rather the point is just to express the state.

The trickiest cases are the declarations. Why can't we have a declaration, "I hereby fry an egg" and thereby an egg is fried? Because the capacities of representation are here exceeded. A supernatural being could do this because such a being could intentionally bring states of affairs about solely by representing them as having been brought about. We can't do that. But we do have a humbler, though still god-like, form of word magic: we can agree in advance that certain kinds of speech acts can bring about states of affairs by way of representing them as having been brought about. Such speech acts have both directions of fit, but not separately and independently. We can't fry eggs this way, but we can adjourn meetings, resign, pronounce people man and wife, and declare war.

III. INTENTIONALITY AND THE INSTITUTION OF LANGUAGE

So far we have described the structure of meaning intentions for people who already have a language, and we tried to isolate the specific character of the meaning intention by imagining that the whole speech act was performed by way of making some simple 'utterance' such as raising one's arm. Our question was, what does the intention add to the physical event to make it a case of meaning something by the Intentional production of the physical event? Given the existence of language as an institution, what is the structure of individual meaning intentions?

But that still leaves unanswered the question of the relation of the institution to Intentionality. Granted that these institutions are sets of constitutive rules, how do they relate to prelinguistic forms of Intentionality?

Suppose there was a class of beings who were capable of having Intentional states like belief, desire, and intention, but who did not have a language, what more would they require in order to be able to perform linguistic acts? Notice that there is nothing fanciful in the supposition of beings in such a state, since as far as we know the human species once was in that state. Notice also that the question is conceptual and not historical or genetic. I am not asking what additions would need to be made to their brains or how language did in fact evolve in the history of the human race.

When we have ascribed to our beings the capacity for having Intentional states, we have already ascribed to them the capacity for relating their Intentional states to objects and states of affairs in the world. The reason for this is that a being capable of having Intentional states must be capable of an awareness of the conditions under which its Intentional states are satisfied. For example, a being capable of having desires must be capable of an awareness of the satisfaction or frustration of its desires, and a being capable of intentions must be capable of recognizing the fulfillment or frustration of its intentions. And this can be generalized: For any Intentional state with a direction of fit, a being that has that state must be able to distinguish the satisfaction from the frustration of that state. This follows from the fact that an Intentional state is a representation of the conditions of its satisfaction. This does not mean that such beings will always or even most of the time get it right, that they won't make mistakes; rather, it means that they must have the capacity for recognizing what it would be to get it right.

Now back to our question: What more would such beings have to have in order to have a language? The question needs to be made narrower, because there are all sorts of features of actual languages that are irrelevant to our present discussion. Presumably, such beings would need a recursive device capable of generating an infinite number of sentences; they would need quantifiers, logical connectives, model and deontic operators, tenses, color words, etc. The question I am asking is much narrower. What would they need in order to get from having Intentional states to performing illocutionary acts?

The first thing that our beings would need to perform

illocutionary acts is some means for externalizing, for making publicly recognizable to others, the expressions of their Intentional states. A being that can do that on purpose, that is, a being that does not just express its Intentional states but performs acts for the purpose of letting others know of its Intentional states, already has a primitive form of a speech act. But it still has nothing as rich as our statements, requests, or promises. A man who makes a statement does more than let it be known that he believes something, a man who makes a request does more than let it be known that he wants something, a man who makes a promise does more than let it be known that he intends something. But again, what more? Each of the speech act categories, even the expressive category, serves social purposes that go beyond just the expression of the sincerity condition. For example, the primary extra-linguistic purpose of directives is to get people to do things; a primary extra-linguistic purpose of assertives is to convey information; a primary purpose of commissives is to create stable expectations of people's behavior.

Such facts will, I think, provide a clue to the relations between the types of speech acts and the corresponding types of Intentional states. As a preliminary formulation one might say that our beings would be capable of making a primitive form of assertion when they could perform actions which were expressions of belief for the purpose of giving information; directives (in this primitive form) would be expressions of desire for the purpose of getting people to do things; commissives (again, in primitive form) would be expressions of intention for the purpose of creating stable expectations in others about the future course of one's own behavior.

The next step would be to introduce conventional procedures for doing each of these things. However, there is no way that these extra-linguistic purposes can be realized by a conventional procedure. They all have to do with the perlocutionary effects which our actions have on our audiences, and there is no way that a conventional procedure can guarantee that such effects will be achieved. The perlocutionary effects of our utterances cannot be included in the conventions for the use of the device uttered, because an effect which is achieved by convention cannot include the subsequent responses and behavior of our audiences. What the conventional procedures can capture is, so to speak, the illocutionary analogue of these various perlocutionary aims. Thus, for example, any conventional device for indicating that the utterance is to have the force of a statement (for example, the indicative mood) will be one which by convention commits the speaker to the existence of the state of affairs specified in the propositional content. Its utterance, therefore, provides the hearer with a reason for believing that proposition, and expresses a belief by the speaker in that proposition. Any conventional device for indicating that the utterance is to have the force of a directive (e.g., the imperative mood) will be one which by convention counts as an attempt by the speaker to get the hearer to do the act specified in the propositional content. Its utterance, therefore, provides a reason for the hearer to do the act and expresses a desire of the speaker that the hearer do the act. Any conventional device for indicating that the utterance is to have the force of a commissive counts as an undertaking by the speaker to do the act specified in the propositional content. Its utterance, therefore, creates a reason for the speaker to do that act, creates a reason for the hearer to expect him to do the act, and expresses an intention by the speaker to do the act.

The steps, then, necessary to get from the possession of Intentional states to the performance of conventionally realized illocutionary acts are: first, the deliberate expression of Intentional states for the purpose of letting others know that one has them; second, the performance of these acts for the achievement of the extra-linguistic aims which illocutionary acts standardly serve; and third, the introduction of conventional procedures which conventionalize the illocutionary points that correspond to the various perlocutionary aims.

Chapter 7

INTENSIONAL REPORTS OF INTENTIONAL STATES AND SPEECH ACTS

In Chapter 1, I made a distinction between Intentionality-with-a-t and intensionality-with-an-s. Though Intentionality is a feature of both speech acts and mental states and intensionality is a feature of some mental states and some speech acts, there is a clear distinction between the two. I have further argued that it is a mistake to confuse features of reports of Intentional states with features of the Intentional states themselves, and in particular it is a mistake to suppose that because reports of Intentional states are intensional-with-an-s that Intentional states themselves must be intensional-with-an-s. This confusion is part of a more pervasive and fundamental confusion, namely, the belief that we can analyze tne character of Intentionality solely by analyzing the logical peculiarities of reports of Intentional states. I believe on the contrary that it betrays a fundamental confusion if we try to get clear about Intentionality by analyzing intensionality. It is important to keep in mind that there are at least three different sets of questions about Intentional states and about how they are reported in utterances of intensional sentences: first, what are the features of the Intentional states? (Chapters 1–3 were devoted to discussing this question); second, how are those features represented in ordinary speech? (this chapter is mostly concerned with this question); and third, how can we best represent these features in a formalized system such as the predicate calculus? (If you can get clear about the answers to the first two questions, the third is considerably easier.)

This chapter is about intensionality and therefore only incidentally about Intentionality. It is about the status of the words following "that" in contexts such as "said that", "believes that", "fears that", etc.; about the words following "whether" in "wonders whether", "asks whether", etc.; the status of words following the verb in "wants to", "intends to", "promises to", etc. In the discussion which follows it is important to keep in mind the distinction between *sentences* (which are syntactical entities to which a literal meaning normally attaches), *utterances* of sentences (which are speech acts of a certain minimal kind, viz., utterance acts), and literal and serious utterances of sentences (which are, when successful, speech acts of a much richer kind, viz., *illocutionary acts* whose illocutionary force and propositional content is a matter of the literal meaning of the sentence uttered). Every illocutionary act is an utterance act, but not conversely. And to each of the three terms of these distinctions the usual type-token differentiation applies.

What exactly is the status of the words following "that" in the report

1. The sheriff believes that Mr. Howard is an honest man

and how do they compare with the status of the words in the statement

2. Mr. Howard is an honest man.

One might say: why is there supposed to be a problem here at all? Isn't it obvious that the words following "that" in 1 mean exactly the same as they do in 2? The reason there is a special problem about these cases is that, on the one hand, we are inclined to say that the words in the dependent clause in 1 must have and be used with the same meaning they ordinarily have and are used with in 2 (how else would we be able to understand 1?); but, on the other hand, we are also inclined to say that in such cases they cannot be used with their ordinary meanings because the logical properties of the words following "that" in 1 seem to be quite different from the same words in 2. On both of our criteria, 2 is extensional; 1 is intensional. Existential generalization is a valid form of inference in 2 (if 2 is true then $(\exists x)$ (x is an honest man)); and the substitution of other expressions referring to the same object will preserve truth value in 2 (e.g., if Mr. Howard is an honest man and Mr. Howard is Jesse James then Jesse James is an honest man). Neither of these conditions holds in general for sentences of form 1. Furthermore, in a serious literal utterance of 2, the proposition that Mr. Howard is an honest man is asserted, while in a serious literal utterance of 1 that proposition is not asserted. In short, if the meaning of the whole is a function of the meaning of the parts, and if the relevant parts in 1 and 2 have the same meaning, and if the logical properties of a literal and serious utterance are determined by the meaning of the sentence uttered, then how can it be the case that 1 and 2 have such different logical properties?

This is a characteristic pattern of philosophical problems: on the one hand, very powerful linguistic intuitions incline us to a certain common sense view, in this case that there is perfect synonymy between the relevant portions of 1 and 2; but, on the other hand, powerful arguments seem to militate against common sense. I believe an application of the theory of speech acts will enable us to satisfy our linguistic intuitions and yet account for the different logical properties of 1 and 2.

At the risk of some repetition I will now make explicit what I take to be the various conditions of adequacy on any account of intensional reports of Intentional states. For purposes of the present discussion I will ignore problems of intensionality arising in modal contexts because they raise certain special issues which go beyond the scope of this book.

A. The analysis should be consistent with the fact that the meanings of the shared words in pairs such as 1 and 2 are the same, and in serious literal utterances of each they are used with these same meanings.

B. It should account for the fact that in 1 the embedded sentence does not have the logical properties it has in 2, viz., 2 is extensional, 1 is intensional.

C. It should be consistent with the fact that it is part of the meanings of 1 and 2 that, in serious literal utterances of 1, the proposition that Mr. Howard is an honest man is not asserted, whereas in 2 it is.

(On a natural interpretation, Frege[1] and his followers reject condition A while accepting B and C; Davidson[2] and his followers accept condition A while rejecting B and C. I will argue that we can accept all three.)

---

1 G. Frege, 'On sense and reference', in P. Geach and M. Black (eds.), *Translations from the Philosophical Writings of Gottlob Frege* (Oxford: Basil Blackwell, 1952), pp. 56–78.
2 D. Davidson, 'On saying that', in D. Davidson and G. Harman (eds.), *The Logic of Grammar* (Encino and Belmont, California: Dickenson, 1975), pp. 143–52.

D. The analysis should account for other sorts of sentences containing "that" clauses, including those where some or all of the logical properties are preserved, such as

3. It is a fact that Mr. Howard is an honest man

(3 admits of both existential generalization and substitution)

4. The sheriff knows that Mr. Howard is an honest man

(4 entails the existence of Mr. Howard but does not permit substitution).

E. The analysis should apply to other sorts of reports of Intentional states and speech acts which do not employ "that" clauses embedding a sentence but use infinitives, interrogative pronouns, the subjunctive, change of tense, etc. Furthermore the analysis should work not just for English but for any language containing reports of Intentional states and speech acts. Some examples are:

5. Bill wants Mr. Howard to be an honest man
6. Bill told Sally to make Mr. Howard be an honest man
7. Sally fears that Mr. Howard is an honest man.

(In many languages, e.g., French, the copula in 7 would have to be in the subjunctive.)

8. Mr. Howard said he would become an honest man

(where the "would" in English is in the subjunctive).

As a step toward an analysis of indirect discourse let us begin by considering a simpler sort of report.

9. The sheriff uttered the words, "Mr. Howard is an honest man".

What is the status of the words in quotation marks in 9? I have argued at length elsewhere[3] against the (still!) orthodox view that quotation marks around a word serve to make a totally new word, the proper name of the word or words being quoted. On my account, the words occurring inside the quotation marks in 9 are exactly the same words as occur in 2. If I were to have any doubts

---

3 See *Speech Acts* (Cambridge: Cambridge University Press, 1969), Chapter 4.

on this score, simple visual inspection would be sufficient to reassure me. On the traditional view, however, the words in 2 do not occur inside the quotation marks in 9 because the whole expression, including the quotation marks, is a new proper name, the proper name of the sentence which occurs in 2. According to this view *no words at all* occur inside quotation marks in 9. To the naive eye, untrained in the subtleties of elementary logic texts, several words do indeed appear to occur in quotation marks in 9, e.g., "Mr.", "Howard", "is", and so on; but, according to the orthodox view, that is a mere orthographic accident, in a way that it is an orthographic accident that "cat" appears to occur in "catastrophe". According to the orthodox view, the whole thing is a proper name, it contains no component words and it has no internal structure.

I find this view, frankly, preposterous. It is hard to imagine any chain of reasoning that could convince me that the words inside the quotation marks in 9 were not the very same words that occur after the numeral "2" in 2, or that there are any proper names in 9, other than the name "Howard". Still, lest this appear to be mere Moore-like stubbornness on my part I shall pause to consider the orthodox view. The only motivation I have ever been able to fathom for this view is the principle that if we want to talk about something we can never put the thing itself into a sentence, but must put its name or some other expression referring to it into the sentence. But this principle is – it seems to me – obviously false. If, for example, you are asked what was the sound made by the bird you saw yesterday, you can say "The bird made this sound —", where the blank space is to be filled by a sound and not the name of the sound. In such a case a token of the sound itself is part of the token utterance and an awareness of that sound token is part of the proposition expressed by the speaker and understood by the hearer. Of course we *can* use words to refer to other words. We could say, "John uttered the words which form the last three in line 7 on page 11 of the book", and here we use a definite description to refer to words; but when we are talking about words, it is seldom necessary to use names or definite descriptions, because we can almost always produce the words themselves. The only exceptions I know to this principle are cases where it is obscene or sacrilegious or otherwise taboo to say the word itself, e.g., "le mot de Cambronne". In such cases we need a name for it, but ordinarily we don't need a name, we simply repeat the word.

There is an additional argument against the view that when we surround expressions with quotation marks we create a new name. Often the syntactical position of the quoted passage will not even permit insertion of a name or other noun phrase. Thus, note the difference between "Gerald said 'I will consider running for the Presidency'" and "Gerald said he would 'consider running for the Presidency'". In the second form, if we regard the interior quotation marks as forming a new name, a noun phrase, the sentence would become ungrammatical, since the context "Gerald said he would" does not permit a noun phrase after "would". The orthodox view turns the original into a sentence having the grammatical form of, for example,

Gerald said he would Henry,

which is ungrammatical.

What then, to return to our question, is the status of the words quoted in 9 and what is their relation to the words in 2? The relation of the quoted words in 9 to the words in 2 is one of identity, the same words occur within the quotes in 9 as occurred in 2. But what then is the difference in their status? In the serious literal utterance of 2 the speaker makes a statement with these words. But in such an utterance of 9 these words are indexically presented and talked about; they are not used to make a statement or to perform any speech act other than an utterance act. In 2 the relevant words are used to perform an utterance act, a propositional act, and an illocutionary act. In an utterance of 9 the reporter *repeats the same* utterance act, but he does not repeat the same propositional act or illocutionary act. I believe this will provide us with a clue to the analysis of indirect discourse in general, because it suggests that the appropriate question to ask is, which of the original speech acts of the original speaker are *repeated* by the reporter and which are merely reported by the reporter? Consider the varying degrees of commitment by the reporter in the following sequence:

10. The sheriff uttered the words, "Mr. Howard is an honest man"

11. The sheriff said that Mr. Howard is an honest man
12. The sheriff said, "Mr. Howard is an honest man"
13. The sheriff said then, and I do now say, Mr. Howard is an honest man.

To have some convenient terms, I will call reports of type 10 *word* reports, those of type 11 *content* reports, and those of type 12 *verbatim* reports. I will call the person uttering a sentence of types 10–13 the *reporter*, and the person being reported the *speaker*.

Now which of the speaker's original acts does the reporter's serious and literal utterance of each of these sentences commit him to repeating? I think the answers are fairly obvious, so I will simply state them baldly and then develop my argument concerning them subsequently.

In 10, the reporter is committed to repeating the speaker's utterance act but not his propositional or illocutionary act.

In 11, the reporter is committed to repeating the speaker's propositional act but not his utterance act or his illocutionary act.

In 12, the reporter is committed to repeating the speaker's utterance act and his propositional act but not his illocutionary act.

In 13, the reporter is committed to repeating the speaker's propositional act and his illocutionary act, but not necessarily his utterance act. We can even construct cases where the reporter is committed to repeating all three, viz., utterance, propositional, and illocutionary acts:

14. As John said, "Mr. Howard is an honest man".

And sometimes, when translating from one language to another, we relax the requirement in the verbatim report that the reporter must repeat the same words as the speaker; we require only that he repeat the speaker's propositional act and an utterance act with the same *meaning* in the translation language as in the original. Thus we say,

15. Proust said, "For a long time I used to go to bed early",

whereas what he actually said was

16. Longtemps je me suis couché de bonne heure.

The picture, then, that emerges on this account is that just as in the word report the reporter repeats the same utterance act as the speaker but not necessarily the same illocutionary or propositional act as the speaker, so in the content report he repeats the same propositional act but not necessarily the same utterance act or illocutionary act as the speaker. To make this idea completely clear let us remind ourselves of the illocutionary structure of 2 in order that we can compare it with the illocutionary structure of its report in 11. It is important to understand the illocutionary structure of what is being reported in order to understand the report; and indeed I believe the reason many philosophers have such heavy going in giving an account of reported speech is that they do not have a coherent account of speech to begin with, just as the reason that so many have such heavy going in giving an account of reports of Intentional states is that they do not have a coherent account of Intentional states to begin with. In the serious and literal utterance of 2, to perform an illocutionary act, a certain propositional content is presented with a certain illocutionary force. Using Frege's assertion sign we can represent these facts in the following form

2′. ⊢(Mr. Howard is an honest man).

Now on my account in, for example, 11, the reporter *repeats* the propositional content but he does not *repeat* the illocutionary force attaching to that propositional content, he only *reports* that illocutionary force. He does not present the proposition with the same illocutionary force as the original speaker, and so he does not make the same assertion as the original speaker. The structure of his report can be exhibited by the following variation on 11:

11′. The sheriff asserted this proposition: Mr. Howard is an honest man.

Here the rest of the sentence makes it clear that the original proposition is repeated and therefore demonstratively presented; but the original illocutionary force is not repeated, it is only reported. The original proposition is presented demonstratively as one might demonstratively present anything else in the context of the utterance.

Since Frege had the elements necessary for the construction of this account, in particular he had a rudimentary theory of the distinction between propositional content and illocutionary force, and since the analysis is Fregean in spirit, it might seem puzzling that he never even considers such an account. But the reason that he could not have accepted the analysis I am presenting is that he accepted the principle underlying the theory of use and mention that we have already seen reason to reject: he thought the only way you could talk about something was to name it or otherwise refer to it. He supposed that if the speaker's proposition is in some sense talked about by the reporter then what occurs in the reporter's utterance must be the name of the proposition and not an expression of the proposition itself. Indeed, Frege's thesis about indirect discourse is precisely that the expressions in question refer to their customary sense and the whole embedded clause refers to a proposition; it is the proper name of a proposition. But once we see the falsity of the traditional account of the quite valid distinction between the use and the mention of expressions, we are in a position to see the falsity of the extension of the same principle to indirect discourse. The mention of a proposition does not require us to name or otherwise refer to it, we can just present the proposition itself. When we report someone else's speech we no more need names for his propositions than we need names for his words, we simply repeat his expression of these propositions in the content report, just as we repeat his words in the word report. Of course we could name or otherwise refer to his propositions. When we say, for example, "Mr. Howard asserted the Copernican Hypothesis", the expression "the Copernican Hypothesis" functions to refer to a proposition, not to express it. But with the exception of a few famous propositions such as the Copernican Hypothesis, propositions neither have nor need names.

This account of reports of speech acts can easily be extended to reports of Intentional states, and it is not at all surprising that it can, given the close parallelism between speech acts and Intentional states that we explored in Chapter 1. In content reports of speech acts of form 11, the reporter repeats the proposition expressed by the speaker; in content reports of beliefs of form 1, the reporter *expresses* the proposition which is the representative content of the believer's belief, but he need not be *repeating* any expression of belief, for the believer may never have expressed his belief. The reporter expresses the proposition which the believer believes, but in so doing he need not be repeating anything the

believer has done. (Often in real life we relax the requirement that
the content expressed must be exactly the same as the content
believed. We say, for example, "The dog believes his owner is at
the door", without thereby attributing to the dog the possession of
the concept of ownership.) And just as the content report of form
11 presents the proposition without its illocutionary force of
assertion, but with a report of that illocutionary force, so the belief
content report of form 1 presents the proposition without its
Intentional mode of belief, but with a report of that mode. Because
the existence of Intentional states does not require any speech at all,
there are very few verbatim reports of Intentional states. Strictly
speaking a verbatim report can only be a report of a speech act (it
may be an internal speech act), and hence a verbatim report of an
Intentional state can only be a report of an Intentional state
expressed in a speech act.

This account will perhaps be clearer if I contrast it with
Davidson's views. According to Davidson, the reporter who says,

17. Galileo said that the earth moves

says something which is equivalent to

18. (a) The earth moves.
    (b) Gallileo said that.

18(a) is completely extensional and since, according to Davidson,
its occurrence in 17 is equivalent to its occurrence in 18, the
subordinate clause in 17 is extensional as well. The reason for a
change in the truth value of 17 under substitution has nothing to
do with any intensionality of the subordinate clause but derives
from the fact that the reference of the demonstrative "that" may
change if co-referring expressions are substituted in the original.
On Davidson's view, if I utter 17, that makes me and Galileo
"samesayers".

On my account we are precisely not samesayers, since in a
serious and literal utterance of 17 I do not *say* that the earth moves,
I only say that Galileo said it. We are not *samesayers*, but *same
proposition expressers*. A serious literal utterance of 18, on the other
hand, does make Gailieo and me samesayers because in such an
utterance of 18 I assert that the earth moves. In 18(a) the assertive
force is part of the literal meaning, but that assertive force is

removed by the embedding in 17 and that is why 18(a) is extensional even though the subordinate clause in 17 is intensional.

I find the account presented in this chapter intuitively fairly obvious, and indeed once the mistake about use and mention is removed, I really do not see any objection to it. Still, I have so far presented, but not argued, in favor of it: How might one argue for it in a way that could convince a skeptic? Perhaps the best way to meet this challenge is to show how the account can meet all of our criteria of adequacy, A through E, in a way that gives a unified account of "that" clauses, whether extensional or intensional, and a unified account of reports of Intentional states and speech acts, whether in "that" clauses or in other forms.

The first step in meeting this challenge is to show how we can resolve the paradox deriving from conditions A, B, and C that gave rise to the puzzle in the first place: How can it be the case that (A) the words in the subordinate clauses of reports such as 1 and 11 have their ordinary meanings and yet, (B) the logical properties of a serious and literal utterance of those same words in 2 are not preserved in a serious and literal utterance of 1 and 11? Furthermore, (C) if the words keep their ordinary meanings, why is the proposition asserted in a serious and literal utterance of 2 not asserted in such an utterance of 1 and 11? I believe the answer to the latter question provides the answer to the former. On my account though the words in the sentence keep their same meanings, those meanings in 1, 2, and 11 determine propositional content but not illocutionary force. In 2 the illocutionary force is not carried by the meanings of any of the words, and the illocutionary force of the original is removed by the embedding as a subordinate clause in 1 and 11. The illocutionary force of a literal and serious utterance of 2 is determined by word order, mood of the verb, sentence boundary, and intonation contour. Now, strictly speaking, the whole sentence of 2 is not repeated in 1 and 11 since it has lost its sentence boundaries. In 1 and 11 the sequence of words, "Mr. Howard is an honest man", is not by itself a sentence though in these contexts it is sufficient to express a propositional content. Modern English is partly misleading in these cases, since it allows us to keep the same mood of the verb in the report as in the

original,[4] but even in modern English the separation of propositional content and illocutionary force is clearly visible in the
reports of utterances of imperative and interrogative sentences,
where the structure of the reports does not permit us to keep the
original mood of the verb in the report. Thus, suppose the sheriff
asks

19. Is Mr. Howard an honest man?

and this is reported by

20. The sheriff *asked whether* Mr. Howard *was* an honest man.

Here it is clear that the interrogative force which *occurs* as part of
the literal meaning in 19 is *reported* in 20, but it does not occur in 20.
The verb "ask" explicitly reports the illocutionary force; and the
sentence expressing the original proposition is presented with a
different word order, a change of the original interrogative mood
of the verb, an (optional) change of tense, and an embedding
within the scope of the interrogative pronoun "whether". I think
what is going on in the surface structure of these forms is quite
revealing about what is happening in the logical structure. The
interrogative force of 19 is removed in 20 because, though the
same proposition occurs in 19 and 20, in 20 it is presented not as a
question but as part of the report of a question. Similar
considerations apply to the reports of directive speech acts. Thus
21, said by the sheriff

21.   Mr. Howard, be an honest man!

is reported by

22. The sheriff ordered Mr. Howard to be an honest man.

In this pair the imperative mood in 21 is removed in 22, replaced by
the infinitive and reported by the verb "ordered".

What we see in each of these pairs, 19/20, 21/22, is that the
reporter *repeats* the propositional content, but *reports* the illocutionary force. In these cases there is a variety of syntactical devices

---

4 Even modern English frequently requires a tense shift in reported speech. Nixon said "I
am not a crook". But the correct content report is: Nixon said he *was* not a crook.

for signalling to the hearer that the proposition has a different illocutionary status in the report from what it had in its original occurrence.

In summary then our answer to the question concerning condition C is that words and other elements repeated in content reports such as 1 and 11 keep their original meanings, but those meanings determine propositional content and not illocutionary force. The illocutionary force of the original is not repeated, but is reported; and English and other languages have a variety of syntactical devices for signalling to the hearer that the illocutionary force of the original no longer attaches to the proposition in the report.

Now since the assertive illocutionary force is removed from the propositional content in 1 and 11, and since it is the commitment involved in *asserting* the proposition, and not just the proposition as such, that commits the speaker to its truth conditions, the reporter can express the same proposition with the same words as the speaker and still not be committed to the truth conditions of that proposition. And that is why the reporter's expression of the proposition is intensional while the speaker's is extensional. In order to show how this account resolves the apparent paradox which results from holding both condition A and condition B, let us consider existential generalization and substitutability in turn.

If the relevant words have the same meaning in 2 and 11 and the proposition in 2 is repeated in 11, why is existential generalization a valid form of inference over 2 but not over 11? The speaker who makes a serious and literal utterance of 2 does not just *express* the propositional content, he actually *asserts* it. That assertion commits him to the truth conditions of the proposition, and those truth conditions include the existence of an object purportedly referred to by the utterance of the referring expression. If 2 is true then there must exist such an object, and that is why existential generalization is a valid form of inference. But the reporter who makes a serious and literal utterance of 11 is committed only to expressing the same proposition as the original speaker of 2, he is not committed to asserting it. The truth conditions to which he is committed include the condition that the report must contain an expression of the same proposition as the proposition expressed by the original speaker, but since he is not asserting that proposition, and thus is not committed to its truth conditions, 11 can be true even if there is no object corresponding to the referring expression; and that is why existential generalization is not a valid form of inference for 11.

Why does substitution fail for 11 and not for 2, if the proposition in each is the same? Substitution fails because the form of 11 commits the reporter to repeating the same proposition as the speaker: taken strictly, the expression "he said that" in 11 commits the reporter to repeating the same proposition as was originally expressed by the speaker, hence any substitution which alters the proposition can alter the truth value of the report. As Frege was aware, in general, substitutions which preserve not only the same reference but also the same sense will preserve truth value even in intensional contexts: as long as the propositional content is preserved by the substitution, the truth value remains constant. But where two terms are ordinarily used to refer to the same object and the sense of the two is different, the substitution of one term for another can alter the content of the proposition and thus alter the truth value of the report. The truth value of 2, on the other hand, does not depend on how the object is identified; other identifications of the same object will preserve truth value.

Often we have partial content reports where the reporter does not commit himself to the whole of the original proposition. Thus we say things of the form

23. I won't tell you exactly what he said, but the sheriff said that Mr. Howard was a certain sort of man.

Here the form of the report makes it clear that the reporter is not committed to repeating the whole of the original.

The analysis I am offering here is really just an expansion of points made in Chapter 1. In reports of Intentional states one represents a representation. Now since the report is of the ground floor representation and not of what is represented by it, the commitments of the ground floor representation may be absent from the report; hence the ontological commitments of the former may be absent from the latter. And since the report proceeds by repeating the propositional content of the original representation, any substitution which alters that propositional content can alter the truth value of the report, since a different representation is then presented in the report.

Condition D: Given our answers to questions concerning conditions A, B, and C, how do we present a unified account of "that" clauses, etc.? That is, if embedded "that" clauses are in general demonstrative presentations of propositional contents, then how do we account for the fact that some are intensional and some are extensional?

Whether or not the embedded proposition is extensional or intensional is entirely a matter of the semantic content of the rest of the sentence. Thus the differences between sentences of forms

1. The sheriff believes that Mr. Howard is an honest man

and

3. It is a fact that Mr. Howard is an honest man

are entirely a matter of the difference in meaning between "The sheriff believes that" and "It is a fact that". Both sentences are used literally to make assertions, but whereas "It is a fact that" commits the speaker to the assertion of the embedded proposition, "The sheriff believes that" does not. The difference between the status of the expressed proposition in the two cases is solely a matter of the rest of the sentence, and does not require us to postulate two different kinds of "that" clauses. Further evidence that the status of the occurrence of the subordinate clause is the same is that the two sentences permit conjunction reductions of the form, "It is a fact that and Jones believes that Mr. Howard is an honest man".

An intermediate case is provided by 4. "Knows that", like "proves that" and "sees that", is indeed an Intentional verb, but in addition to marking the Intentionality of the state or act of the person being reported, they are all 'success' verbs. For these contexts, inference to the existence of the objects purportedly referred to in the subordinate clause is a valid form of inference; and statements of the form "X knows that p, X sees that p, X proved that p" all entail p. For these contexts, however, substitution is not truth preserving because the identity of the content of what is known, proved, or seen, is at least in part a matter of the aspect under which the referents are known, proved, or seen.

A full answer to the question concerning condition E is really for linguists and not philosophers of language: How does this account square with the variety of devices in English and in other languages for indicating intensionality? I have already considered some of the ways in which English reports indicative, interrogative and imperative speech acts, and in each case we saw, though more strikingly for interrogative and imperative reports, a separation between *reported* illocutionary force and *repeated* propositional content. In order to extend – and thus test – the account in this chapter, one would want to know how illocutionary force and propositional content are indicated in a variety of other languages, and how the distinction between propositional content and illocutionary force is represented in reports of utterances in those languages. An especially interesting syntactical form, which exists in English and in several other languages, is the form the French call "style indirecte libre". Consider

> She [Louisa] could not bear to think of her lofty, spiritual sister degraded in the body like this. Mary was wrong, wrong, wrong: she was not superior, she was flawed, incomplete.
>
> (D. H. Lawrence, *Daughters of the Vicar*)

The second sentence is a report of an Intentional state; the author is not telling us that Mary was wrong, wrong, wrong, but that Louisa thought that she was wrong, wrong, wrong. The complexity of the example derives from three features: first, though the sentence is a report of an Intentional state, it stands alone and is not embedded (hence "libre" in "style indirecte libre"); secondly, it has some features of direct discourse – we are to think of the "wrong, wrong, wrong" as what Louisa is thinking to herself in those words; but third, it also has some features of indirect discourse such as the tense shift – we are to think of Louisa as saying to herself "Mary *is* wrong, wrong, wrong", but this is reported as "Mary *was* wrong, wrong, wrong".

This chapter has been mostly concerned with intensional reports of Intentional states and speech acts, the so-called *de dicto* reports. But what about those reports where the occurrence of some of the expressions in the report is extensional, the so-called *de re* reports?

"Bush believes that Reagan is President" is *de dicto* and intensional. It can be true even if it turns out that Reagan never existed. But what about

Reagan is believed by Bush to be President

or

Reagan is such that Bush believes him to be President?

Such reports are *de re*, and in them the occurrence of "Reagan" is extensional. The endemic mistake in the history of linguistic philosophy has been to infer from the fact that the *de dicto* report is intensional that therefore the states reported must themselves be intensional. I have claimed in Chapter 1 that such a view is a massive confusion, and in this chapter I have tried to analyze sentences used to make *de dicto* reports. The parallel confusion in the case of *de re* reports has been to infer from the fact that there are two kinds of reports, *de re* and *de dicto*, that therefore there are two kinds of states reported, that the states themselves are either *de re* or *de dicto*. But from the fact that there are two different kinds of reports it simply does not follow, nor is it the case that, there are two different kinds of states. To this and related confusions we will turn in the next chapter.

Chapter 8

ARE MEANINGS IN THE HEAD?

The fundamental question of the philosophy of language has always been: How does language relate to reality? The answer I proposed to that question in *Speech Acts* was that language relates to reality in virtue of the fact that speakers so relate it in the performance of linguistic acts. The original question then reduces to one of analyzing the nature and conditions of the possibility of these acts. In this book I have tried to ground that analysis further in the Intentionality of the mind: the question, "How does language relate to reality?" is only a special case of the question, "How does the mind relate to reality?", and just as the question about language reduced to one about various sorts of speech acts, so the question about the mind reduces to one about the various forms of Intentionality, the representational capacities of speech acts being simply a special case of derived Intentionality.

On one interpretation of Frege, my general approach to Intentionality is a matter of revising and extending Frege's conception of "*Sinn*" to Intentionality in general, including perception and other forms of self-reference; and my approach to the special problem of reference is in some respects Fregean in spirit, though, of course, not in detail. Specifically, it is possible to distinguish at least two independent strands in Frege's account of the relations between expressions and objects. First, in his account of the *Sinn* and *Bedeutung* of *Eigennamen*, an expression refers to an object because the object fits or satisfies the *Sinn* associated with the expression. Second, in his fight against psychologism Frege felt it necessary to postulate the existence of a "third realm" of abstract entities: senses, propositions, etc. Communication in the utterance of an expression is possible only because both the speaker and the hearer can grasp a common abstract sense associated with the expression. My own account is Fregean in accepting the first of these strands, but I reject the second. Linguistic reference is a special case of Intentional reference, and Intentional reference is always by way of the relation of fitting or satisfaction. But it is not necessary to postulate any special metaphysical realms in order to account for communication and shared Intentionality. If you think about the Evening Star under the mode of presentation "Evening Star", and I think about the same planet under the same mode of presentation, the sense in which we have an abstract entity in common is the utterly trivial sense in which, if I go for a walk in the Berkeley hills and you go for exactly the same walk, we share an abstract entity, the same walk, in common. The possibility of shared Intentional contents does not require a heavy metaphysical apparatus any more than the possibility of shared walks.

Both the Fregean and the present account of meaning are internalist in the sense that it is in virtue of some mental state in the head of a speaker and hearer – the mental state of grasping an abstract entity or simply having a certain Intentional content – that speaker and hearer can understand linguistic references. At the time of this writing, the most influential theories of reference and meaning reject a Fregean or internalist analysis. There is a variety of reasons for which the anti-internalist position has become fashionable, and there is considerable disagreement among the anti-internalists as to what the correct analysis of reference and meaning is. In this chapter and the next I will consider and answer at least some of the more influential attacks on the internalist, Fregean, or Intentionalistic tradition. These chapters, therefore, are more argumentative than those which preceded them: my aim is not only to present an Intentionalistic account of reference but to do so by way of answering what I believe is a family of mistaken doctrines in contemporary philosophy. Here, in no special order, are some of the most influential theses urged against the internalist picture.

1. There is supposed to be a fundamental distinction between *de re* and *de dicto* beliefs and other sorts of propositional attitudes. *De re* beliefs are relations between agents and objects, they cannot be individuated solely in terms of their mental contents (*de dicto*), because the object itself (*res*) has to be part of the principle of individuation of the belief.

2. There is supposed to be a fundamental distinction between the "referential" and the "attributive" use of definite descrip-

tions. Only in the case of attributive uses of definite descriptions does a speaker "refer" to an object in virtue of the fact that his Intentional content sets conditions which the object satisfies, but these are not genuine cases of referring at all; in the referential use of definite descriptions the speaker need not use an expression that the object referred to satisfies.[1]

3. Indexical expressions, e.g., "I", "you", "this", "that", "here", "now", are supposed to be impossible for an internalist theory to account for, since their utterance lacks a "completing Fregean sense".

4. Exponents of the so-called causal theory of names and the causal theory of reference are supposed to have refuted something called the "descriptivist theory" of names and of reference, and thereby to have refuted any internalist or Fregean account, and to have shown that reference is achieved in virtue of some *external* causal relations.

5. The causal theory of reference is supposed to be applicable to a large class of general terms, the natural kind terms and perhaps others; and for these terms there are supposed to be decisive arguments showing that knowing their meanings cannot consist in being in psychological states of any sorts, but must involve some more direct causal relations with the world. It is supposed to have been shown that "meanings are not in the head".

I believe that all these views are false. Furthermore, they share a family resemblance; they suggest a picture of reference and meaning in which the speaker's internal Intentional content is insufficient to determine what he is referring to, either in his thoughts or in his utterances. They share the view that in order to account for the relations between words and the world we need to introduce (for some? for all? cases) external contextual, non-conceptual, causal relations between the utterance of expressions and the features of the world that the utterance is about. If these views are correct then the account I have given of Intentionality must be mistaken. At this point then I see no alternative to mounting a series of set piece philosophical arguments. The

---

1 I will not discuss this view further in this book since I have attempted to refute it elsewhere; see, 'Referential and attributive', in J. R. Searle, *Expression and Meaning* (Cambridge: Cambridge University Press, 1979), pp. 137–61.

justification for making such a fuss over views I believe are false anyway has to do with the size of the issues involved. If we are unable to account for the relation of reference in terms of internal Intentional contents, either the contents of the individual speaker or the linguistic community of which he is a part, then the entire philosophical tradition since Frege, both the analytic and the phenomenological strands, is mistaken and we need to start over with some external causal account of reference in particular, and the relation of words to the world in general.

I. MEANINGS IN THE HEAD

I shall begin by considering Hilary Putnam's argument that "meanings are not in the head".[2] I think in the relevant sense that meanings are precisely in the head – there is nowhere else for them to be – and that Putnam's arguments fail to show anything to the contrary.

Putnam considers two views:

(1) Knowing the meaning of a word or expression consists in being in a certain psychological state.

(2) Meaning (intension) determines extension.

Appropriately construed these two entail a third:

(3) Psychological states determine extension.

Putnam tries to show that we cannot hold both (1) and (2) together and that (3) is false. He proposes to reject (1) and (3) while accepting a revised version of (2). In the discussion which follows it is important to point out that nothing hangs on accepting the traditional analytic–synthetic distinction; for the purposes of this discussion both Putnam and I accept holism, and nothing in our dispute turns on that issue.

Putnam's strategy is to try to construct intuitively plausible cases where the same psychological state will determine different extensions. If type-identical psychological states can determine different extensions, then there must be more to the determination of extension than psychological states, and the traditional view is, therefore, false. Putnam offers two independent arguments to

---

2 H. Putnam, 'The meaning of meaning', in *Philosophical Papers*, vol. 2, *Mind, Language and Reality* (Cambridge: Cambridge University Press, 1975), pp. 215–71.

show how the same psychological state can determine different extensions. He sometimes talks as if they were part of the same argument but, in fact, they are quite independent and, I believe, only the second is really serious. I will, therefore, deal rather briefly with the first.

The first argument concerns what he calls the principle of "the linguistic division of labor", i.e., the principle that in any linguistic community some people have more expertise in applying certain terms than others do. For example, in our community some people know more about trees than others and so can tell which trees are, for example, beeches and which are elms. Others, such as myself, don't know much about the difference between beech trees and elm trees, so insofar as there is any *concept* attaching to the words "beech" and "elm" for me, they are pretty much the same concept. In both cases I have the concept of a big, deciduous tree growing in the Eastern part of the United States. Therefore, according to Putnam, in my idiolect the concept or "intension" is the same, but the extension is clearly different. "Beech" denotes beech trees and "elm" denotes elm trees: same psychological state, different extensions.

I really don't believe any defender of the traditional view would be worried by this argument. The thesis that meaning determines reference can hardly be refuted by considering cases of speakers who don't even know the meaning or know it only imperfectly. Or to put the same point another way, the notions of intension and extension are not defined relative to idiolects. As traditionally conceived, an intension or Fregean *Sinn* is an abstract entity which may be more or less imperfectly grasped by individual speakers. But it does not show that intension does not determine extension to show that some speaker might not have grasped the intension, or grasped it only imperfectly; for such a speaker hasn't got a relevant extension either. The notion of the "extension in my idiolect" has no application for cases where one does not know the meaning of the word.

To make out the case, Putnam would have to argue that the collectivity of speakers' Intentional states, including those of all the ideal experts, does not determine the correct extensions. But if the argument is to be based on linguistic and factual ignorance, the very doctrine of the linguistic division of labor would seem to refute the argument from the start, because the doctrine is that where one speaker is ignorant he can appeal to the experts: what is and what is not an elm is for the experts to decide. That is, where *his* intension is inadequate he lets *their* intension determine extension. Furthermore, if we assume that Putnam *knows* this argument to be valid we get something very much like an inconsistency as follows:

    1. My (Putnam's) concept of "elm" = my concept of "beech"

but

    2. The extension of "elm" in my idiolect ≠ the extension of "beech" in my idiolect.

How do I know 2 to be true? Obviously because

    3. I know that beeches are not elms and elms are not beeches.

And how do I know that? I know that because I know that elms and beeches are two *different* species of trees. Imperfect as my grasp of the relevant concepts is, at least I have enough conceptual knowledge to know that the two are distinct species. But for this very reason,

    4. Number 3 states conceptual knowledge.

If such knowledge is not conceptual knowledge, nothing is. Therefore,

    5. Contrary to 1, my concept of "elm" ≠ my concept of "beech".

In his more important and influential second argument Putnam tries to show that even the collectivity of speakers' Intentional states might be insufficient to determine extension, for there might be two communities with the same set of collective intensions but with different extensions. Imagine that in a distant galaxy there was a planet very similar to ours with people like ourselves speaking a language indistinguishable from English. Imagine, however, that on this twin earth the stuff they call "water" is perceptually indistinguishable from what we call "water", but in fact it has a different chemical composition. What is called "water" on twin earth is a very complicated chemical compound, the formula for which we will abbreviate as "XYZ". According to

Putnam's intuitions, the expression "water" on earth in 1750, before anything was known about the chemical composition of water referred to H_2O; and "water" on twin earth in 1750 referred to XYZ. Thus, even though the people on both earth and twin earth were all in the same psychological state relative to the word "water", they had different extensions and therefore Putnam concludes that psychological states do not determine extension.

Most people who have criticized Putnam's argument have challenged his intuitions about what we would say concerning the twin earth example. My own strategy will be to accept his intuitions entirely for the purpose of this discussion, and then argue that they fail to show that meanings are not in the head. But I want to digress for a moment and consider what the traditional theorists would say about the example as presented so far. I think it would go something like this: Up to 1750 "water" meant the same on both earth and twin earth and had the same extension. After it had been discovered that there were two different chemical compositions, one for earth and one for twin earth, we would have a choice. We could *define* "water" as H_2O, which is what we have, in fact, done; or we could just say that there are two kinds of water, and that water on twin earth is constructed differently from water on earth. There is, indeed, some support for these intuitions. Suppose, for example, there had been a great deal of going and coming between earth and twin earth, so that speakers were likely to have encountered both. Then it seems likely that we would construe water as we now construe jade. Just as there are two kinds of jade, nephrite and jadeite (Putnam's example), so there would be two kinds of water, H_2O and XYZ. Furthermore, it looks like we pay a high price for accepting his intuitions. A very large number of things have water as one of their essential components, so if the stuff on twin earth is not water then presumably their mud is not mud, their beer is not beer, their snow is not snow, their ice cream is not ice cream, etc. If we take it really seriously, indeed, it looks as if their chemistry is going to be radically different. On our earth if we drive cars we get H_2O, CO and CO_2 as products of the combustion of hydrocarbons. What is supposed to come out of the cars on twin earth? I think that a defender of the traditional view might also point out that it is odd that Putnam assumes that "H_2O" is fixed and that "water" is problematic. We could equally well imagine cases where H_2O is slightly different on twin earth from what it is on earth. However, I don't want to pursue these alternative intuitions to Putnam's, rather I want to accept his intuitions for the purpose of the argument and continue with his positive account of how extension is determined.

On Putnam's theory the extension of a general term like "water", and indeed on his theory just about any general term, is determined *indexically* as follows. We identify a kind of substance such as water by certain surface features. These are such things as that water is a clear, tasteless, colorless liquid, etc. The crucial point is that the extension of the word "water" is then determined as whatever is identical in structure with this stuff, whatever that structure is. Thus, on his account the reason that "water" on twin earth has a different extension from "water" on earth is that the stuff identified indexically has a different structure on twin earth from the structure that it has on earth, and "water" is simply defined as whatever bears the relation "same L" to this stuff.

Now from the point of view of a traditional theorist what exactly does this argument achieve? Even supposing Putnam is right about his intuitions, all he has done is substitute one Intentional content for another. For the traditional cluster-of-concepts Intentional content, Putnam has substituted an indexical Intentional content. In each case it is a meaning in the head that determines extension. In fact, Putnam's suggestion is a rather traditional approach to natural kind terms: a word is defined ostensively as whatever bears the right relation to the denotation of the original ostension. "Water" has simply been defined as whatever is identical in structure to this stuff whatever that structure is. And this is simply one case among others in which intensions, which are in the head, determine extensions.

On the traditional Lockean view, water is defined (nominal essence) by a check list of concepts: liquid, colorless, tasteless, etc. On the Putnam proposal, water is defined (real essence) indexically by identifying something that satisfies the nominal essence and then declaring that water is to be defined as whatever has the same real essence as the stuff so identified. This may be an improvement on Locke but it certainly does not show that meanings are not in the head.

I believe Putnam would not regard this as an adequate response, since the whole tone of his writings on this topic is to suggest that he takes himself not to be proposing a variation of the traditional view that meanings are in the head but to be rejecting the tradition altogether. The interest of this discussion for the present work only becomes clear when we examine the underlying assumptions about Intentionality that lead him to suppose that the alternative account of meaning that he proposes is somehow fundamentally inconsistent with the view that meanings are in the head. Let us try to state his position a little more precisely. We can distinguish three theses:

(1) The associated cluster of concepts does not determine extension,

(2) The indexical definition does determine extension,

(3) What is in the head does not determine extension.

Now (3) does not follow from (1) and (2). To suppose that it does one must assume that the indexical definition is not in the head. Putnam uses (1) and (2) to argue for (3) and thereby assumes that the indexical definition is not in the head. Now, why does he think that? Why does he think that in the case of these indexical definitions what is in the head does not determine extension? I believe that there are two reasons why he makes this fallacious move. First, he supposes that since we don't know the micro-structure, and since it is the micro-structure that determines extension, then what is in the head is insufficient to determine extension.

But that, I believe, is simply a mistake; and we can illustrate the way it is a mistake by considering the following example. The expression, "The murderer of Brown", has an intension which determines as its extension the murderer of Brown.[3] The intension, "The murderer of Brown", fixes the extension even though it is a fact about the world who murdered Brown. For someone who does not know who murdered Brown the extension of the expression, "The murderer of Brown", is still the murderer of Brown even though he does not know who it is. Now analogously, the Intentional content "identical in structure with this (indexically identified) stuff" is an Intentional content that would determine an

---

3 Strictly speaking it determines the unit class whose sole member is the murderer of Brown, but for the purposes of this argument we can ignore this distinction.

extension, even if we don't know what that structure is. The theory that intension determines extension is the theory that intensions set certain conditions which anything has to meet in order to be part of the extension of the relevant intension. But that condition is satisfied by Putnam's example: the indexical definition of water has an Intentional content, that is, it sets certain conditions which any potential sample has to meet if it is to be part of the extension of "water", in exactly the same sense that the expression "The murderer of Brown" sets certain conditions which any potential candidate has to meet if he or she is to be the extension of "The murderer of Brown". But in both cases it is a matter of fact about the world, whether or not some existing entities satisfy the Intentional content. It is, therefore, just a mistake to suppose that because we define "water" in terms of an unknown micro-structure, that intension does not determine extension.

But there is a second and deeper reason why Putnam supposes that his analysis shows that meanings are not in the head. He makes certain assumptions about the nature of Intentional contents and the nature of indexical expressions and especially about the way Intentional contents relate to indexical expressions, which we must now explore. The assumptions emerge when he says:

> For these (indexical) words no one has ever suggested the traditional theory that 'intension determines extension'. To take our Twin Earth example: if I have a *Doppelgänger* on Twin Earth, then when I think, 'I have a headache', *he* thinks 'I have a headache'. But the extension of the particular token of 'I' in his verbalized thought is himself (or his unit class, to be precise), while the extension of the token of 'I' in *my* verbalized thought is *me* (or my unit class, to be precise). So the same word, 'I', has two different extensions in two different idiolects; but it does not follow that the concept I have of myself is in any way different from the concept my *Doppelgänger* has of himself.[4]

This passage makes it clear that Putnam supposes both that the traditional view that what is in the head determines extension cannot be applied to indexicals and that if two speakers, I and my "*Doppelgänger*", have type-identical mental states our states must

4 *Op. cit.* p. 234.

have the same conditions of satisfaction. I believe both these assumptions are false. I want to argue, first, that if by "intension" we mean Intentional content then the intension of an utterance of an indexical expression precisely does determine extension; and, second, that in perceptual cases two people can be in type-identical mental states, indeed we can even suppose that a man and his *Doppelgänger* can be type-identical down to the last microparticle, and their Intentional contents can still be different; they can have different conditions of satisfaction. Both perceptual Intentionality and indexicality are cases of self-referentiality of Intentional or semantic content. We will explore the self-referentiality of in-dexical propositions later in this chapter. For present purposes it is sufficient to remind ourselves of the causal self-referentiality of perceptual experience that we explored in Chapters 2 and 4 and to show how it is relevant to the twin earth argument.

Let us suppose that Jones on the earth in 1750 indexically identifies and baptizes something as "water" and twin Jones on twin earth also indexically identifies and baptizes something as "water". Let us also suppose that they have type-identical mental contents and type-identical visual and other sorts of experiences when they make the indexical identification. Now, since they give the same type-identical definitions, namely, "water" is defined as whatever is identical in structure with this stuff, and since they are having type-identical experiences, Putnam supposes that we cannot account for how "water" has a different extension on earth from the extension on twin earth in terms of their mental contents. If their experiences are the same, how can their mental contents be different? On the account of Intentionality presented in this book the answer to that problem is simple. Though they have type-identical visual experiences in the situation where "water" is for each indexically identified, they do not have type-identical Inten-tional contents. On the contrary, their Intentional contents can be different because each Intentional content is causally self-referential in the sense that I explained earlier. The indexical definitions given by Jones on earth of "water" can be analyzed as follows: "water" is defined indexically as whatever is identical in structure with the stuff causing *this* visual experience, whatever that structure is. And the analysis for twin Jones on twin earth is: "water" is defined indexically as whatever is identical in structure with the stuff causing *this* visual experience, whatever that structure is. Thus, in each case we have type-identical experiences, type-identical utterances, but in fact in each case something different is meant. That is, in each case the conditions of satisfaction established by the mental content (in the head) is different because of the causal self-referentiality of perceptual experiences.

This account does not have the consequence that different speakers on earth must mean something different by "water". Most people do not go around baptizing natural kinds; they just intend to use words to mean and refer to whatever the community at large, including the experts, use the words to mean and refer to. And even when there are such public baptisms they would normally involve on the part of the participants shared visual and other experiences of the sort that we discussed in Chapter 2. But the account does have the consequence that, in making indexical definitions, different speakers *can* mean something different because their Intentional contents are self-referential to the token Intentional experiences. I conclude, then, that even if we accept all of his intuitions – which many of us will not – Putnam's arguments do not show that meanings are not in the head. Quite the contrary, what he has done is to offer us an alternative Intentionalistic account, based on indexical presentations, of the meanings of a certain class of general terms.

II. ARE THERE IRREDUCIBLY *DE RE* BELIEFS?[5]

I have never seen a clear and precise statement of what exactly the *de dicto/de re* distinction as applied to propositional attitudes is supposed to be. Perhaps there are as many versions of it as there are authors on the subject, and certainly the notions have gone far beyond the literal Latin meanings, "of words" and "of things". Suppose one believes, as I do, that all Intentional states are entirely constituted by their Intentional content and their psychological mode, both of which are in the head. On such an account all beliefs are *de dicto*. They are entirely individuated by their Intentional

---

5 Like other authors who write on this topic I will use belief as an example for the whole class of propositional attitudes.

content and psychological mode. Some beliefs, however, are also actually about real objects in the real world. One might say that such beliefs are *de re* beliefs, in the sense that they refer to actual objects. *De re* beliefs would then be a subclass of *de dicto* beliefs, in the same way that true beliefs are a subclass of *de dicto* beliefs, and the term *"de dicto* belief" would be redundant since it just means belief.

On such a view, the belief that Santa Claus comes on Christmas Eve and the belief that de Gaulle was President of France are both *de dicto*, and the second is also *de re* since it is about real objects, de Gaulle and France.

With such an account of the *de re/de dicto* distinction I would have no quarrel. But several accounts in the philosophical literature since Quine's original article[6] advance a much stronger thesis: The intuitive idea is that in addition to the class of *de dicto* beliefs which are entirely individuated by their content and mode, by what is in the head, there is a class of beliefs for which what is in the head is insufficient to individuate the beliefs because such beliefs involve relations between believers and objects as part of the identity of the belief. Such beliefs are not a subclass of *de dicto* beliefs, but are irreducibly *de re*. Purely *de dicto* beliefs could be held by a brain in a vat; they are independent of how the world is in fact. But *de re* beliefs, on this view, are relations between believers and objects; for them, if the world were different in certain ways, the beliefs themselves would be different even though what is in the head remained unchanged.

There are as near as I can tell three sets of considerations that incline people to the view that there are irreducibly *de re* beliefs. First, there just does seem to be a class of beliefs which are irreducibly *about* objects, that is, beliefs which relate the believer to an object and not just to a proposition and in that sense are *de re* rather than *de dicto*. For example, suppose that George Bush believes that Ronald Reagan is President of the United States. Now that is clearly a fact about Bush, but under the circumstances isn't it equally clearly a fact about Reagan? Isn't it just a plain fact about Reagan that Bush believes him to be President? Furthermore, there

---

6 W. V. Quine, 'Quantifiers and propositional attitudes', in *Ways of Paradox* (New York: Random House, 1966), pp. 183–94.

is no way to account for the fact simply in terms of facts about Bush, including facts which relate him to propositions. The fact in question is stated by a proposition of the form

> About Reagan, Bush believes him to be President of the United States

or, more pretentiously,

> Reagan is such that Bush believes of him that he is President of the United States.

Such propositions, describing *de re* beliefs, permit quantification into "belief contexts"; that is, each permits an inference to

$$(\exists x) \text{ (Bush believes (} y \text{ is President of the United States) of } x)$$

According to received opinion, both our logical theory and our theory of mind compel us to such an analysis.

Second, there is clearly a distinction between propositional attitudes which are directed at particular objects and those which are not. In Quine's example, we need to make a distinction between the desire a man might have for a sloop where any old sloop will do, and the desire a man might have which is directed at a particular sloop, the sloop *Nellie* parked at the Sausalito Yacht Harbor. In the first or *de dicto* desire, the man seeks – as Quine says – mere "relief from slooplessness", in the second or *de re* desire the man's desire relates him to a particular object. The difference according to Quine is expressed in the following two sentences:[7]

> *de dicto:* I wish that $(\exists x)$ $(x$ is a sloop & I have $x)$
> *de re:* $(\exists x$ $(x$ is a sloop & I wish that I have $x)$

Third, and I believe most important, there is supposed to be a class of beliefs which contain a "contextual", "nonconceptual" element, and for that reason are not subject to an internalist or *de dicto* account. As Tyler Burge writes,[8] "A *de re* belief is a belief whose correct ascription places a believer in an appropriate *nonconceptual* contextual relation to objects the belief is about . . . The crucial point is that the relation not be merely that of concepts

---

7 See Quine, *op. cit.*, p. 184.
8 T. Burge, 'Belief de re', *Journal of Philosophy*, vol. 74, no. 6 (June 1977), pp. 338–62.

being concepts *of* the object – concepts that denote or apply to it" (first italics mine). According to Burge such beliefs cannot be completely or exhaustively characterized in terms of their Intentional contents, because, as he puts it, there are contextual, nonconceptual elements which are crucial to the identity of the belief.

I believe that all three of these reasons can be answered rather swiftly, and that all three embody various confused notions of Intentionality. I begin with the third set of reasons, as a discussion of them prepares the way for a discussion of the earlier two; and I will confine my remarks to Burge because he gives the strongest statement of the *de re* thesis known to me.

Implicit in Burge's account is a contrast between the conceptual and the contextual. A fully conceptual belief is *de dicto* and completely analyzable in general terms. A contextual belief is individuated in part by relations between the believer and objects in the world and is therefore *de re*. His strategy is to argue by way of examples that there are beliefs that are not fully conceptual but are contextual. I agree that there are beliefs that are not fully conceptual in the sense that they do not consist in verbal descriptions in general terms but that does not show that they are contextual or *de re* in his sense. In addition to the two options of "conceptual" or "contextual" there is a third possibility, there are forms of Intentionality which are not general but particular and yet are entirely in the head, entirely internal. Intentionality may contain self-referential elements both of the causal kind that we considered in our discussion of perception, memory, intention, and action, and of the indexical kind that I alluded to briefly in the discussion of Putnam and will say more about later in this chapter. A proper understanding of the self-referentiality of certain forms of Intentionality is, I believe, sufficient to account for all of Burge's examples of allegedly *de re* beliefs, since in each case the Intentional content can be shown to account completely for the content of the belief. And that is just another way of saying that, in the relevant sense, the belief is *de dicto*.

His first example is of a man seen coming from the distance in a swirling fog. Of this example he says, "We may plausibly be said to believe of him that he is wearing a red cap, but we do not see the man well enough to describe or image him in such a way as to individuate him fully. Of course, we could individuate him ostensively with the help of the descriptions that we can apply but there is no reason to believe that we can always describe or conceptualize the entities or spatio-temporal positions that we rely on in our demonstration."

I find this passage very revealing, since it says nothing at all about the Intentional content of the visual experience itself which in this case is part of the content of the belief. Once you understand that the visual experience has a causally self-referential propositional content you don't need to worry about "describing" or "conceptualizing" anything in words in order to individuate the man: the Intentional content of the visual experience has already done it. On my account the (*de dicto*) Intentional content of the visual experience individuates the man, and that content is part of the (*de dicto*) content of the belief. The relevant *de dicto* Intentional content of the belief can be expressed as follows:

(There is a man there causing this visual experience and that man is wearing a red cap.)

In such a case the "contextual" elements are indeed present, but they are fully internalized in the sense that they are part of the Intentional content. Notice that this *de dicto* belief is quite sufficient to individuate any alleged *de re* analogue but at the same time it is consistent with the hypothesis that there is no man there at all. Such a belief as this could be held by a brain in a vat. It might be objected that this analysis has the consequence that it is in principle impossible for two different people to have the same perceptual belief. But that consequence does not follow, for the same man may be part of the conditions of satisfaction of two different perceptual beliefs; and it may be even part of the content of two perceptual beliefs that they should have exactly the same man as part of their conditions of satisfaction. Thus, in the case of shared visual experiences, I may believe not only that I am seeing a man and that you are seeing a man but that we are both seeing the *same* man. In such a case, the conditions of satisfaction will require not only that there is a man causing my visual experience, but that the same man is also causing your visual experience. Of course our beliefs will be different in the trivial sense that any self-referential perceptual content makes reference to a particular token and not to qualitatively similar tokens, but that is a result we want anyway, since, when you and I share a visual experience, what we share is a common set of conditions of satisfaction and not the same token visual experiences. Your experience will be numerically different from mine even though they may be qualitatively similar.

The next class of cases considered by Burge are indexicals. His example is that of a man who believes of the present moment that it is in the twentieth century. But this is subject to Intentionalistic analysis formally similar to that we gave in the perceptual case. The method here as before is always to ask what must be the case in order that the Intentional content is satisfied. In the case of visual perception, the visual experience itself must figure causally in the conditions of satisfaction. In the case of the indexicals, there is an analogous self-referentiality though this time it is not causal. The truth conditions of "This moment is in the twentieth century", are that the moment of this utterance is in the twentieth century. Just as the perceptual case is self-referential to the experience, so the indexical case is self-referential to the utterance. I hasten to add that this statement of the conditions of satisfaction is not meant as a *translation* of the original sentence: I am not saying that "this moment" just *means* "the moment of this utterance". Rather, what I am arguing is that the indexical operator in the sentence *indicates*, though does not represent or describe, the form of the self-referentiality. The self-referentiality of indexical expressions is in that sense *shown* but not *said*, just as the self-referentiality of visual experience is 'shown' but not 'seen'. In the case of the statement of the conditions of satisfaction, I describe or represent or say what was indicated or shown in the original.

I conclude, then, that there is nothing irreducibly *de re* about either perceptual or indexical beliefs. They are subject to an Intentionalistic or *de dicto* analysis and the mistake of supposing there must be irreducibly *de re* sets of perceptual or indexical beliefs seems to rest on the assumption that all *de dicto* Intentionalistic analyses must be given using purely general words. Once the self-referential forms of indexicality and perceptual experience are explicated it is easy to see that there are forms of Intentionality where the Intentional contents are sufficient to determine the entire sets of conditions of satisfaction but they do not do so by setting purely general conditions, but rather by indicating relations in which the rest of the conditions of satisfaction must stand to the Intentional state or event itself.

The diagnosis, then, of the mistake made by the *de re* theorists who rely on perceptual and indexical beliefs is the following: they correctly see that there is a class of beliefs that cannot be accounted for in purely general terms. They also see that these beliefs depend on contextual features, and they then mistakenly suppose that these contextual features cannot themselves be entirely represented as part of the Intentional content. Having contrasted the conceptual (in general terms) with the contextual (involving the real world) they then ignore the possibility of a completely internalist account of nonconceptual beliefs. I am arguing for forms of Intentionality that are not conceptual but not *de re* either.

Part of the difficulty here, I am convinced, comes from this archaic terminology which seemingly forces us to choose between the views that all beliefs are in words (*dicta*) and that some involve things (*res*). We can sort this out if we distinguish between several different questions. The question, "Are all beliefs *de dicto*?", tends to oscillate between at least four different interpretations.

1. Are all beliefs expressible using purely general terms?
2. Do all our beliefs occur to us in words which are sufficient to exhaust their content?
3. Do all of our beliefs consist entirely in an Intentional content?
4. Do some beliefs relate the believer directly to an object without the mediation of an Intentional content which is sufficient to individuate the object? Are they such that a change in the world would necessarily mean a change in the belief even if what is in the head remained constant?

The answer to the first two questions is no: the first, because many beliefs contain singular terms essentially, as we will see in our discussion of indexicals; and the second, because many beliefs contain, for example, a perceptual content, as we saw in the case we considered where a belief contains a visual experience as part of its content. But a negative answer to the first two questions does not entail a negative answer to the third: a belief can be exhaustively characterized by its Intentional content, and in that sense be a *de dicto* belief, even though it is not characterizable in general terms and contains nonverbal forms of Intentionality. If by *de dicto* we mean *verbal*, *in words*, then not all beliefs are *de dicto*, but it does not follow from that that there are irreducibly *de re* beliefs, because a negative answer to the first two questions does not entail an affirmative answer to the fourth. If the answer to 3 is yes, that is, if, as I believe, all beliefs consist entirely in their Intentional content, then it is consistent to claim that the answer to 1, 2, and 4 is no. In once sense of *de dicto*, there are some beliefs that are not *de dicto* (in words), but that does not show that there are any irreducibly *de re* beliefs, because in another sense of *de dicto* (Intentional content) all beliefs are *de dicto* (which illustrates, among other things, that this terminology is muddled).

Using these results we can now turn to the other two arguments for the belief in irreducibly *de re* attitudes. The first argument says correctly that it is a fact about Ronald Reagan that Bush believes him to be President. But in what does this fact consist? On my account it consists simply in the fact that Bush believes the *de dicto* proposition that Ronald Reagan is President of the United States, and that Ronald Reagan satisfies the Intentional content associated with Bush's use of the name "Ronald Reagan". Some of this content is perceptual, some indexical, much of it is causal; but all of it is *de dicto* in the sense that it consists entirely in an Intentional content. Bush could have had exactly the same belief if Ronald Reagan had never existed and the whole thing, perceptions and all, had been a massive hallucination. In such a case Bush would have had a lot of perceptual, indexical, and causal Intentional contents which nothing satisfied.

Quine's argument I believe rests on confusing the distinction between particular and general propositional attitudes with a distinction between *de re* and *de dicto* propositional attitudes. There really is a distinction between those Intentional states that make reference to a particular object and those that do not. But in each case the state is *de dicto*. On this view, the sentence that Quine gives to express the *de re* attitude cannot be correct, because the sentence expressing the desire for a particular sloop is incomplete: there is no way an agent can have a desire for a *particular* object without representing that object to himself in some way, and Quine's formalization does not tell us how the object is represented. In the example as stated the agent would have to have a belief in the existence of a particular sloop and a desire to have that very sloop.

The only way to express the relation between the belief in the existence of a particular sloop and the desire to have it in the quantifier notation is to allow the scope of the quantifier to cross over the scope of the Intentional operators. That this is the correct way to represent the facts is at least suggested by the fact that we would so express the man's mental state in ordinary language. Suppose the man who wants a particular sloop gave expression to his whole mental state including his representation of the sloop. He might say,

> There is this very nice sloop in the yacht harbor and I sure wish I had it.

The mental states he expressed here are, first, a belief in the existence of a particular sloop and, then, a desire to have that sloop. In English,

> I *believe* that there is this very nice sloop in the yacht harbor and I *wish* I had it.

Notice that in this formulation the scope of the quantifier in the content of the belief extends to the content of the desire even though the desire is not within the scope of the belief. Thus, using square brackets for the scope of the Intentional verbs and round brackets for the quantifier and F for the Intentional content which identifies the sloop in question, we have:

> Bel $[(\exists x) ((\text{sloop } x \ \& \ Fx) \ \& \ (\forall y) (\text{sloop } y \ \& \ Fy \rightarrow y = x)] \ \&$
> Des $[\text{I have } x])$

This *de dicto* form represents the entire content of the desire directed at a particular object.

We have so far considered and rejected some arguments in favor of the belief in *de re* propositional attitudes. I want to conclude with a Wittgensteinian diagnosis of what I believe to be the deepest but unstated motives for the belief in irreducibly *de re* attitudes. The belief in two fundamentally different kinds of propositional attitudes, *de re* and *de dicto*, derives from the possibility that our language provides of giving two different kinds of reports of propositional attitudes, *de re* reports and *de dicto* reports. Suppose, for example, that Ralph believes that the man in the brown hat is a spy.[9] Now about Ralph's belief we can either say, "About the man in the brown hat, Ralph believes he is a spy", or, "Ralph believes that the man in the brown hat is a spy". The first report commits us, the reporters, to the existence of the man in the brown hat. The second report commits us only to reporting the content of Ralph's belief. Now since sentences about beliefs can differ in this way, and indeed can have different truth conditions, we are inclined to think that there must be a difference in the phenomena reported. But notice that the distinction we can make between the *de re* report of Ralph's belief and the *de dicto* report is not a distinction that Ralph can make. Suppose Ralph says, "About the man in the brown hat, I believe he is a spy", or he says, "I believe that the man in the brown hat is a spy". From Ralph's point of view these amount to exactly the same belief. Imagine the craziness of the following conversation:

> Quine: About the man in the brown hat, Ralph, do you believe he is a spy?
>
> Ralph: No Quine, you've asked me if I hold a *de re* belief, but it is not the case that *about* the man in the brown hat I believe that he is a spy. Rather, I believe the *de dicto* belief, I believe *that* the man in the brown hat is a spy.

Just as the belief that Intentional-with-a-t states are somehow intrinsically intensional-with-an-s entities is founded on the confusion between logical properties of reports of Intentional states with logical properties of the Intentional states themselves, so the belief that there are two different kinds of Intentional states, *de re* and *de dicto*, is founded on confusing two different kinds of reports of Intentional states, *de re* and *de dicto* reports, with logical features of the Intentional states themselves. I conclude, then, that there is a genuine *de re/de dicto* distinction, but it is only a distinction in kinds of reports. If *de re* propositional attitudes are supposed to be those in which Intentional content is insufficient to individuate the mental state, then there are no such things as *de re* propositional attitudes; though there are *de re reports* of propositional attitudes in the sense that there are reports that commit the reporter to the existence of objects that the propositional attitudes are about.

9 The example is, of course, Quine's, 'Quantifiers and propositional attitudes'.

III. INDEXICAL EXPRESSIONS

In both our discussion of Putnam's attack on internalism in semantics and our discussion of the alleged existence of irreducibly *de re* beliefs, we have suggested an account of indexical expressions and it is now time to make that account fully explicit.

There is at least one big difference between the problem of *de re* attitudes and the problem of indexicals: there are no such things as irreducibly *de re* propositional attitudes, but there really are indexical expressions and indexical propositions. The strategy therefore in this section will differ from that of the previous sections. First, we need to develop a theory of indexicals; second, to do it in such a way as to show how it fits in with the general account of Intentionality developed in this book; and, third, in so doing to answer those accounts of indexicals which claim that it is impossible to assimilate indexicals to an internalist or Fregean account of language. I begin with some of the arguments of the opposition.

Various authors, notably Perry[10] and Kaplan[11] maintain that there are thought contents which are essentially indexical. Consider, for example, the belief I might have if I come to believe that I am inadvertently making a mess in a supermarket by spilling sugar out of my cart. If I come to believe that I am making a mess, the content of my Intentional state seems to contain an essential indexical element; and this is shown by the fact that no paraphrase of my belief into any nonindexical terms will capture exactly the belief I have when I believe that I am making a mess. If I try to specify the belief using space and time coordinates, I will not be able to specify the content of my belief. For example, my possession of the belief that person p is making a mess at location l and at time t would not explain how my behavior changes when I discover that it is *me* that is making the mess, since I might have the belief that some person satisfying certain space–time coordinates is making a mess without realizing that it is me. Analogous remarks apply to definite descriptions and proper names: the belief that I am

---

10 J. Perry, 'The problem of the essential indexical', *NOUS*, vol. 13, no. 1 (March 1979), pp. 3–21.
11 D. Kaplan, 'Demonstratives', mimeo, UCLA, 1977.

making a mess is not the same as the belief that the only non-bearded philosopher in the Berkeley Co Op is making a mess or the belief that JS is making a mess, for I might have these latter beliefs without knowing that I am the only non-bearded philosopher in the Berkeley Co Op or that I am JS. The content of my belief seems, then, to be essentially indexical.

As I am sure both Perry and Kaplan are aware, there is nothing so far that is anti-Fregean or anti-internalist about this point. In fact, it looks like a paradigm example of Frege's distinction between sense and reference. Just as the proposition that the Evening Star shines near the horizon is different from the proposition that the Morning Star shines near the horizon, so the proposition that I am making a mess is different from the proposition that JS is making a mess. So far, so Fregean.

The anti-Fregean point comes next. According to Perry[12] and Kaplan[13] there is no way a Fregean can account for such essentially indexical Intentional contents, because in such cases there is no "completing Fregean sense" which is sufficient by itself to determine the conditions of satisfaction. To illustrate and support this claim Perry introduces the following sort of example. Suppose David Hume believes "I am David Hume". Suppose also that Heimson believes "I am David Hume", and just to make the strongest case let us suppose that Heimson is David Hume's *Doppelgänger* on twin earth and that he has type-identical mental states with David Hume, and indeed we can suppose that he is type identical with Hume down to the last microparticle. Now the sentence that Hume and Heimson both utter (or think), "I am David Hume", has the same Fregean sense on both occasions and Heimson and Hume are in type-identical mental states. But the propositions expressed must be different because they have different truth values. Hume's is true, Heimson's is false. There is a Fregean sense to the sentence, "I am David Hume", but it is not sufficient to determine which proposition is expressed. Kaplan and Perry conclude from such examples that the Fregean account of sense and reference and the Fregean account of propositions must

12 J. Perry, 'Frege on demonstratives', *The Philosophical Review*, vol. 86, no. 4 (October 1977), pp. 474–97.
13 *Op. cit.*

be inadequate to explain indexicals. Since what is expressed in such utterances is essentially indexical and since there is no completing Fregean sense, we need another theory of propositions at least for such cases.

At this point they adopt what I believe is a desperate expedient, the theory of "direct reference" and "singular propositions". According to them, in such cases the proposition is not the Intentional content in the mind of the speaker but rather the proposition must contain the actual objects referred to. Hume's proposition contains Hume, the actual man and not some representation of him, and Heimson's proposition contains Heimson, the actual man and not some representation of him. Expressions which (like Russell's logically proper names) introduce objects themselves into propositions are said to be "directly referential" and the propositions in question are (misleadingly) said to be "singular propositions".

I am, frankly, unable to make any sense of the theory of direct reference and singular propositions, but for the purposes of this argument I am not attacking its intelligibility but its necessity to account for the data: I think that the arguments for it are inadequate and rest on a misconception of the nature of Intentionality and of the nature of the functioning of indexicals.

(i) How do indexical expressions work?

We need to develop an account of indexicals which will show how the utterance of an indexical expression can have a "completing Fregean sense":[14] that is, we need to show how in the utterance of an indexical expression a speaker can express an Intentional content which is sufficient to identify the object he is referring to in virtue of the fact that the object *satisfies* or *fits* that Intentional content.

In what follows I will confine the discussion to indexical *referring* expressions such as "I", "you", "this", "that", "here", "now",

14 Though remember, the account is not Fregean in postulating a third realm of abstract entities. Ordinary Intentional contents will do the job. When I say "completing Fregean sense" I do not mean to imply that such senses are abstract entities, but rather that they are sufficient to provide adequate "modes of presentation".

"he", "she", etc. But it is worth pointing out that the *phenomenon* of indexicality – the phenomenon of the conditions of satisfaction being determined in virtue of relations things have to the realization of the Intentional content itself – is quite general and extends beyond just referring expressions and indeed even beyond cases of indexical *expressions*. Various forms of indexicality are part of the nonrepresentational Background. For example, I now believe that Benjamin Franklin was the inventor of bifocals. Suppose that it was discovered that 80 billion years before Benjamin Franklin's discovery, in a distant galaxy, populated by organisms somewhat like humans, some humanoid invented the functional equivalent of bifocals. Would I regard my view that Benjamin Franklin had invented bifocals as false? I think not. When I say Benjamin Franklin invented bifocals there is a concealed indexical in the background: the functioning of the Background in such cases assigns an indexical interpretation to the sentence. Relative to *our* earth and *our* history, Benjamin Franklin invented bifocals; the statement that Benjamin Franklin invented bifocals is, therefore, like most statements, indexical; even though there are no indexical *expressions* (other than the tense of the verb) contained in the *sentence* used to make the statement.

Let us begin by asking what indexical referring expressions have in common that makes them indexical? What is the essence of indexicality? The defining trait of indexical referring expressions is simply this: In uttering indexical referring expressions, speakers refer by means of indicating relations in which the object referred to stands to the utterance of the expression itself. "I" refers to the person uttering the expression, "you" refers to the person addressed in the utterance of the expression, "here" refers to the place of the utterance of the expression, "now" refers to the time of the utterance of the expression, and so on. Notice that in every case the speaker will refer to a particular entity because his utterance expresses an Intentional content that indicates relations that the object he is referring to has to the utterance itself. The utterance of indexical expressions, therefore, has a form of self-referentiality which is similar to the self-referentiality of certain Intentional states and events, and we will need to explore it in more detail. But at this point we need only note that this self-referential feature is sufficient to account for how the utterance of an indexical expression can have a completing Fregean sense. The problem for a Fregean (internalist or Intentionalist) account of reference is to show in every case how reference succeeds in virtue of the fact that the utterance sets conditions of satisfaction and an object is referred to in virtue of the fact that it meets those conditions. An object is referred to in virtue of satisfying an Intentional content, normally expressed by a speaker in the utterance of an expression. This is the basic idea of Frege's notion of the "*Sinn*" of "*Eigennamen*". His favorite examples are cases such as "the Morning Star", where the lexical meaning of the expression is supposedly sufficient to determine which object is referred to. What is special about indexical expressions is that the lexical meaning of the expression by itself does not determine which object it can be used to refer to, rather the lexical meaning gives a rule for determining reference relative to each utterance of the expression. Thus the same unambiguous expression used with the same lexical meaning can be used to refer to different objects because the lexical meaning determines that the conditions laid down by the utterance of the expression, viz., the completing sense expressed by the speaker in its utterance, is always self-referential to the utterance itself. Thus, for example, "I" has the same lexical meaning when uttered by you or me, but the reference in each case is different because the sense expressed by my utterance is self-referential to that very utterance and the sense expressed by your utterance is self-referential to your utterance: in any utterance "I" refers to the person who utters it.

There are, then, three components to the Fregean sense expressed by a speaker in the utterance of indexical expressions: the self-referential feature which is the defining trait or essence of indexicality; the rest of the lexical meaning, which can be expressed in general terms; and for many indexical utterances, the awareness by the speaker and the hearer of the relevant features of the actual context of the utterance, as in, for example, perceptual demonstratives, e.g., "that man over there". We need to explore each of these features in turn.

Self-referentiality. How does it work? Recall that for visual experiences the specification of the conditions of satisfaction makes reference to the visual experience itself. If I see my hand in front of my face then the conditions of satisfaction are

Vis Exp (there is a hand there and the fact that there is a hand there is causing this Vis Exp).

The form of the conditions of satisfaction of indexical propositions is analogously self-referential; though there is a difference in that the self-referentiality of the indexical cases is not causal. The sense in which the indexical cases are self-referential, like the case of Intentional self-reference, does not imply that the speaker in making the utterance performs a *speech act of referring* to the utterance, nor is the utterance explicitly *represented* in itself. Rather, the specification of the conditions of satisfaction, e.g., the truth conditions, requires reference to the utterance itself. Consider any utterance of the sentence, "I am now hungry". That utterance will be the making of a true statement iff the person uttering the sentence is hungry at the time of the utterance of the sentence. The conditions of satisfaction can therefore be represented as follows:

(the person making this utterance, "I", is hungry at the time of this utterance, "now").

This analysis does not imply that "I" is *synonymous* with "the person making this utterance", nor is "now" synonymous with "the time of this utterance". They could not be synonymous because the self-referentiality of the original is shown but not stated, and in the statement of the truth conditions we have stated it and not shown it. Just as we do not see the visual experience even though the visual experience is part of its own conditions of satisfaction, and is in that sense self-referential, so we do not refer to (in the speech act sense) the utterance of the indexical expression, even though the utterance is part of its own truth conditions and is in that sense self-referential. The self-referentiality of the visual experience is *shown* but not *seen*; the self-referentiality of the indexical utterance is *shown* but not *stated*. If we wanted to introduce a synonym which *showed* the indexicality we could introduce an arbitrary device, such as the asterisk symbol (*) to indicate the indexicality, i.e., to express the fact without stating it that the expression was being used to refer by way of indicating relations in which the referred to object stood to the utterance of the expression itself. Such a form of expression would give a canonical notation for isolating the self-referentiality of indexical expressions:

I = *person uttering
you = *person addressed
here = *cospatial
now = *cotemporal

and so on. All of these equivalences give us a *display* of the meaning of expressions, and consequently a display of the meanings of sentences containing these expressions. Thus, for example, the meaning of the sentence "I am hungry" is given by

*person uttering is hungry at *cotemporal.

Nonindexical descriptive content. We will deepen our understanding of the self-referential feature of indexical expressions if we see how it latches on to the rest of the lexical meaning, the nonindexical descriptive content, of the expression. I said that all indexical referring expressions refer by indicating relations in which the object referred to stands to the utterance of the expression. This naturally raises the question, how many kinds of relations are indicated in this manner? In English and in other languages known to me there are certainly four, and possibly five, relations indicated by the literal meaning of indexical expressions. These four are:

(1) time: examples of such expressions are "now", "yester-day", "tomorrow", and "later on";
(2) place: e.g., "here" and "there";
(3) utterance directionality: "you" refers to the person being addressed in the utterance, "I" refers to the person uttering;
(4) discoursal relations: anaphoric pronouns and expressions such as "the former" and "the latter" refer to something in virtue of its relation to the rest of the discourse in which the indexical utterance is embedded.

Notice that in each of these examples the nonindexical descriptive lexical meaning contains two elements: a sense which expresses the particular determinate form of the determinable relation indicated, and a sense which expresses the sort of entity being referred to. Thus, "yesterday" expresses the determinate time indication "one day before", and the type of entity referred to is a day. Thus the entire set of conditions of satisfaction expressed by "yesterday" are: the day which is one day before the day of this utterance. Not all indexicals have a lexical meaning which is in this way complete, for example, the demonstratives "this" and "that" usually require an extra expression ("this man" or "that tree"), as well as an awareness of the context in order to express a completing Fregean sense in a given utterance. More about this later.

These four are certainly forms of indexical relations expressed in the literal meaning of English indexical expressions. It has been argued that another relation is indicated by such words as "actual" and "real", the idea being that the word "actual" expresses its sense indexically by referring to *the world* in which it is uttered; and thus among *possible* worlds the *actual* world is picked out indexically. I think this claim is completely false; however, since it involves modal issues that go beyond the scope of this book I will not discuss it further here.[15]

Though there are only four (or arguably five) forms of indexical relations indicated in the lexical meaning of expressions in actual languages such as English, there is no limit in principle to introducing new forms of indexicality. We might, for example, have an expression which when uttered at a certain pitch would indicate sounds of a higher or lower pitch or of the same pitch. That is, we could imagine a class of indexical expressions that are used to refer to tonal qualities by indicating relations in which the tonal qualities stand to the tonal quality of the utterance analogously to the way that "today", "yesterday", and "tomorrow" refer to days by indicating relations in which they stand to the day of the utterance of the expression itself.

Awareness of the context of utterance. Often the literal utterance of an indexical expression will not by itself carry a completing Fregean sense, but the completing Fregean sense is provided by the Intentional content of the indexical utterance together with the Intentional content of the awareness by the speaker and the hearer of the context of the utterance. One sees this most clearly in the case of the utterance of the demonstratives "this" and "that".

15 For a criticism of the view see P. van Inwagen, 'Indexicality and actuality', *The Philosophical Review*, vol. 89, no. 3 (July 1980), pp. 403–26.

Suppose upon seeing a man behave strangely at a party I say "That man is drunk". Now, in this case the descriptive content of "man" together with the indexical does not provide the completing Fregean sense because the utterance is only meant and understood in the context of an accompanying visual perception of which man is meant, and the proposition expressed has to contain the Intentional content of the perceptual experience that accompanied the utterance. The argument for this is simply that somebody who doesn't have the relevant perceptual experiences, e.g., because he is listening to me on the telephone or is blind or overhears me from the next room, cannot fully grasp the proposition I express; without the perceptual experience, he literally doesn't understand the entire proposition even though he understands all the words uttered.

In such cases a complete analysis of the proposition which makes the completing Fregean sense fully explicit would have to include both the Intentional content of the utterance and the Intentional content of the visual experience, and it would have to show how the latter is nested in the former. Here is how it works. The indexical expression refers by indicating relations in which the object stands to the utterance of the expression itself. In this case, then, there is some relation R such that the truth conditions of the utterance are expressible as

The man who stands in relation R to this utterance is drunk.

And, in the case as described, R is perceptual and temporal; the man who is referred to is the man we are *seeing* at the *time* of this utterance. But if we are seeing someone at the time of this utterance each of us will also have a visual experience with its own present-tense propositional content:

Vis exp (there is a man there and the fact that there is a man there is causing this visual experience).

Now that Intentional content simply plugs into the Intentional content of the rest of the utterance to give us the completing Fregean sense which identifies the man uniquely in virtue of both the self-referentiality of the utterance and the self-referentiality of the visual experience. The entire conditions of satisfaction of the whole proposition (with the self-referential parts italicized) are expressible as follows:

> ((there is a man, x, there, and the fact that x is there is causing *this vis exp*) and x is the man visually experienced at the time of *this utterance* and x is drunk).

This may look strange, but I think that the reader who is prepared to recognize the Intentionality of the visual experience, its role in the Intentionality of the proposition expressed by the utterance, the self-referentiality of the visual experience, and the self-referentiality of the indexical utterance, will see that something like this formulation has to be right. It is intended to capture both the indexical and the perceptual content of the proposition and the relations between them. In the case of the perceptual use of the demonstratives, both the sense of the indexical expression and the Intentional content contained in the perceptual experience that accompanies the utterance contribute to the propositional content expressed in the utterance. Notice that in these cases we have a completing Fregean sense sufficient to identify the object. Notice, further, that there is no twin earth problem for these cases. I, on this earth, and my *Doppelgänger*, on twin earth, will express different Fregean senses in our use of the demonstrative "That man", even though our utterances and our experiences are qualitatively type identical. His perception and his utterance are both self-referential, as are mine.

Let us now summarize the account. We need to distinguish between an indexical expression with its literal meaning, the literal utterance of an indexical expression, and the sense expressed by a speaker in the literal utterance of the expression. Analogously, we need to distinguish the indexical sentence (i.e., any sentence containing an indexical expression or morpheme, such as the tense of a verb) with its literal meaning, the literal utterance of an indexical sentence, and the proposition expressed by the speaker in a literal utterance of an indexical sentence. The meaning of the indexical expression by itself is not sufficient to provide the completing Fregean sense, since the same expression with the same meaning can be used to refer to different objects, e.g., different people refer to themselves by uttering "I". But the literal indexical meaning is such as to determine that when a speaker makes an utterance of that expression the sense he expresses will be relative to that utterance. So the sense of the expression can become a completing Fregean sense relative to an utterance because the lexical sense determines that any utterance is self-referential to that very utterance. And this explains how two different speakers can utter the same sentence with the same meaning, e.g., "I am hungry", and still express different Fregean propositions: each proposition expressed is self-referential to the utterance in which it is expressed. It is the completing Fregean sense expressed which determines the reference and it is the Fregean sense and not the reference which is a constituent of the proposition. It cannot be emphasized too strongly that there is nothing reductionist or eliminative about this account of indexicality. I am not trying to show that indexicality is really something else, but rather I am trying to show what it is and how it works in utterances to express Intentional contents.

(ii) How this account answers the objection to an internalist account of indexicals

In the course of developing an independently motivated account of indexicals we have, in passing, answered the objection of Perry and Kaplan that no Frege-like account of indexicals can provide a completing Fregean sense. Hume and Heimson utter the same sentence with the same literal meaning but each utterance expresses a different Intentional content; and each, therefore, has a different completing Fregean sense, because each proposition expressed is self-referential to the utterance which expresses the proposition. In every case we have shown how the self-referentiality of the indexical utterance, as determined by the rule for using the indexical expression, sets the conditions which an object has to meet in order to be the referent of that utterance. Perry argues correctly that there are essentially indexical thought contents (propositions, in my sense), but he argues, in my view incorrectly, that there is no completing Fregean sense for essentially indexical thought contents. And from these two premises he concludes that the propositions expressed in such cases can only be accounted for on a direct reference theory. I accept the first of his premises but reject the second and his conclusion. Indexical expressions are not counterexamples to the claim of the theory of Intentionality that objects are referred to by utterances only in virtue of the sense of the utterance, only by virtue of the fact that the utterance sets conditions of satisfaction which the objects referred to must meet.

Two concluding remarks: First, I have called my account of indexicals "Fregean" in spirit, but it is quite different from Frege's few actual remarks about indexicals. What little Frege did say seems both mistaken and inconsistent with his general account of sense and reference. About "I" he says that since each of us is aware of himself in a special, private way, "I" has both a public and a private sense. About "yesterday" and "today" he says that if we want to express today the same proposition that was expressed yesterday by an utterance containing "today" we must use the word "yesterday",[16] thus he seems to adopt a *de re* account of such indexical propositions. What is one to make of these remarks? The idea of incommunicable senses of expressions is profoundly anti-Fregean, since the notion of sense was introduced, in part, to provide a publicly graspable content to be shared by speaker and hearer. And the example of "yesterday" and "today" looks like a stock example of the sort of case where different senses can determine the same reference. Just as "the Evening Star" and "the Morning Star" can have the same reference with different senses because the referent is presented in each case with a different "mode of presentation", so "today" said yesterday and "yesterday" said today have different senses and hence are parts of the expression of different Fregean propositions, even though they both are used to refer to the same day. I believe Frege failed to see that it was possible to give a Fregean account of indexicals because he failed to see their self-referential character, and this failure is part of a larger failure to see the nature of Intentionality.

Second, discussions like this can tend to degenerate into a kind of fussy scholasticism which conceals the basic 'metaphysical' assumptions at issue, and, as far as possible, I believe, we should allow those assumptions to surface. My basic assumption is simply

16 G. Frege, 'The thought: a logical inquiry', reprinted in P. F. Strawson (ed.) *Philosophical Logic* (Oxford: Oxford University Press, 1967), pp. 17–38.

this: causal and other sorts of natural relations to the real world are only relevant to language and other sorts of Intentionality insofar as they impact on the brain (and the rest of the central nervous system), and the only impacts that matter are those that produce Intentionality, including the Network and the Background. Some form of internalism must be right because there isn't anything else to do the job. The brain is all we have for the purpose of representing the world to ourselves and everything we can use must be inside the brain. Each of our beliefs must be possible for a being who is a brain in a vat because each of us is precisely a brain in a vat; the vat is a skull and the 'messages' coming in are coming in by way of impacts on the nervous system. The necessity of this internalism is masked from us in many of these discussions by the adoption of a third-person point of view. By adopting a God's eye view we think we can see what Ralph's real beliefs are even if he can't. But what we forget when we try to construct a belief that is not entirely in Ralph's head is that we have only constructed it in our head. Or, to put the point another way, even if there were a set of external semantic concepts they would have to be parasitic on and entirely reducible to a set of internal concepts.

Paradoxically, then, the point of view from which I defend a 'Fregean' account of reference is one Frege would have found utterly foreign, a kind of biological naturalism. Intentionality is a biological phenomenon and it is part of the natural world like any other biological phenomenon.

Chapter 9

PROPER NAMES AND INTENTIONALITY

I. THE NATURE OF THE PROBLEM

The problem of proper names ought to be easy, and at one level I think it is: we need to make repeated references to the same object, even when the object is not present, and so we give the object a name. Henceforward this name is used to refer to that object. However, puzzles arise when we reflect on the following sorts of considerations: objects are not given to us prior to our system of representation; what counts as one object or the same object is a function of how we divide up the world. The word does not come to us already divided up into objects; we have to divide it; and how we divide it is up to our system of representation, and in that sense is up to us, even though the system is biologically, culturally, and linguistically shaped. Furthermore, in order that someone can give a name to a certain object or know that a name is the name of that object, he has to have some *other* representation of that object independently of just having the name.

For the purposes of this study we need to explain how the use of proper names fits in with our general account of Intentionality. Both definite descriptions and indexicals serve to express at least a certain chunk of Intentional content. The expression may not by itself be sufficient to identify the object referred to, but in cases where the reference succeeds there is enough other Intentional content available to the speaker to nail down the reference. This thesis holds even for "referential" uses of definite descriptions, where the Intentional content that is actually expressed in the utterance may not even be true of the object referred to.[1] But what about proper names? They obviously lack an explicit Intentional content, but do they serve to focus the speaker's and hearer's

---

1 See J. R. Searle, 'Referential and attributive', in *Expression and Meaning* (Cambridge: Cambridge University Press, 1979), pp. 137–61.

Intentionality in some way; or do they simply refer to objects without any intervening Intentional content? On my account the answer is obvious. Since linguistic reference is always dependent on or is a form of mental reference and since mental reference is always in virtue of Intentional content including Background and Network,[2] proper names must in some way depend on Intentional content and it is now time to make that way – or those ways – fully explicit.

The problem of proper names used to be put in the form, "Do proper names have senses?", and in contemporary philosophy there are supposed to be two competing answers to that question: an affirmative answer given by the "descriptivist" theory, according to which a name refers by being associated with a description or perhaps a cluster of descriptions, and a negative answer given by the "causal" theory according to which a name refers because of a "causal chain" connecting the utterance of the name to the bearer of the name or at least to the naming ceremony in which the bearer of the name got the name. I believe that neither side should be satisfied with these labels. The causal theory would be better described as the external causal chain of communication theory,[3] and the descriptivist theory would be better described as the Intentionalist or internalist theory, for reasons which will emerge in this discussion.

Labels apart, it is important to get clear at the start about what exactly is at issue between these two theories. Almost without exception, the accounts I have seen of the descriptivist theory are more or less crude distortions of it, and I want to make explicit four of the most common misconceptions of the issues in order to set them aside so that we can get at the real issues.

First, the issue is most emphatically not about whether proper names must be exhaustively analyzed in completely general terms. I do not know of any descriptivist theorist who has ever maintained that view, though Frege sometimes talks as if he might

---

2 In what follows in this chapter I will use "Intentional content" broadly so as to include relevant elements of the Network and Background.

3 K. Donnellan recognizes the inappropriateness of the label for his views. Cf. 'Speaking of nothing', *The Philosophical Review*, vol. 83 (January 1974), pp. 3–32; reprinted in S. P. Schwartz (ed.), *Naming, Necessity and Natural Kinds* (Ithaca and London: Cornell University Press, 1977), pp. 216–44.

be sympathetic to it. In any case it has never been my view, nor, I believe, has it ever been the view of Strawson or Russell.

Second, as far as I am concerned the issue is not really about analyzing proper names in *words* at all. In my earlier writings on this subject[4] I pointed out that in some cases the only "identifying description" a speaker might have that he associates with the name is simply the ability to recognize the object.

Third, some authors[5] think that the descriptivist holds that proper names are associated with a 'dossier' in the speaker's mind and that the issue is between this dossier conception and the conception of the use of a proper name as analogous to pointing. But that again is a misconception of descriptivism. On the descriptivist account, pointing is precisely an example that fits his thesis, since pointing succeeds only in virtue of the intentions of the pointer.

Fourth, Kripke claims that on the descriptivist picture "some man really gives a name by going into the privacy of his own room and saying that the referent is to be the unique thing with certain identifying properties".[6] But that is not the view any descriptivist known to me ever espoused and it is not surprising that Kripke gives no source for this strange view.

But if these four accounts misrepresent descriptivism and the issues between descriptivist and causal theories, what exactly are these views and the issues between them? The issue is simply this: Do proper names refer by setting *internal* conditions of satisfaction in a way that is consistent with the general account of Intentionality that I have been providing, or do proper names refer in virtue of some *external* causal relation? Let us try to state this issue a little more precisely. The descriptivist is committed to the view that in order to account for how a proper name refers to an object we need to show how the object *satisfies* or *fits* the "descriptive" Intentional content that is associated with the name in the minds of speakers; some of this Intentionality will normally be expressed or

---

4 In, e.g., *Speech Acts* (Cambridge: Cambridge University Press, 1969), p. 90.

5 The term, I believe, was first used by H. P. Grice in 'Vacuous names', in Davidson and Hintikka (eds.), *Words and Objections* (Dordrecht: Reidel, 1969), pp. 118–45.

6 S. Kripke, 'Naming and necessity', in G. Harman and D. Davidson (eds.), *Semantics of Natural Language* (Dordrecht: Reidel, 1972), p. 300.

at least be expressible in words. The causal theorist is committed to the view that no such Intentionalist analysis will ever do the job and that in order to account for the relation of successful reference between the utterance of a name and the object referred to we need to show some sort of external causal connection between the utterance of a name and the object. Both theories are attempts to answer the question, "How in the utterance of a name does the speaker succeed in referring to an object?" The answer given by the descriptivist is that the speaker refers to the object because and only because the object satisfies the Intentional content associated with the name. The causal theorist answers that the speaker refers to an object because and only because there is a causal chain of communication connecting the speaker's utterance with the object or at least with the baptism of the object – an important qualification we will come to later.

II. THE CAUSAL THEORY

There are different versions of the causal theory and I shall not try to discuss all of them. The most influential have been those of Kripke and Donnellan, and I shall confine most of my discussion to their views. They are not identical, but I will call attention to the differences between them only when necessary to avoid confusion.

I begin with Kripke's version.

> A rough statement of a theory might be the following. An initial baptism takes place. Here the object may be named by ostension, or the reference of the name may be fixed by a description. When the name is "passed from link to link", the receiver of the name must, I think, intend when he hears it to use it with the same reference as the man from whom he heard it.[7]

There are several things to notice about this passage. First, the account of the introduction of the name in the baptism is entirely descriptivist. The baptism either gives us an Intentional content in verbal form, a definite description (Kripke gives the example of the introduction of the name "Neptune" for a then as yet unperceived planet), or it gives the Intentional content of a perception when an

---

7 Kripke, *op. cit.*, p. 302.

object is named ostensively. In the perceptual case, there is indeed a causal connection, but as it is Intentional causation, internal to the perceptual content, it is useless to the causal theorist in his effort to give an external causal account of the relation of name to object. Of course, in such cases there will also be an external causal account in terms of the impact of the object on the nervous system, but the external causal phenomena will not by themselves give an ostensive definition of the name. To get the ostensive definition the perceiver has to perceive the object and that involves more than the physical impact of the object on his nervous system. So it is an odd feature of Kripke's version of the causal theory that the external causal chain does not actually reach up to the object, it only reaches to the baptism of the object, to the name introduction ceremony, and from that point on what fixes the reference is an Intentional content which may or may not also have an external causal connection to the object. Many, perhaps most, philosophers think of the causal theory of names as asserting a causal connection between the referring use of names and the object they name, but in Kripke's case at least that isn't really true. An interesting point and one we will come back to later.

Some authors, e.g., Devitt,[8] are disappointed with this aspect of Kripke's account and want to reserve the notion of genuinely "designational" names to those that are causally connected to the object itself. But this seems quite arbitrary. There is nothing to prevent us from introducing a name by description and using it to refer, even as a "rigid designator"; and in any case, there are lots of proper names of abstract entities, e.g., numerals are names of numbers, and abstract entities are incapable of initiating physical causal chains.

A second feature to notice about Kripke's account is that the causal chain isn't, so to speak, *pure*. In addition to causation and baptism, an extra Intentionalistic element is allowed to creep in: each speaker must intend to refer to the same object as the person from whom he learned the name. So this does give us some Intentional content associated with each use of a name "N" in the causal chain, viz., "N is the object referred to by the person from

---

8 M. Devitt, *Designation* (Chicago: University of Chicago Press, 1981), esp. chapter 2, 25–64.

whom I got the name". Now this is an odd requirement for the
following reason: if everybody in the chain actually had this
restricted intention, and if the Intentional content were in fact
satisfied, i.e., if each speaker really did succeed in referring to the
same object, then it would follow trivially that the reference would
go right back to the target of the initial baptism and the talk about
causation would be redundant. But that is presumably not
Kripke's idea, since that would have no explanatory power and
would in fact be circular. We would explain successful reference in
virtue of a chain of successful references. Kripke's idea is clearly
this: you will account for how the Intentional content is satisfied,
that is, how the reference is successful, in terms of external
causation plus the intention that it should be successful. So Kripke
sets three conditions to account for how each token utterance
refers to the initial target: initial baptism, causal chain, restricted
Intentional content. And the account is still external in this sense:
though each link in the chain of communication is perceived by
both speaker and hearer, "It is not how the speaker thinks he got
the reference but the actual chain of communication which is
relevant".[9]

Before criticizing Kripke's account let us turn to Donnellan's.

> The main idea is that when a speaker uses a name intending to
> refer to an individual and predicate something of it, successful
> reference will occur when there is an individual that enters into
> the historically correct explanation of who [sic] it is that the
> speaker intended to predicate something of. That individual will
> then be the referent and the statement made will be true or false
> depending on whether it has the property designated by the
> predicate.[10]

The passage has two key elements: (a) "historically correct
explanation of" (b) "who it is that the speaker intended to
predicate something of". To help us with (a) Donellan introduces
the idea of an "omniscient observer of history". The omniscient
observer will see whom or what we meant even if we can't give any
Intentional content that fits whom or what we meant. But then in

9 Kripke, *op. cit.*, p. 300.
10 Donnellan, *op cit.*, p. 229.

what did our satisfying (b) consist? What fact about *us* makes it the case that when we said, for example, "Socrates is snub nosed", it was *Socrates* that we "intended to predicate something of"? Evidently, on Donnellan's account, no fact about us at all – except for the causal chain connecting our utterance to Socrates. But, then, what is the nature of this chain; what does the omniscient observer look for and why? Rorty assures us that the causal theory needs only "ordinary physical causation", the banging of object against object, as it were. I think Donnellan's observer is going to have to look for Intentional causation and Intentional content. I will come back to this point.

Kripke insists, and I take it that Donnellan would agree, that the causal theory is not intended as a complete theory but rather as a "picture" of how proper names work. Still, we want to know if it is an accurate picture and one way to proceed is to try to get counterexamples, examples of names that don't work according to the picture. Does the causal theory (or picture) as stated, for example, by Kripke give us sufficient conditions of successful reference using proper names? The answer, I think, is clearly no. There are numerous counterexamples in the literature, but perhaps the most graphic is from Gareth Evans.[11] "Madagascar" was originally the name of a part of Africa. Marco Polo, though he presumably satisfied Kripke's condition of intending to use the name with the same reference as "the man from whom he heard it", nonetheless referred to an island off the coast of Africa, and that island is now what we mean by "Madagascar". So, the use of the name "Madagascar" satisfies a causal condition that connects it with the African mainland, but that is not sufficient to enable it to refer to the African mainland. The question we need to come back to is how and why does it refer to Madagascar instead of the African mainland, given that the causal chain goes to the mainland?

If a Kripkean causal chain picture does not give us a sufficient condition does it at least give us a necessary condition? Here again the answer seems to me clearly no. In general it is a good idea to use examples that have been presented against one as examples that

---

11 G. Evans, 'The causal theory of names', *Proceedings of the Aristotelian Society*, suppl. vol. 47, pp. 187–208; reprinted in Schwartz (ed.), *op. cit.*, pp. 192–215.

actually work in one's favor, so let us consider the following from Kaplan.[12] He writes that the description theory couldn't be right because, for example, it says in the *Concise Biographical Dictionary* (Concise Publications: Walla Walla, Washington) that "Rameses VIII" is "One of a number of ancient pharaohs about whom nothing is known". But surely we can refer to him even though we do not satisfy the description theory for using his name. Actually what the example shows is that a great deal is known about Rameses VIII, and indeed he is a rather ideal case even for the most naive version of the description theory since we seem to have a perfect identifying description. Rameses VIII is the pharaoh named "Rameses" who ruled Egypt after a pharaoh named "Rameses VII".[13] That is, imagine, as I suppose is the case, that we have at least some knowledge of the history of ancient Egypt, including the knowledge that pharoahs with the same name are numbered sequentially. Suppose for the sake of argument that we know quite a bit about Rameses VII and Rameses IX. We could then use, without any hesitation, the name "Rameses VIII" to refer to the Rameses who came between Rameses VII and Rameses IX, even though the various causal chains stretching back from us to ancient Egypt miss Rameses VIII. What we have in this case is an example of the Network in operation; in this case, it is that part of the Network containing knowledge about the past.

In general one can say that the whole Network of Intentionality is nailed down causally, *via* Intentional causation, to the real world at various points, but it would be a serious mistake to suppose that the Network must nail down, by any kind of causation, at every single point that reference is made using a proper name.[14] I believe the reason that causal theorists make this mistake is that they overdraw the analogy between reference and perception, an analogy that is made explicitly by Donnellan.[15] Perception does nail down to the world in this way at every point, because every perceptual experience has the causal self-referentiality of Inten-

---

12 D. Kaplan, 'Bob and Carol and Ted and Alice', in K. J. Hintikka, et al. (eds.), *Approaches to Natural Language* (Dordrecht and Boston: Reidel, 1973), pp. 490–518.
13 For reasons we will shortly investigate this description is parasitic on other speakers, but it is nonetheless sufficient to identify about whom we are talking.
14 I am indebted to Jim Stone for discussion of this point.
15 In Schwartz (ed.), *op. cit.*, p. 232.

tional content that we have discussed earlier. But proper names do not carry that kind of causation, even of Intentional causation. It is possible to satisfy the conditions for successfully using a proper name even though there is no causal connection, either Intentional or external, between the utterance of the name and the object referred to. Indeed, this will be the case for any system of names where one can identify the bearer of the name from the position of the name in the system. I can, for example, refer to M Street in Washington simply because I know that there is in that city an alphabetical sequence of street names, "A", "B", "C", etc. I needn't have any causal connection with M Street in order to do that.[16] And the point is even clearer if we consider names of abstract entities: if I count up to 387, the numeral names the number without any causal chain connecting me and any alleged baptismal ceremony of that number.

There are plenty of acknowledged counterexamples to the claim that the causal theory gives us either necessary or sufficient conditions for the use of a proper name to refer to its bearer. Why are the authors of these theories not impressed by these examples? There is, by the way, an odd asymmetry in the role of counterexamples in these discussions: alleged counterexamples to the descriptivist theory are generally regarded as disastrous for the theory; counterexamples to the causal theory are cheerfully accepted as if they did not matter. The reason why the causal theorists are not impressed, I suspect, is that they feel that, as Kripke says explicitly, the causal theory offers a more adequate *picture* of how names work even if it cannot account for every case. After all, the counter-examples may just be odd and marginal cases and what we really want to know is what is central and essential to the operation of the institution of proper names. Furthermore, the counterexamples are not really very important to us theoretically unless they are backed by some independently motivated theory, some account of why they are counterexamples. I am in sympathy with both of these impulses and I believe we should look for the essential character of the institution and not be too impressed by odd examples, and I believe the counterexamples are only interesting if backed by a theory that explains them. Indeed, I

16 Evans, *op. cit.*, gives several examples of this sort.

would like to see counterexamples to both the causal and descriptivist theory treated with these same attitudes. The difficulty is that the counterexamples I have presented do seem to raise serious difficulties for the causal theory (or picture) and they are backed by a theory of Intentionality. In the Madagascar case the Intentionality that attaches to the name shifts the reference from the terminus of the causal chain to the object that satisfies the associated Intentional content, and in the case of locating names in systems of names the position of a name as an element in the Network gives sufficient Intentionality to secure reference for the name without any causal chain.

Let us then turn to the more important question: Does the causal theory or picture give the essential character of the institution of proper names? I think the answer is clearly no. To see this, imagine a primitive hunter-gatherer community with a language containing proper names. (And it is not at all implausible to imagine a language used by a primitive community; as far as we know it was in such communities that human languages evolved in the first place.) Imagine that everybody in the tribe knows everybody else and that newborn members of the tribe are baptized at ceremonies attended by the entire tribe. Imagine, furthermore, that as the children grow up they learn the names of people as well as the local names of mountains, lakes, streets, houses, etc., by ostension. Suppose also that there is a strict taboo in this tribe against speaking of the dead, so that no one's name is ever mentioned after his death. Now the point of the fantasy is simply this: As I have described it, this tribe has an institution of proper names used for reference in exactly the same way that our names are used for reference, but *there is not a single use of a name in the tribe that satisfies the causal chain of communication theory.* As I have described it there is not a single chain of communication of the sort favored by Kripke, Donnellan, and others. Every use of the name in this tribe as I described it satisfies the descriptivist claim that there is an Intentional content associating the name with the object. In this case we are to suppose that the people are taught the names by ostension and that they learn to recognize their fellow tribe members, mountains, houses, etc. The teaching sets up an Intentional content which the object satisfies.[17]

17 It does not, of course, set up a definition, for reasons I gave in 'Proper names', *Mind*, vol. 67 (1958), pp. 166–73.

It seems to me that the causal theorist might make the following reply: The spirit of the causal theory is kept in this example, because though there is no chain of *communication* there is nonetheless a *causal* connection between the acquisition of the name and the object named because the object is presented ostensively. The answer to that is twofold. First, the kind of causal connection that teaches the use of the name is straightforward Intentional causation; it is not externalist at all. That is, the kind of causal connection that is set up in these cases is a descriptivist causal connection. When I say "Baxter", I mean the man I am able to *recognize as* Baxter or the man to whom I was *introduced as* Baxter, or the man whom I *saw* baptized as Baxter, and in each of these cases the causal element implied by the italicized term is Intentional causation. In every case the causal condition is part of the Intentional content associated with the name. And notice that what counts is not the fact that I give a *verbal* description, but that there is an Intentional content.

If the causal theory is to be an alternative to the descriptivist theory, the causation in question must not be descriptivist, it must not be internal, otherwise the causal theory is just a variant of the descriptivist theory. It just amounts to the claim that descriptivism includes some, e.g., perceptual, elements in the Intentional content associated with the use of the name. But, secondly, we needn't even suppose that all of the names in the community are introduced by ostension. As Kripke concedes, there may be names in the community that are introduced purely by description. Suppose that the astronomers and meteorologists of the community are able to predict storms and astronomical events in the future and that they attach proper names to these future events and phenomena. These names are taught to all the members of the community purely by description and there isn't any question of the events causing the names because the events are in the future. Now here it seems to me is a community that satisfies all of the conditions essential for having proper names and having the institution of proper names that function to refer in the way that our proper names function to refer, but there is not a single use of a proper name that satisfies the story, picture, or theory of the causal theorists.

If we so easily describe an example of an entire community that satisfies the conditions for using proper names but does not satisfy the conditions laid down by the causal theory, how are we to account for the fact that the theory has seemed so plausible to so many philosophers? What are we to make of this dispute? Notice that in neither Donnellan nor in Kripke was the causal theory presented as the result of some independently motivated account of the use of names, rather it was presented as a briefly sketched alternative to the descriptivist theory. The main thrust of both arguments was in attempting to refute descriptivism, and if we are to understand what is going on in this dispute we must now turn to that theory.

III. THE DESCRIPTIVIST ACCOUNT OF PROPER NAMES

You will not understand the descriptivist theories unless you understand the views they were originally opposed to. At the time I wrote 'Proper names'[18] in 1955 there were three standard views of names in the philosophical literature: Mill's view that names have no connotation at all but simply a denotation, Frege's view that the meaning of a name is given by a single associated definite description, and what might be called the standard logic textbook view that the meaning of a name "N" is simply "called N". Now the first and third of these views seem to be obviously inadequate. If the problem of a theory of proper names is to answer the question, "In virtue of what does the speaker in the utterance of a name succeed in referring to a particular object?", then Mill's account is simply a refusal to answer the question; it simply says that the name refers to the object, and that's that. But the third answer is also defective. As I wrote in *Speech Acts*,

> the description, "The man called X" will not do, or at any rate will not do by itself, as a satisfaction of the principle of identification. For if you ask me, "Whom do you mean by X?" and I answer, "The man called X", even if it were true that there is only one man who is called X, I am simply saying that he is the man whom other people refer to by the name "X". But if they refer to him by the name "X" then they must also be prepared to substitute an identifying description for "X" and if they in turn

18 *Op. cit.*

substitute "the man called X", the question is only carried a stage further and cannot go on indefinitely without circularity or infinite regress. My reference to an individual may be parasitic on someone else's but this parasitism cannot be carried on indefinitely if there is to be any reference at all.

For this reason it is no answer at all to the question of what if anything is the sense of a proper name "X" to say its sense or part of its sense is "called X". One might as well say that part of the meaning of "horse" is "called a horse". It is really quite amazing how often this mistake is made.[19]

Perhaps equally amazing is that Kripke makes this same point,[20] even using the same example of "horse" as if it were an objection or difficulty for the description theory, when in fact it was one of the fundamental theses of the theory, at least in its recent formulations. Notice, however, that the above passage does not imply that one cannot refer to an object by a name "N" when the only identifying description one has of the object is "called 'N'", rather it says that this by itself cannot be a complete account of how proper names refer, for such identifying descriptions are dependent on there being some other identifying descriptions of a completely different sort. The polemical aim of the passage was to attack the standard logic textbook view, not for giving a false account of how reference is secured but for giving an account which is incomplete and lacking in explanatory power. Often, in fact, one does make what I called parasitic references using a proper name: often the only identifying description one associates with a name "N" is simply the "object called N in my community or by my interlocutors". In such a case, my use of the name is parasitic on other speakers' use of the name in the sense that my reference, using a name to which I can attach only the Intentional content "called N", is successful only if there are now or have been other people who use or have used the name "N" and attach a semantic or Intentional content of a completely different sort. (And remember, "identifying description" does not imply "in words", it simply means: Intentional content, including Network

19 *Op. cit.*, pp. 170–1.
20 Kripke, *op. cit.*, pp. 283–4.

and Background, sufficient to identify the object, and that content may or may not be in words.) Thus, for example, if all I know about Plotinus is that I have heard other people talk about somebody using the name "Plotinus", I can still refer to Plotinus using "Plotinus", but my ability to do that is parasitic on other speakers.

Frege's account, then, is the most promising, and it was that account I sought to develop. Its chief merit is that Frege sees that with proper names, as with any term capable of referring, there must be some Intentional content in virtue of which it refers. Its chief demerits are that he seems to have thought that semantic content was always in words, specifically definite descriptions, and that the description gave a definition or sense of the name. One additional virtue of the Fregean account, and the account I tried to develop, is that they enable us to answer certain puzzling questions concerning the occurrence of proper names in identity statements, in existential statements, and in intensional-with-an-s statements about Intentional states, and, as far as I can see, no causal theorist to date has given a satisfactory answer to these questions.

Now in the light of this brief sketch of the motivations for the descriptivist theory let us have another look at the causal theory. From the point of view of the descriptivist theory, what the causal analysis amounts to is the following: *the "causal chain of communication" is simply a characterization of the parasitic cases seen from an external point of view.* Let me try to make this clear. Kripke says that at each link in the chain of communication the speaker must have the intention, "when I utter 'N' I mean to refer to the same object as the person from whom I got the name 'N'". The descriptivist says that one sort of identifying description that one can attach to a name "N" is "the person referred to by others in my linguistic community as 'N'". Both sides agree that this is not enough by itself: Kripke insists that the chain must terminate in an initial baptism; the descriptivist allows for a variety of ways in which it can terminate, of which an initial baptism is one. Where is the difference? As far as the issue between descriptivism and the causal theory is concerned there is no difference: Kripke's theory is just a variant form of descriptivism. But what about the causal chain? Doesn't the causal theory require an external causal chain that guarantees successful reference? *The external causal chain plays no explanatory role whatever in either Kripke's or Donnellan's account,* as I will explain shortly. The only chain that matters is a transfer of Intentional content from one use of an expression to the next, in every case reference is secured in virtue of descriptivist Intentional content in the mind of the speaker who uses the expression. This will become clearer when we turn to the alleged counterexamples, but you can see it already in Kripke's characterization: Suppose that there is an initial baptism of a mountain with the name "N" and then a chain with ten links, each of a person who utters "N" intending to use it to refer to whatever the person he got it from used it. Assuming there is no intervening Intentionality, no other beliefs, etc., about N, this by itself is sufficient to guarantee that each person refers to the initial target of the baptism solely in virtue of the fact that there is one and only one object that satisfies or fits his or her Intentional content. After the speaker who made the initial baptism, subsequent Intentional contents are parasitic on the prior ones for achieving reference. Of course there will be an external causal characterization of the chain, and an omniscient observer could observe Mr. One talking to Mrs. Two and so on down to Mr. Ten, and he could describe a sequence of events without mentioning any Intentionality, without any mention of descriptive content. But the sequence of features characterized by the external observer are not what secures reference. Reference, for Kripke, is secured entirely by descriptive content.

The way to test which feature is doing the work, descriptive content or causal chain, is to vary one while holding the other constant and see what happens. Suppose that Miss Seven decides to use the name not to refer to the same thing as the person from whom she got it but to refer to her pet poodle instead. Externally described, the chain of communication can be exactly the same: the name "N" goes from One to Ten, but the shift in Intentional content means that Seven, Eight, Nine, and Ten are referring to a poodle and not a mountain, solely because the poodle and not the mountain satisfies their identifying description (this is much like the Madagascar example). Or, conversely, imagine that the chain is one of constant descriptive content, each parasitic on the prior speaker back to the initial baptism, but vary the external causal story in any way you like and this still will not affect the reference. Now which is doing the work, Intentionality or "ordinary physical causation"?

In response to the suggestion that the descriptivist can easily accommodate their account, Kripke, Donellan, and Devitt all insist that on the descriptivist view the speaker would have to remember from whom he got the name. But this seems to me plainly false. I can (and do), for example, make parasitic references using the name "Plotinus" in the manner I considered above without remembering from whom I got the name. I just intend to refer to the same person as the person (whoever that may be) from whom I got the name, in accordance with Kripke's version of descriptivism.

But why does it matter? What difference does it make whether the chain is described by way of Intentional content or external physical causation? Because the issue, to repeat, is whether reference succeeds in virtue of the fact that the object referred to fits or satisfies some associated description or whether reference is achieved by virtue of some facts about the world quite in-dependently of how those facts are represented in the mind: some condition which the utterance of the expression meets which is independent of the contents of any associated description. Kripke and Donellan claim to be arguing against the conception of reference by way of associated Intentional content and in favor of external causal conditions. I am arguing that to the extent that their account works, it works because it is descriptivist; the external causal chain plays no explanatory role. And I am not saying that their account can be forced into the descriptivist mould, but that when closely scrutinized the very account they offer is descriptivist on its face. We should not be surprised that they have so little to say about causation. It plays no role in their accounts. To see this further let us turn to Donnellan.

> Suppose someone says 'Socrates was snub-nosed', and we ask to whom he is referring. The central idea is that this calls for a historical explanation; we search not for an individual who might best fit the speaker's descriptions of the individual to whom he takes himself to be referring . . . but rather for an individual *historically related* to his use of the name 'Socrates' on this occasion. It might be that an omniscient observer of history would see an individual related to an author of dialogues, that one of the central characters of these dialogues was *modelled* upon that individual, that these dialogues have been handed

down and that the speaker has read translations of them, that the speaker's now predicating snub-nosedness of something is *explained by* his having read these translations. . . . 'What individual, if any, would the speaker describe in this way, even perhaps mistakenly?' (my italics).[21]

This passage seems to me to give a very reasonable account – the question it leaves us is: What is the omniscient observer supposed to look for and why? What considerations does he make in deciding "what individual, if any, would the speaker describe in this way"? Since there are an indefinite number of "historical relations" there must be some principle for selecting those that are relevant. What is it? I think that the answer is implicit in the passage. We are to take two sets of Intentional contents as decisive. First, the author of the dialogues *modelled* one of the central characters on an actual individual, that is, the author had a representation of the individual in question and intended the name "Socrates" in the dialogue to refer to him. Second, the speaker, having read the dialogues, intended his use of "Socrates" to refer to the same person that the author of the dialogues referred to. The speaker in his turn will pick up a lot of extra descriptions from the dialogues and these may or may not be true of the man he is referring to.

Now, if we ask the man, "Whom do you mean by 'Socrates'?", he might give us some of these descriptions, and, as Donnellan points out, these descriptions might not be true of the man referred to as "Socrates" by the author of the dialogues but true of someone else, say the author himself. Suppose the man says, "By 'Socrates' I mean the man who invented the method of dialogue", and suppose the author of the dialogues invented it himself and modestly attributed it to Socrates. Now if we then say, "All the same the man was really referring to the person referred to by the author as 'Socrates' and not to the man who *in fact* invented the dialogue method", we are committed to the view that the speaker's Intentional content, "I am referring to the same man as the author of the dialogues referred to", takes precedence over his content, "I am referring to the inventor of the dialogue method". When he gave us the latter answer, he gave it to us on the assumption that one and the same man satisfied both. If they come apart, that is, if each Intentional content is satisfied by a different person, it is up to the speaker which one takes precedence. The speaker expressed a fragment of his Network of Intentional contents. If that fragment doesn't fit the object which satisfies the rest of the Network, the omniscient observer will, quite reasonably, suppose that the rest of the Network takes precedence. He is referring to the historical Socrates even if he gave a false description, but that supposition is a supposition about how the man's Intentional content determines reference. Thus on both Kripke's and Donnellan's accounts the conditions of successful reference are descriptivist right down to the ground.

IV. DIFFERENCES BETWEEN THE TWO ACCOUNTS

Though both the "descriptivist" and the "causal" theories are at bottom descriptivist, there are still several important differences between them.

1. According to the causal theory the transfer of Intentionality in the chain of communication is really the essence of the institution of proper names. According to the descriptivist it is just an incidental feature. It is not the essential or defining trait of the institution at all. And the purpose of the parable of the hunter-gatherer community was to make just this point: the tribe has the institution of proper names to refer, but there are no chains of communication, no parasitic references. Another way to make the same point is to see that though parasitic reference is always possible for proper names this sort of parasitism is also possible for any word at all that expresses an Intentional content, including general terms. Consider, for example, the words "structuralism" and "structuralist". For a long time I had only the haziest of ideas what these words meant. I knew that structuralism was some kind of fashionable theory, but that was about the limit of my knowledge. Still, given my Network and Background, I could use the word "structuralism" in a parasitic way; I could, for example, ask, "Are there still a lot of structuralists in France?", or, "Is Pierre a structuralist?" And notice that this parasitism is not restricted to natural kind terms of the sort Putnam talks about. It wasn't a case

of identifying passing structuralists ostensively by their surface appearance and hoping that one day scientific investigation would reveal their true nature. As far as this difference between the descriptivist and causal theory is concerned, the argument would appear to favor the descriptivist claim that chains of communication are not the essential feature of the institution of proper names, though both sides would agree that they do in fact commonly occur.

2. The descriptivist finds it very implausible to suppose that in the chains of communication, when they do occur, the only Intentionality which secures reference is that each speaker intends to refer to the same object as the previous speaker. In real life a whole lot of information gets transferred in the chain of communication and some of this information will be relevant to securing reference. For example, the *type* of thing named by the name – whether it is a mountain or a man or a moose or whatever – is generally associated with the name even in the parasitic cases; and if the speaker is wildly mistaken about this we are disinclined to say that he really succeeded in referring. Suppose, for example, that he hears a discussion about Socrates's philosophy of mathematics and he confusedly supposes that "Socrates" is the name of an odd number. Suppose he says "I think Socrates is not a prime but is divisible by 17". He satisfies Kripke's version of the causal theory, but he is not successful in referring to Socrates. Furthermore, where the initial target of the baptism is not identical with the object that satisfies the associated nonparasitic content we don't always construe the reference as going to the initial target. In the Madagascar case, each speaker we suppose intended to refer to the same object as the previous speaker, but Marco Polo introduced some new Intentional content that took precedence over the chain of communication. He identified an island and not a portion of the African continent.

It is a little-noticed but absurd consequence of Kripke's view that it sets no constraints at all on what the name might turn out to refer to. Thus, for example, it might turn out that by "Aristotle" I am referring to a bar stool in Joe's Pizza Place in Hoboken in 1957 if that is what the causal chain happened to lead to. I want to say: by "Aristotle" I couldn't be referring to a bar stool, because that is not what I mean by "Aristotle". And Kripke's remarks about essentialism are not enough to block this result for they are all *de re* necessities attaching to objects themselves but not attaching any restrictive Intentional content to the use of the name. Thus, even if it is a *de re* metaphysical necessity that the actual man had a certain mother and father, that tells us nothing at all about how the name refers to that man and not to a bar stool.

3. In general the descriptivist is inclined to prefer the first order Intentional content and see the parasitic cases as less important; the causal theorist emphasizes the parasitic identifying description. The germ of truth in the causal theory seems to me this: For names of objects where we are not directly acquainted with the object we will often tend to give precedence to the parasitic Intentional content. For example, for names of remote historical figures, e.g., Napoleon or Socrates, or famous people, e.g., Nixon, given a conflict between the first order Intentional content and the parasitic we will usually prefer the latter. Why? Because the chain of parasitic Intentionality will get us back to the original target of the baptism and that we are usually, though not always, inclined to think is what matters. In this respect, proper names differ from general terms. Since the point of having proper names is just to refer to objects, not to describe them, it often doesn't really matter to us much what descriptive content is used to identify the object as long as it identifies the right object, where the "right object" is just the one that other people use the name to refer to.

V. ALLEGED COUNTEREXAMPLES TO DESCRIPTIVISM

With this discussion in mind let us turn to the counterexamples. The counterexamples I have seen to the descriptivist theory fail in general because the authors look only at what the agent might *say* and not at the *total Intentional content* he has in his head, and also because they neglect the role of the Network and the Background. Each counterexample is designed to show that a speaker will refer to an object in the utterance of a name even though the associated definite description is not satisfied by that object or is satisfied by something else or by nothing. I will show that in each case reference is achieved only because the object satisfies the Intentional content in the mind of the speaker.

Example 1: The Gödel/Schmidt case (Kripke)

The only thing Jones knows or thinks he knows about Kurt Gödel is that he is the author of the famous incompleteness proof. But suppose, in fact, that the proof was written by another man, Schmidt. Now when we ask Jones for an identifying description of "Gödel" he says, "the author of the proof of the incompleteness of arithmetic". But in fact when Jones uses "Gödel" he is referring to Gödel and not to the man who satisfies his description. It is obvious from what I have said that the correct account of this case is that Jones has quite a bit more Intentional content than just the description he gives. At the very least he has "the man called 'Gödel' in my linguistic community or at least by those from whom I got the name". The reason he doesn't give this as an answer when asked for an identifying description is that he assumes that something more than this is wanted. This much Intentionality is already possessed by whoever asked him for the identifying description.

It is characteristic of these discussions that the authors too seldom give us the sentences in which we are supposed to imagine the name occurring, but if we consider actual sentences, this example could go in either direction. Suppose Jones says, "On line 17 of his proof, Gödel makes what seems to me to be a fallacious inference", and suppose we ask him who he means by "Gödel". He responds, "I mean the author of the famous incompleteness theorem", and we, then, say, "Well, in fact, Gödel did not prove that theorem, it was originally proven by Schmidt". Now what does Jones say? It seems to me that he might well say that by "Gödel" he just means the author of the incompleteness proof regardless of what he is, in fact, called. Kripke concedes that there could be such uses. They involve what I have called secondary aspect uses of proper names.[22] But Jones needn't say that. He might say, "I was referring to the man whom I have heard called 'Kurt Gödel', regardless of whether or not he proved the incompleteness of arithmetic". On the other hand suppose Jones says, "Kurt Gödel lived in Princeton". In this case, it seems to me

---

22 'Referential and attributive', in *Expression and Meaning*, p. 148.

much more likely that if he finds that Gödel does not satisfy the non-parasitic definite description that he attached to the name he would simply fall back on the parasitic Intentional content that he attaches to the name. But in either case it is the speaker's Intentional content that determines reference. It is not enough to look just at what a speaker says in response to a particular question, one has to look at his total Intentional content, as well as Background capacities associated with a name and at what he would say if informed that different parts of that content were satisfied by different objects. There seems to me nothing in this example that need bother the descriptivist.

Example 2: Thales the well digger (Donnellan)[23]

Suppose that all that a certain speaker knows or thinks he knows about Thales is that he is the Greek philosopher who said that all is water. But suppose there never was a Greek philosopher who said such a thing. Suppose that Aristotle and Herodotus were referring to a well digger who said, "I wish all were water so I wouldn't have to dig these damned wells". In such a case, according to Donnellan, when the speaker uses the name "Thales" he is referring to that well digger. Furthermore, suppose there was a hermit who never had any dealings with anyone, who actually held that all was water. Still, when we say "Thales" we are plainly not referring to that hermit.

There are really two aspects to this argument: one about the hermit, the other about the well digger. On the surface, the well digger case is formally similar to the Gödel/Schmidt case. The speaker always has his parasitic Intentional content to fall back on if his associated description is satisfied by some object that doesn't fit the rest of his Intentional content. However, this case also raises the separate issue of how the Network of the speaker's beliefs will set some further constraints on the chain of parasitic Intentionality. Suppose that Herodotus had heard a frog at the bottom of a well making croaking noises that sounded like the Greek for "all is water"; suppose further that this frog is a family pet named "Thales", and that this incident is the origin of the view that somebody held that all is water. When I use the name "Thales",

23 'Proper names and identifying descriptions', *Synthese*, vol. 21 (1970), pp. 335–58.

taking myself to be referring to a Greek philosopher, am I referring to that frog? I think not. Similar doubts could be raised about the well digger: I can think of sentences where I would be inclined to say that I was referring to the well digger and other sentences in which I would be inclined to say that I failed to refer to anyone because there was no such person as Thales the philosopher.

But in the cases in which I am referring to a well digger I do so because the well digger satisfies enough of my descriptive content; in particular, he satisfies the content, "The person referred to as 'Thales' by the people from whom I got this use of the name", that is, he satisfies the parasitic Intentional content of the sort we mentioned before. In the case of the hermit, the reason we feel no inclination at all to say we are referring to him with the name "Thales" is that he does not satisfy the condition of fitting into the relevant Network of Intentionality. When we say "Thales is the Greek philosopher who held that all is water", we don't just mean *anybody* who held that all is water, we mean that person who was known to other Greek philosophers as arguing that all is water, who was referred to in his time or subsequently by some Greek variant or predecessor of the expression we now pronounce as "Thales", whose works and ideas have come down to us posthumously through the writings of other authors, and so on. Now, to repeat, in all these cases there will be an external causal account of how we got that information, but what secures reference is not the external causal chain, but the sequence of the transfer of Intentional contents. The reason we are not tempted to allow the hermit to qualify as Thales is that he simply does not fit into the Network and the Background. This example is somewhat analogous to the example of the humanoid who invented bifocals 80 billion years before Benjamin Franklin was ever alive. When he said Franklin invented bifocals, we meant: relative to our Network and Background.

Example 3: The two patches (Donnellan)[24]

Suppose a man sees two identical colored patches on a screen, one above the other. Suppose he names the top one "*A*" and the bottom one "*B*". The only identifying description he can give for

---

24 'Proper names and identifying descriptions', *op. cit.*, pp. 347ff.

A is "the one on top". But suppose that, unknown to him, we have given him inverting lenses so that the one he thinks is on top is really on the bottom and vice versa. In such a case the identifying description he can give is actually false of the object referred to, yet his reference to A is nonetheless successful.

I will deal with this example rather swiftly. A is the one he actually sees right *there*. It is the one causing *this* visual experience. You couldn't ask for a better 'identifying description' than that. Expressions like "the one on top" are strictly for public consumption, and though one can imagine cases in which they would take precedence over the Intentional presentation, in most cases the presentational content is primary. In short, his Intentional content either in perception or in memory is sufficient to pick out A. But suppose that he forgets that he saw it. Suppose he even forgets that he thought it was on top. He just remembers that the name named a patch. Can't he still use the name to refer to the patch? Of course. There is no reason why a parasitic Intentional content might not depend on one's own earlier Intentional contents. Now A is just identified as "the one I was previously able to identify as 'A'", a limiting case, perhaps, but nonetheless a possible one.

Example 4: The twin earth (Putnam et al.)[25]

The correct account of how a name secures reference for us here on earth cannot be that it does it by way of an associated descriptive content, because if there were a twin earth our names would still refer to objects on our earth and not to objects on twin earth, even though any description of an object on earth would equally well fit its *Doppelgänger* on twin earth. In order to account for how reference thus succeeds unambiguously on earth we have to recognize the role of external causal links between utterances and objects.

I have already answered this sort of objection in Chapter 2 concerning perception and in Chapter 8 concerning indexical expressions. For the case of proper names it suffices to say that the

25 H. Putnam, 'The meaning of meaning', in *Philosophical Papers*, vol. 2, *Mind, Language and Reality* (Cambridge: Cambridge University Press, 1975), pp. 215–71.

causal self-referentiality of all perceptual forms of Intentionality, the self-referentiality of indexical forms of Intentionality, and in general the way we are indexically related to our own Intentional contents, including the Network and Background, is sufficient to block any possible twin earth ambiguities. We can see this even in the parasitic cases. When, for example, I say that the only description I associate with "Plotinus" is "called Plotinus", I don't mean just any object ever called "Plotinus" by someone. I mean, inter alia, rather the *person* that *I* have heard and read referred to as Plotinus. The fact that a *Doppelgänger* on twin earth could also be called "Plotinus" is as irrelevant as the fact that somebody might have (and no doubt somebody has) named his dog "Plotinus", or that many other people have been called "Plotinus".

VI. MODAL ARGUMENTS

This book is about Intentionality and not about modality, and I have therefore avoided the modal issues up to this point. However, some philosophers think that Kripke's modal arguments are decisive against any version of descriptivism, so I will therefore digress at least briefly to consider them.

Frege had argued that the definite description that a speaker associated with a proper name provided the "sense", in his technical meaning of that word, of the proper name for that speaker. I argued against Frege that the associated definite description couldn't provide a sense or definition of the proper name because that would have as consequence that, for example, it was an analytic necessity that Aristotle was the most famous teacher of Alexander, if a speaker associated the definite description, "the most famous teacher of Alexander the Great", as the sense of the proper name "Aristotle". I argued that the associated cluster of Intentional contents that speakers associate with a proper name is related to the name by some much weaker relation than definition, and that this approach would preserve the virtues of Frege's account while avoiding its absurd consequences. Kripke begins his criticism of my account by distinguishing descriptivism construed as a theory of reference from descriptivism construed as a theory of meaning, and by claiming that if descriptivism is construed only as a theory of reference, a theory of how reference with proper names is secured, then it is unable to provide a Fregean solution to the puzzles concerning proper names in identity statements, existential statements, and statements concerning propositional attitudes. He doesn't say anything in support of this latter claim, and in any case it seems to me plainly false. I try to show that proper names don't have definitions in the usual sense but that reference is secured by an associated Intentional content. Thus, in Kripke's terms I am providing a theory of reference but not a theory of meaning. However, the distinction is not as sharp as he suggests, for the following reason: the Intentional content associated with a proper name can figure as part of the *propositional content* of a statement made by a speaker using that name, even though the speaker's associated Intentional content is not part of the *definition* of the name. And that is why one can provide a descriptivist theory of how proper names secure reference (and hence give a theory of reference and not a theory of meaning for proper names) while at the same time showing that the methods by which proper names secure reference explain how the meaning of utterances made using those names contains descriptive content (and hence give an account of names which has consequences for the meanings of propositions containing those names). For example, on the descriptivist account a speaker can believe that Hesperus shines near the horizon while not believing that Phosphorus shines near the horizon, even though Hesperus and Phosphorus are identical. A speaker can consistently believe this if he associates independent Intentional contents with each name, even though in neither case does the Intentional content provide a definition of the name. The cluster theory, so-called, is able to account for such puzzles while at the same time advancing the theory as an account of how reference is secured and not as an account of meaning in the strict and narrow Fregean sense.

Indeed the account I am providing suggests the direction for a solution to Kripke's "puzzle about belief".[26] Here is the puzzle: Suppose a bilingual speaker, not knowing that "Londres" and "London" name the same city, sincerely asserts in French

---

26 S. Kripke, 'A puzzle about belief', in A. Margalit (ed.), *Meaning and Use* (Dordrecht: Reidel 1976), pp. 239–83.

"Londres est jolie" and yet also sincerely asserts in English "London is not pretty". Does he or does he not believe that London is pretty? The first step in solving the puzzle is to note that because the speaker associates different Intentional contents with "Londres" and "London" the contribution that each word makes to the proposition in the man's head is different and therefore he believes two propositions which, though they cannot both be true (because they refer to the same object and attribute inconsistent properties to it), are not contradictories. The case is analogous to the Hesperus–Phosphorus example.[27]

The main modal argument used against my account is the rigid designator argument. In its crudest versions the argument goes as follows:

(1) Proper names are rigid designators

(2) Definite descriptions are not rigid designators; and, by parity of reasoning, Intentional contents are not rigid designators,

therefore,

(3) Proper names are not equivalent in meaning or sense or functioning to definite descriptions or Intentional contents of any sort.

Even if we grant the first premise for the sake of the discussion, it seems to me the argument fails for two reasons. First, some definite descriptions are indeed rigid designators. Indeed, any definite description that expresses identity conditions for the object, that is, any description which specifies features which determine the

---

27 Kripke considers the approach I suggest but rejects it on what I believe are inadequate grounds. He thinks that the same puzzle could arise if the speaker associated the same "identifying properties" with each name without knowing that they were the same. The speaker thinks, for example, in English "London is in England", and in French "Londres est en Angleterre", without knowing that England is Angleterre. But once again if we look at the total Intentional content we suppose is in the man's head in order to imagine him saying "Londres est jolie" and simultaneously "London is not pretty", we must suppose that he has different Intentional contents associated with "London" and "Londres". At the very least we must suppose that he thinks they are two *different* cities and that, by itself, has all sorts of ramifications in his Network: e.g., he thinks "is identical with Londres" to be false of the town he refers to as "London", while true of that town he refers to as "Londres"; he thinks London and Londres have different locations on the surface of the earth, different inhabitants, etc. The moral as usual is: to resolve the puzzle don't just look at the sentences he utters, look at the total Intentional content in the man's head.

identity of the object will be a rigid designator. Any description expressing properties necessary and sufficient for, for example, being identical with Aristotle, will be a rigid designator. Indeed, it was this feature that I was trying to get at in my earliest discussion of proper names when I said the question of the rule for using a name must be connected to the question of the *identity* of the object.[28] But second, and more important for this discussion, any definite description at all can be treated as a rigid designator by indexing it to the actual world. I can, by simple fiat, decide to use the expression "The inventor of bifocals" in such a way that it refers to the actual person who invented bifocals and continues to refer to that very person in any possible world, even in a possible world in which he did not invent bifocals.[29] Such a use of the definite description will always take wide scope or will be in a sense scopeless in the way that is characteristic of proper names. Since any definite description whatever can be made into a rigid designator, it does not show that the functioning of proper names differs from the function of definite descriptions to show that proper names are always (or almost always) rigid designators and definite descriptions are in general not rigid designators.

VII. HOW DO PROPER NAMES WORK?

I said at the beginning that the answer to this question ought to be fairly easy, and I think it is provided that we keep certain principles in mind. The facts we seek to explain are: Names are used to refer to objects. In general, the contribution that a name makes to the truth conditions of statements is simply that it is used to refer to an object. But there are some statements where the contribution of the name is not, or is not solely, that it is used to refer to an object: in identity statements, in existential statements, and in statements about Intentional states. Furthermore, a name is used to refer to the same object in different possible worlds where it has different properties from those it has in the actual world.

---

28 In *Mind* (1958), *op. cit.*

29 A similar point is made by D. Kaplan with his notion of "Dthat" ('Dthat', in P. Cole (ed.), *Syntax and Semantics*, vol. 9 (New York, 1978)) and by A. Plantinga with his notion of an "Alpha transform" (in 'The Boethian compromise', *American Philosophical Quarterly*, vol. 15, no. 2 (April 1978), pp. 129–38).

The principles we need to keep in mind when we explain these facts are:

1. In order that a name should ever come to be used to refer to an object in the fist place there must be some independent representation of the object. This may be by way of perception, memory, definite description, etc., but there must be enough Intentional content to identify which object the name is attached to.

2. Once the connection between name and object has been set up, speakers who have mastered the Background practice of using names may make use of the fact that the connection between name and object has been set up, without knowing anything more about the object. Provided they don't have any Intentional content wildly inconsistent with the facts about the object, their only Intentional content might be that they are using the name to refer to what others are using it to refer to, but such cases are parasitic on the non-parasitic forms of identification of the object.

3. All reference is a virtue of Intentional content (broadly construed), whether the reference is by way of names, descriptions, indexicals, tags, labels, pictures, or whatever. The object is referred to only if it fits or satisfies some condition or set of conditions expressed by or associated with the device that is used to refer to it. In the limiting case these conditions may be simple Background capacities for recognition, as, for example, in the case we considered in Chapter 2 where the only Intentional content that a man had associated with the name was simply his capacity to recognize the bearer, or they may be parasitic Intentional contents of the sort described in principle 2. Principles 1 and 2 are simply applications of principle 3.

4. What counts as an object and hence as a possible target for naming and referring is always determined relative to a system of representation. Given that we have a system rich enough to individuate objects (e.g., rich enough to count one horse, a second horse, a third horse . . .), and to identify and reidentify objects (e.g., rich enough to determine what must be the case if that is to be the *same horse* as the one we saw yesterday), we can then attach names to objects in such a way as to preserve the attachment of the same names to the same objects, even in counterfactual situations where the Intentional content associated with the name is no longer satisfied by the object. Principles 1, 2, and 3 only have

application in a representational system which satisfies principle 4.

I believe these principles explain the facts we mentioned above. The whole purpose of having the institution of proper names is to enable us to refer to objects, but since there will be some Intentional content associated with a name this Intentional content can figure as part of the propositional content of a statement made using a name in identity statements, in existential statements, and in statements about Intentional states, even though the normal and primary function is not to express Intentional content but just to refer to objects, and even though the associated Intentional content is not part of the definition of the name. And the explanation of the fact that names can be introduced by and used with an Intentional content which is not a rigid designator, and still the name can be used as a rigid designator, is simply that we have a notion of the identity of an object which is separable from those particular Intentional contents which are used to identify the object. Thus, for example, we have a notion of *the same man* which is independent of such descriptions as the author of the *Odyssey*. We can then use the name "Homer" to refer to the man who was the actual author of the *Odyssey* even in possible worlds where Homer did not write the *Odyssey*.

Part of the appearance that there is something especially problematic about these rather simple explanations is that there is a family of different sorts of cases in which these principles operate. First, the central cases. The most important and extensive use of names for each of us is of people, places, etc., with which we are in daily, or at least frequent, personal contact. Baptism apart, one originally learns these names from other people, but, once learned, the name is associated with such a rich collection of Intentional contents in the Network that one does not depend on other people to determine which object one is referring to. Think, for example, of the names of your close friends and family members, of the town where you live or the streets in your neighborhood. Here there is no question of any chain of communication. Examples of such names for me would be "Berkeley, California" or "Alan Code".

Second, there are names which have prominent uses, where the uses are not based on acquaintance with the object. The Intentional content associated with these names is for the most part derived from other people, but it is rich enough to qualify as *knowledge about* the object. Examples for me would be such names as "Japan" or "Charles de Gaulle". In such cases, the Intentional content is rich enough so that it sets very strong constraints on the sort of things that could be referred to by my uses of the names. For example, regardless of the chain of communication, it couldn't turn out that by "de Gaulle" I am referring to a Florentine tapestry, or by "Japan" I am referring to a butterfly.

Third, there are uses of names where one is almost totally dependent on other people's prior usage to secure reference. It is these cases that I have described as parasitic, for in these cases the speaker does not have enough Intentional content to qualify as knowledge about the object. The object may not even be generally referred to by the name that he has acquired for it. For me such a name would be "Plotinus". Even in these cases the limited Intentional content places some constraints on the type of object named. In my use, Plotinus couldn't have turned out to be a prime number.

Chapter 10

EPILOGUE: INTENTIONALITY AND THE BRAIN

Throughout this book I have avoided discussing the issues that are most prominent in contemporary discussions of the philosophy of mind. I have said next to nothing about behaviorism, functionalism, physicalism, dualism, or any of the other attempts to solve the "mind–body" or "mind–brain" problem. Still, there is in my account an implicit view of the relation of mental phenomena to the brain, and I want to end by making it explicit.

My own approach to mental states and events has been totally realistic in the sense that I think there really are such things as intrinsic mental phenomena which cannot be reduced to something else or eliminated by some kind of re-definition. There really are pains, tickles and itches, beliefs, fears, hopes, desires, perceptual experiences, experiences of acting, thoughts, feelings, and all the rest. Now you might think that such a claim was so obviously true as to be hardly worth making, but the amazing thing is that it is routinely denied, though usually in a disguised form, by many, perhaps most, of the advanced thinkers who write on these topics. I have seen it claimed that mental states can be entirely defined in terms of their causal relations, or that pains were nothing but machine table states of certain kinds of computer systems, or that correct attributions of Intentionality were simply a matter of the predictive success to be gained by taking a certain kind of "intentional stance" toward systems. I don't think that any of these views are even close to the truth and I have argued at length against them elsewhere.[1] This is not the place to repeat those criticisms, but I do want to call attention to some peculiar

---

1 'Minds, brains and programs', *Behavioral and Brain Science*, vol. 3 (1980), pp. 417–24; 'Intrinsic Intentionality', *Behavioral and Brain Science*, same issue, pp. 450–6; 'Analytic philosophy and mental phenomena', *Midwest Studies in Philosophy*, vol. 5 (1980), pp. 405–23.

features of these views which ought to arouse our philosophical suspicions. First, no one ever came to these views by a close scrutiny of the phenomena in question. No one ever considered his own terrible pain or his deepest worry and concluded that they were just Turing machine states or that they could be entirely defined in terms of their causes and effects or that attributing such states to themselves was just a matter of taking a certain stance toward themselves. Second, no one would think of treating other biological phenomena in this way. If one were doing a study of hands or kidneys or of the heart, one would simply assume the existence of the entities in question, and then get on with the study of their structure and function. No one would think of saying, for example, "Having a hand is just being disposed to certain sorts of behavior such as grasping" (manual behaviorism), or "Hands can be defined entirely in terms of their causes and effects" (manual functionalism), or "For a system to have a hand is just for it to be in a certain computer state with the right sorts of inputs and outputs" (manual Turing machine functionalism), or "Saying that a system has hands is just adopting a certain stance toward it" (the manual stance).

How, then, are we to explain the fact that philosophers have said such apparently strange things about the mental? An adequate answer to that question would trace the history of the philosophy of mind since Descartes. The short answer is that each of these views was not designed as much to fit the facts as to avoid dualism and to provide a solution to the apparently unsolvable mind–body problem. My brief diagnosis of the persistent anti-mentalistic tendency in recent analytic philosophy is that it is largely based on the tacit assumption that, unless there is some way to eliminate mental phenomena, naively construed, we will be left with a class of entities that lies outside the realm of serious science and with an impossible problem of relating these entities to the real world of physical objects. We will be left, in short, with all the incoherence of Cartesian dualism.

Is there another approach that does not commit one to the view that there is some class of mental entities lying outside the physical world altogether, and yet does not deny the real existence and causal efficacy of the specifically mental aspects of mental phenomena? I believe there is. In order to see that there is, we have to rid ourselves of various *a priori* pictures about how mental phenomena must be related to physical phenomena in order to describe how, as far as we know, they actually are related. And, as usual in philosophy, our problem is one of removing one set of inadequate models or paradigms of the relationship in question and substituting more adequate models and paradigms. As the first step toward doing this, I want to try to state as strongly as I can what some of the traditional difficulties for a view such as mine are supposed to be.

On my account, mental states are as real as any other biological phenomena, as real as lactation, photosynthesis, mitosis, or digestion. Like these other phenomena, mental states are caused by biological phenomena and in turn cause other biological phenomena. If one wanted a label one might call such a view "biological naturalism". But how would such a biological naturalism deal with the famous mind–body problem? Well, there is not just one mind–body problem but several – one is about other minds, one about free will, etc. – but the one that has seemed most troublesome concerns the possibility of causal relations between mental and physical phenomena. From the point of view of someone who takes this problem seriously the objection to my account could be stated as follows: "You say, for example, that an intention in action causes a bodily movement, but if the former is mental and the latter physical how could there possibly be any causal relation between them? Are we supposed to think that the mental event pushes against the axons and the dendrites or that somehow it sneaks inside the cell wall and attacks the cell nucleus? The dilemma you face is simply this: If the specifically mental aspects of mental states and events function causally as you claim, then the causal relation is totally mysterious and occult; if, on the other hand, you employ the familiar notion of causation according to which the aspects of events which are causally relevant are those described by causal laws, and according to which all causal laws are physical laws, then there can't be any causal efficacy to the mental aspects of mental states. At most there would be a class of physical events which satisfy some mental descriptions, but those descriptions are not the descriptions under which the events instantiate causal laws, and therefore they do not pick out causal aspects of the events. Either you have dualism and an unintelligible account of causation or you have an intelligible account of causation and abandon the idea of the causal efficacy of the mental in favor of some version of the identity thesis with an attendant epiphenomenalism of the mental aspects of psycho-physical events."

The picture that I have been suggesting, and the picture that I believe will eventually lead to a resolution of the dilemma, is one according to which mental states are both *caused by* the operations of the brain and *realized in* the structure of the brain (and the rest of the central nervous system). Once the possibility of mental and physical phenomena standing in both these relations is understood we have removed at least one major obstacle to seeing how mental states which are caused by brain states can also cause further brain states and mental states. One of the assumptions shared by many traditional dualists and physicalists is that by granting the reality and causal efficacy of the mental we have to deny any identity relation between mental phenomena and the brain; and, conversely, if we assert an identity relation we have to deny any causal relations between mental and physical phenomena. In J. J. C. Smart's comparison, if the burglar is *identical* with Bill Sikes, then the burglar can't be *causally correlated* with Bill Sikes[2] (but compare: the burglar's tendency to crime can be causally correlated with Bill Sikes's upbringing). As a first step to removing the dilemma we have to show how mental phenomena can satisfy both conditions.

In order to demythologize the whole mind–body problem a bit I want to start by considering some completely trivial and familiar examples of these same sorts of relations. The examples are deliberately chosen for their banality. Consider the relation of liquid properties of water to the behavior of the individual molecules. Now we cannot say of any individual molecule that it is wet, but we can say both that the liquid properties of the water are *caused by* the molecular behavior, and that they are *realized in* the collection of molecules. Let us consider each relation in turn. *Caused by:* the relation between the molecular behavior and the surface physical features of the water is clearly causal. If, for

---

2 'You cannot correlate something with itself. You correlate footprints with burglars, but not Bill Sikes the burglar with Bill Sikes the burglar.' J. J. C. Smart, 'Sensations and brain processes', in Chappell (ed.) *The Philosophy of Mind* (Englewood Cliffs, N.J.: Prentice-Hall, 1962), p. 161.

example, we alter the molecular behavior we cause the surface features to change; we get either ice or steam depending on whether the molecular movement is sufficiently slower or faster. Furthermore, the surface features of the water themselves function causally. In its liquid state water is wet, it pours, you can drink it, you can wash in it, etc. *Realized in:* the liquidity of a bucket of water is not some extra juice secreted by the H_2O molecules. When we describe the stuff as liquid we are just describing those very molecules at a higher level of description than that of the individual molecule. The liquidity, though not epiphenomenal, is realized in the molecular structure of the substance in question. So if one asked, "How can there be a causal relation between the molecular behavior and the liquidity if the same stuff is both liquid and a collection of molecules?", the answer is that there can be causal relations between phenomena at different levels in the very same underlying stuff. In fact, such a combination of relations is very common in nature: the solidity of the table I am working on and the elasticity and puncture resistance of the tires on my car are both examples of causal properties that are themselves caused by and realized in an underlying microstructure. To generalize at this point, we might say that two phenomena can be related by both causation and realization provided that they are so at different levels of description.

Now let us apply the lessons of these simple examples to the mind–body problem. Consider, for a start, the standard contemporary account of the neurophysiology of visual perception. Of course, the account is at present incomplete and our existing theory might prove to be mistaken in all sorts of fundamental ways. But the difficulties in giving a correct account are the incredible empirical and conceptual difficulties in understanding the operation of a system as complicated as the human (or mammalian) brain; there is not, in addition, a metaphysical obstacle to any such account ever being correct, or at least so I shall argue. The story *begins* with the assault of the photons on the photoreceptor cells of the retina, the familiar rods and cones. These signals are processed through at least five types of cells in the retina-photoreceptor, horizontal, bipolar, amacrine and ganglion cells. They then pass through the optic nerve to the lateral geniculate nucleus, and from there the signals are relayed to the striate cortex and then are diffused through the remarkably specialized cells of the rest of the visual cortex, the simple cells, complex cells, and hypercomplex cells of at least the three zones, 17 (the striate), 18 (visual area II), and 19 (visual area III).

Notice that this story is a causal account, it tells us how the visual experience is caused by the firing of a vast number of neurons at literally millions of synapses. But where, then, is the visual experience in this account? It is right there in the brain where these processes have been going on. That is, the visual experience is caused by the functioning of the brain in response to external optical stimulation of the visual system, but it is also realized in the structure of the brain. A story similar in form, though quite different in content, can be told about thirst. Kidney secretions of renin cause the synthesis of angiotensin, and it seems likely that this substance in turn acts on the neurons of the hypothalamus to cause thirst. There is even a certain amount of evidence that at least some kinds of thirst are localized in the hypothalamus. On such an account, thirst is caused by neural events in the hypothalamus and realized in the hypothalamus. It doesn't matter for our purposes if this account is actually the correct account of thirst, the point is that it is a possible account.

The empirical and conceptual problems of describing the relations between mental phenomena and the brain are incredibly complex, and progress, in spite of much optimistic talk, has been agonizingly slow. But the logical nature of the *kinds* of relations between the mind and the brain does not seem to me in that way at all mysterious or incomprehensible. Both visual experiences and feelings of thirst, like the liquidity of water, are genuine features of the world not to be explained away and redefined or branded as illusory. And again, like liquidity, they link on both sides of causal chains. They are both caused by underlying microphenomena, and in turn cause further phenomena. Just as the liquidity of a bucket of water is causally accounted for by the behavior of the microparticles but is nonetheless capable of functioning causally, so thirst and visual experiences are caused by series of events at the microlevel and are nonetheless capable of functioning causally.

Leibniz considers the possibility of an account such as this and rejects it on the following grounds:

And supposing that there were a machine so constructed as to think, feel, and have perception, we could conceive of it as enlarged and yet preserving the same proportions, so that we might enter it as into a mill. And this granted, we should only find on visiting it, pieces which push against another, but never anything by which to explain perception. This must be sought for, therefore, in the simple substance and not in the composite or in the machine.[3]

An exactly parallel argument to Leibniz's would be that the behavior of H_2O molecules can never explain the liquidity of water, because if we entered into the system of molecules "as into a mill we should only find on visiting it pieces which push one against another, but never anything by which to explain" liquidity. But in both cases we would be looking at the system at the wrong level. The liquidity of water is not to be found at the level of the individual molecule, nor are the visual perception and the thirst to be found at the level of the individual neuron or synapse. If one knew the principles on which the system of H_2O molecules worked, one could infer that it was in a liquid state by observing the movement of the molecules, but similarly if one knew the principles on which the brain worked one could infer that it was in a state of thirst or having a visual experience.

But this model of "caused by" and "realized in" only raises the next question, how can Intentionality function causally? Granted that Intentional states can themselves be caused by and realized in the structure of the brain, how can Intentionality itself have any causal efficacy? When I raise my arm my intention in action causes my arm to go up. This is a case of a mental event causing a physical event. But, one might ask, how could such a thing occur? My arm going up is caused entirely by a series of neuron firings. We do not know where in the brain these firings originate, but they go at some point through the motor cortex and control a series of arm muscles which contract when the appropriate neurons fire. Now what has any mental event got to do with all of this? As with our previous questions, I want to answer this one by appealing to different levels of description of a substance, where the phenomena at each of the different levels function causally; and as with our previous question I want to make clear the relations involved by considering completely banal and unproblematic examples. Con-

3 G. W. Leibniz, *Monadology*, paragraph 17.

sider the explosion in the cylinder of a four-cycle internal combustion engine. The explosion is caused by the firing of the spark plug even though both the firing and the explosion are caused by and realized in phenomena at a microlevel, at which level of description, terms like "firing" and "explosion" are entirely inappropriate. Analogously I want to say that the intention in action causes the bodily movement even though both the intention in action and the bodily movement are caused by and realized in a microstructure at which level terms like "intention in action" and "bodily movement" are inappropriate. Let us try to describe the case a little more carefully – and again it is not the particular case or its details that matter but the type of relations that are exemplified. The aspect of the spark plug firing which is causally relevant is the rise in temperature in the cylinder between the electrodes to the kindling point of the air fuel mixture. It is this rise in temperature which causes the explosion. But the rise in temperature is itself caused by and realized in the movement of individual particles between the electrodes of the spark plug. Furthermore the explosion is caused by and realized in the oxidization of individual hydrocarbon molecules. Diagrammatically it looks like this:

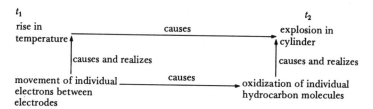

The phenomena at t_1 and t_2 respectively are the same phenomena described at different levels of description. For that reason we could also draw diagonal arrows showing that the movement of the electrons causes the explosion and the rise in the temperature causes the oxidization of hydrocarbon molecules.

Though we know little about how intentional action originates in the brain[4] we do know that neural mechanisms stimulate muscle

4 But see L. Deecke, P. Scheid, and H. H. Kornhuber, 'Distribution of readiness potential, pre-motion positivity, and motor potential of the human cerebral cortex preceding voluntary finger movements', *Experimental Brain Research*, vol. 7 (1969), pp. 158–68.

movements. Specifically they stimulate calcium ions to enter into the cytoplasm of a muscle fiber, and this triggers a series of events that result in the movement of the myosin cross bridges. These cross bridges connect myosin filaments to actin filaments. They alternately attach to actin strands, exert pressure, detach, bend back, reattach and exert more pressure.[5] This contracts the muscle. At the microlevel then we have a sequence of neuron firings which causes a series of physiological changes. At the microlevel the intention in action is caused by and realized in the neural processes, and the bodily movement is caused by and realized in the resultant physiological processes. Diagrammatically it is formally similar to the diagram of an internal combustion ignition:

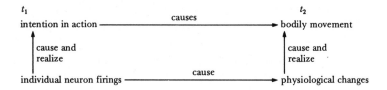

Notice that on this model, as with our earlier model, we could also draw diagonal arrows which in this case would show that the intention in action causes physiological changes and that the neuron firings cause bodily movements. Notice also that on such a model the mental phenomena are no more epiphenomenal than the rise in temperature of the firing of a spark plug.

Of course the analogies I have been using, like most analogies, are imperfect. Specifically, it might be objected that the accounts of liquidity, solidity, etc., fit into a well-established spatio-temporal conception of how the world works in a way that any account of mental states and events could not; that in making the analogy I pretend that mental states have a feature that in fact they lack, namely, well-defined spatial locations. But is this objection really so devastating? I think it rests on our present ignorance of how the brain works. Suppose we had a perfect science of the brain, so that we knew in detail how brain functions produced mental states and events. If we had a perfect knowledge of how the brain produced,

---

5 Neil R. Carlson, *Physiology of Behavior* (Boston: Allen and Bacon, Inc., 1977), pp. 256ff.

for example, thirst or visual experiences, we would have no hesitation in assigning these experiences locations in the brain, if the evidence warranted such assignments. And assuming there were some mental states and events for which there was no evidence of precise localization, but rather evidence that they were global features of the brain or of some large brain area such as the cortex, they would still be treated as global features of a spatial entity, viz., the *brain* or some brain area such as the *cortex*.

Let us now return to our 'dilemma'. The first horn claims that if we think of the relation between the mental and the physical as causal we are left with a mysterious notion of causation. I have argued that this is not so. It only seems so if we think of mental and physical as naming two ontological categories, two mutually exclusive classes of things, mental things and physical things, as if we lived in two worlds, a mental world and a physical world. But if we think of ourselves as living in one world which contains mental things in the sense in which it contains liquid things and solid things, then there are no metaphysical obstacles to a causal account of such things. My beliefs and desires, my thirsts and visual experiences, are real causal features of my brain, as much as the solidity of the table I work at and the liquidity of the water I drink are causal features of tables and water.

The second horn of the dilemma articulates the widely held view that an ideal causal account of the world must always make reference to (strict) causal laws and those laws must always be stated in physical terms. There are many different arguments for such views and I have not even begun to answer them, but I have tried to provide some reasons for thinking that the conclusions are false: our account of Intentional causation provides both the beginnings of the theoretical framework and many instances where Intentional states function causally as Intentional states. And while there are no 'strict' laws, there are lots of causal regularities in the operation of Intentional causation, e.g., prior intentions cause actions, thirst causes drinking, visual experiences cause beliefs. It remains an open empirical question how these higher-level states are realized in and caused by the operations of the brain, and an open question which of the realizations are "type-type" and which are "token-token". The *a priori* arguments that I have seen against the possibility of type, rather than of token, realizations tend to neglect a crucial point: what counts as a type is always relative to a description. The fact that we can't get type-type realizations stated in, for example, chemical terms, does not imply that we can't have type-type realizations at all. If we always insisted on realizations in chemical terms then the reduction of the Boyle–Charles Law to the laws of statistical mechanics – one of the all time successes of type reductions – would fail because the reduction makes no mention of any specific chemical composition of gases. Any old gas will do. For all we know the type of realizations that Intentional states have in the brain may be describable at a much higher functional level than that of the specific biochemistry of the neurons involved. My own speculation, and at the present state of our knowledge of neurophysiology it can only be a speculation, is that if we come to understand the operation of the brain in producing Intentionality, it is likely to be on principles that are quite different from those we now employ, as different as the principles of quantum mechanics are from the principles of Newtonian mechanics; but any principles, to give us an adequate account of the brain, will have to recognize the reality of, and explain the causal capacities of, the Intentionality of the brain.

SUBJECT INDEX

accordion effect, 98–100
action (act), 95, 107, 119
  basic action, 98, 100
  as composite entity, 107
  as conditions of satisfaction, 81, 82, 92,
    94, 108
  explanations of, 105f.
  Intentional account of, Chapter 3
    passim
  and intervening Intentionality, 110
  mental acts, 103
  unintentional action, 100, 101, 102, 108

Background, 19, 20, 54, 65–71, 133f. 139,
  Chapter 5 passim, 143, 147, 151,
  154, 230, 232, 248, 252, 253, 255,
  259
  deep Background, 143, 144
  functioning of, 158
  local Background, 144, 153
  as mental, 154
  and rules, 149, 152
  as skills, 144, 150f., 154, 155
  and truth conditions of sentences, 146
  as world, 144, 155
bodily (physical) movement, Chapter 3
  passim, 106, 130, 162
  as conditions of satisfaction, 87, 88
brain, 15, 20, 102, 154, 230, Chapter 10
  passim, 262, 270, 272

Cartesianism, 14, 74, 263
causal concepts, 75
causal explanations, 117, 120, 121
  and counterfactuals, 118f.
causal inference, 72f.
causality, Chapter 4 passim, 112
  traditional view of, 112
causal laws, Chapter 4 passim, 113, 118,
  120, 122, 126, 134, 264

linguistic version, 113, 120
  metaphysical version, 113
causally relevant aspects, 117, 137, 138,
  139
causal necessity, 116
causal regularities, 113, 118, 132ff., 138
  Background presumptions of, 113f.,
  139
  vs. contingent regularities, 115
  vs. logical regularities, 114
causal relations, Chapter 4 passim, 113,
  262, 264, 266
  vs. causings, 116
  perceived causal relations, 114f., 125,
  130
causal self-reference, 49, 76, 122, 169
  of intentions, 85, 86n
  and type-identical visual experiences,
  50
causal theories
  empiricist, 131f.
  intellectualist, 131f.
  of perception, 63f.
  realistic, 120, 130
  see also, meaning, proper names,
  reference
causation, Chapter 4 passim, 135
  agent vs. event causation, 115
  efficient causation, 135
  as experienced, 124, 125, 129, 130f.
  Intentional account of, Chapter 4
  passim, 123f., 128, 132
  regularity theory of 114, 119, 128
  statements of as intensional, 117, 123
  traditional account of, 118, 119, 123
cause, 123
  as internally related to effect, 121, 126
cognition (Bel)
  as basic category, 30, 33, 35, 104
communication, Chapter 6 passim, 165,

273

Index

NAME INDEX